DAYTRIPS
IN
FRANCE

—— 45 ——

One Day Adventures
by Rail, Bus, or Car

W9-DES-981

To Jo!
Here's wishing you a
year full of adventures
and wonderful memories!

Love from
Karen
Aug/91

Amiens

Deauville
Honfleur
Rouen
Bayeux
Caen
Giverny
Senlis
Chantilly
Reims
Versailles
PARIS
Provins
Chartres
Fontainebleau
Moret
Auxerre
Angers
Blois
Amboise
Dijon
Bourges
Beaune

Lyon

Var
Vence
St. Paul
Menton
Monaco
Grasse
NICE
Nîmes
Avignon
Antibes
Cagnes
Arles
Aix
Cannes
St. Tropez
MARSEILLE

DAYTRIPS
— IN —
FRANCE

— 45 —

One Day Adventures
by Rail, Bus, or Car

Revised Edition

by
Earl Steinbicker

HASTINGS HOUSE
MAMARONECK, NEW YORK

The author would like to thank the following people, whose
generous help and encouragement made this book possible:

George L. Hern, of the French Government Tourist Office.

Rosario G. Mariani and Bruce Haxthausen, both of Air France.

Dagobert M. Scher, of the French National Railroads.

All photos are by the author.

Distributed to the trade by Publishers Group West, Emeryville, CA.

Copyright © 1990 by Earl Steinbicker

All rights reserved. No part of this publication may be reproduced,
stored in a retrieval system, or transmitted, in any form or by any
means, electronic, mechanical, photocopying, recording or otherwise, without the prior permission of the copyright owner or the
publishers.

Library of Congress Cataloging-in-Publication Data
Steinbicker, Earl, 1934–
    Daytrips in France.

    Includes index.
    1. France—Description and travel—1975—Guide-books.
I. Title.
DC16.S73   1985   914.4'04838   85-14030
ISBN 0-8038-9326-4

Printed in the United States of America
10 9 8 7 6 5 4 3 2 1

Contents

Introduction

Visitors to France can choose from an enormous range of experiences. There are magnificent cities and medieval towns to explore, splendid châteaux and quaint fishing villages to visit, history to be relived and wines to be tasted. Few nations can match its scope of art, architecture, cuisine, or natural splendor. What's more, the overwhelming majority of France's most exciting attractions can easily be enjoyed on a daytrip basis with absolutely no need for frequent hotel changes. This book takes a careful look at 45 of the most intriguing destinations and tells you, in step-by-step detail, exactly how to go about probing them on your own.

Daytrips in France is not intended to be a comprehensive guide to the entire nation. It focuses, instead, on four broad areas of maximum tourist interest—walking tours of Paris, daytrips from Paris, daytrips in Provence, and daytrips along the Riviera. The most logical bases for these one-day adventures are Paris, Marseille, and Nice; although other towns could be substituted as suggested in the text.

Daytrips have many advantages over the usual point-to-point touring, especially for short-term visitors. You can sample a far greater range in the same time by seeing only those places that really interest you instead of "doing" the regions town by town. This can lead to a more varied diet of sights, such as spending one day on a Normandy beach, the next back in Paris, and the third in medieval Beaune. They are also ideal for business travelers with a few free days interspersed between meetings.

The benefits of staying in one hotel for a while are obvious. Weekly rates are often more economical than overnight stays, especially in conjunction with airline package plans. You also gain a sense of place, of having established a temporary home-away-from-home in a city where you can get to know the restaurants and enjoy the nightlife. Then, too, you won't waste time searching for a room every night. Your luggage remains in one place while you go out on carefree daytrips.

There is no need to pre-plan every moment of your vacation since with daytrips you are always free to venture wherever you please. Feel like seeing Antibes today? Ah, but this is Tuesday, when its sights are closed, so maybe it would be better to head for Monaco instead, or take a glorious rail excursion through the Var Valley. Is rain predicted for the entire day? You certainly don't want to be in Deauville in a shower, so why not try the wonderful museums in Dijon? The operative word here is flexibility; the freedom of not being tied to a schedule or route.

All of the daytrips in this book may be taken by public transportation, and all but those within the base cities themselves by private car. Full information for doing this is given in the "Getting There" section of each trip. A suggested do-it-yourself tour is outlined in both the text and on the local map provided. Time and weather considerations are included, along with price-keyed restaurant recommendations, background data, and sources of additional information.

The trips have been arranged in a geographic sequence following convenient transportation routes. In several cases it is possible to combine two trips in the same day. These opportunities are noted whenever they are practical.

Destinations were chosen to appeal to a wide variety of interests, and include some new discoveries along with the proven favorites. In addition to the usual cathedrals, castles, and museums there are wine centers, boat cruises, Roman ruins, elegant resorts and major cities, great seaports and quaint fishing villages, preserved medieval towns, caves, exquisite gardens, splendid châteaux, places where history was made, homes of famous artists, natural beauty spots and even an exciting railfan excursion.

Many of the attractions have a nominal entrance fee—those that are free will come as a pleasant surprise. Cathedrals and churches will appreciate a small donation in the collection box to help pay their maintenance costs.

Finally, a gentle disclaimer. Places have a way of changing without warning, and errors do creep into print. If your heart is absolutely set on a particular sight, you should check first to make sure that it isn't closed for renovations, or that the opening times are still valid. Phone numbers for the local tourist information offices are included for this purpose.

One last thought—it isn't really necessary to see everything at any given destination. Be selective. Your one-day adventures in France should be fun, not an endurance test. If it starts becoming that, just stroll over to the nearest sidewalk café, sit down, and enjoy yourself. There will always be another day.

Happy Daytripping!

Getting Around

Getting around France on your own is really quite easy once you know a few of the practicalities. This first section discusses such matters as transportation, package deals, holidays, food and drink, some hints on the suggested tours, and sources of additional information. After that, Section II is devoted to an exploration of Paris. The book then goes on to describe 40 of the most exciting daytrip possibilities in other parts of France. Nearly all of these adventures can be made by rail, all by car, and some by bus. In choosing a form of transportation, you should consider the following information:

BY RAIL:

The French love to travel by rail, which comes as no surprise as they are blessed with the fastest and some of the most modern trains in the world. Rail is almost invariably the quickest way to cover the medium distances outlined in the following chapters. The **French National Railroads** (*Société Nationale des Chemins de Fer Français*, or **SNCF**) operates an average of 1,500 passenger trains a day over a dense network of more than 20,000 miles of track, serving some 4,000 stations. Many of its lines radiate in all directions from Paris, making daytrips from the capital exceptionally fast and easy. In an energy-conscious age it has been the policy of the French government to encourage rail travel by constantly improving the service with expanded schedules and state-of-the-art technology; and by making it readily affordable for both citizens and visitors.

A new era of rail transportation dawned in 1981 when the first **TGV** trains began service between Paris and Lyon. Presently operating at speeds of 186 mph on their own dedicated lines, one of these speed demons has actually been clocked during trials at a phenomenal 255 mph, a new world record! The expanded TGV fleet now serves many other destinations as well, sometimes running partly on regular tracks at reduced speed. The new TGV *Atlantique*, operating from Montparnasse Station in Paris, now runs to Angers and Nantes, as well as Toulouse and the Spanish border. As this becomes fully operational it will expand the number of destinations within daytrip range of Paris. A northern TGV is expected to connect Paris with London via the new Channel Tunnel sometime in 1993, with a branch service to Brussels by 1995. After that, it's on to Amsterdam and Cologne, then Strasbourg and Frankfurt. Meanwhile, the running times of other express trains have been improved, with some routinely cruising at 125 mph.

Seasoned travelers often consider riding trains to be one of the best ways of meeting the local people and making new friends. It is not unusual to strike up an engaging conversation that makes your trip all the more memorable. You also get a marvelous view of the passing countryside from the large windows, and have time to catch up on your reading. Then too, you are spared the worries of driving, especially after having a few glasses of wine with your meals.

All trains operated by the SNCF belong to one of the following categories, as indicated on schedules and departure platforms:

TGV—*Train à Grande Vitesse*. The world's fastest trains offer a smooth, quiet air-conditioned ride between Paris and Lyon in just two hours flat. Frequent daily departures also serve Dijon, Avignon, Marseille, Nîmes, Nice, Geneva, Lausanne and other places. Both first- and second-class accommodations are available. Reservations are an **absolute requirement**, and these may be made for a small fee up until five minutes before departure, either at the reservation window or from special machines in the stations. There is a surcharge during peak travel times, which is waived for railpass users. Meal service at your seat is available for first-class passengers, but must be arranged for when you reserve your seat. A bar car for both classes provides light meals, sandwiches, snacks and beverages.

EC—*EuroCity*. High-speed international expresses with special comforts. Both first- and second-class seating is offered, and there is a supplementary fare that is covered by the various Eurailpasses and by the France Railpass within France only. Those EC trains going to Geneva, Lausanne, or Bern are often of the TGV type, above, which require reservations. Reservations may be made for other EC trains if desired.

IC—*Intercité*. Fast international trains serving many towns in France with modern equipment. Both first- and second-class seating is available. A supplemental fare is charged, but not to users of railpasses. Reservations can be made if desired.

Turbotrain—These modern, high-speed turbine-operated trains link Paris with the Normandy coast, and are frequently used on other major non-electrified lines. Turbotrains carry both first- and second-class cars, as well as a dining car. Reservations are desirable due to the somewhat limited seating capacity.

Corail—Very modern, air-conditioned locomotive-hauled express trains carrying both first- and second-class cars. Reservations are available if desired but are usually not really necessary. A supplemental fare, waived for railpass holders, may be charged on some departures.

A TGV Train at St.-Charles Station, Marseille

Express—These trains make more stops and frequently use modern Corail equipment. The category also includes a number of foreign trains that may or may not measure up to French standards of comfort. Both classes of seating are available.

Omnibus—Often not given any particular designation, these locals make many stops and can take you to smaller, off-beat destinations. Much of the equipment is old and sometimes rather quaint, although there are modern omnibus trains. First class is not always offered.

In addition you may also want to use these services:

RER—Commuter trains operating on a very frequent schedule in and around Paris, which connect with the Métro subway system. Some lines are operated by **SNCF** *(railpasses valid, but ask for a free ticket to operate the turnstiles)* and others by **RATP**—Paris Transit Authority *(Paris Sesame Pass valid)*. The equipment is modern and consists of both first- and second-class cars.

Buses—*Autocars,* operated by or for the French National Railroads and marked "SNCF," connect certain rural areas with train stations in larger towns; and fill in for some rail services during off-peak hours. Railpasses are valid on these—*but not other*—buses.

SCHEDULES for all SNCF services are available at the stations. Generally, the easiest way is to ask at the train information window, usually marked *Renseignements.* The personnel there may not always speak English, but you will have no trouble if you write out the name of your destination and the time you would like to leave. Doing this avoids the confusion caused by towns with similar-sounding names, such as Cannes, Cagnes or Caen. It also prevents misunderstandings of day-to-day variations when, for example, a particular train only runs on Saturdays in summer. At the same time, always check the return schedule so you don't wind up stranded in some quaint village.

There is now a **telephone number** for **train information in English.** In Paris, dial **43-80-50-50.** From other parts of France, first dial 16, wait for a tone, then continue on with 1-43-80-50-50.

All schedules are stated in terms of the 24-hour clock, thus a departure at 3:32 p.m. would be shown as 15.32. Free printed pocket schedules *(Fiches-Horaires)* are available for popular destinations, and schedules are also posted throughout the stations. Be careful of any footnotes on these, as they often refer to variations. The **glossary** on page 16 will be helpful in making translations, as will a pocket French-English dictionary. The regional schedule books *(Indicateur Officiel)*, available at station newstands, are complete but very bulky to use. The smaller **Thomas Cook European Timetable**, sold in some travel book stores in America, by mail from the Forsyth Travel Library (P.O. Box 2975, Shawnee Mission, Kansas 66201–1375, phone toll-free 1-800-FORSYTH for credit-card orders), or at Thomas Cook offices in Britain, is very useful although it does not list *every* local service.

RESERVATIONS are required for all TGV trains and can be made up to two months in advance of, and until five minutes before, departure time if seats are still available. There is a nominal charge for this. Travelers who can read simple French may prefer the handy coin-operated TGV reservation machines, which are valid only for departures within the next hour. You may want to make reservations for other rail trips, particularly on the often-crowded Turbotrains to the Normandy coast in high season. One advantage to reservations is that you can specify a smoking or non-smoking section, and a window or aisle seat. Otherwise, reservations are really not necessary for the daytrips in this book other than those by TGV. Passengers traveling without them should be careful not to sit in someone else's reserved seat, which is marked by a card at the compartment entrance or above the seat.

PARIS has many train stations, a legacy from the days before nationalization when just about every route was operated by a different company. The map on page 13 shows the general location of those that are of interest to tourists. All of them are connected by the Métro subway system and can be easily reached. An inter-station bus service—free to holders of tickets or passes—is provided by the SNCF.

MAJOR RAILWAY
STATIONS IN
PARIS

Gare
de Lyon

Bastille

SEINE

Gare
de l'Est

Gare
du Nord

Gare
d'Austerlitz

RIGHT BANK

Pompidou
Center

Notre
Dame

Forum
des Halles

Pantheon

Opéra

Louvre

Luxembourg
Gardens

St. Germain
des Prés

Tuileries

Gare
St. Lazare

Gare
Montparnasse

Gare des Invalides
& Air Terminal

LEFT BANK

Invalides

Champs Élysées

Tourist
Info.

Eiffel
Tower

Arc de
Triomphe

N

Porte Maillot
Air Terminal

Be sure you know which station you are leaving from before starting out on the day's adventures.

It is always best to arrive at the station *(Gare)* a little early in order to acquaint yourself with its layout. On the departure platform *(Quai)* you will usually find a sign marked *Composition des Trains* that shows the make-up of each express leaving from that platform, including the location of each car. This serves two purposes. First, you won't have to make a last-minute dash when you discover that the first-class cars stop at the opposite end of a long platform. Secondly, and more important, it shows which—if any—cars are dropped off en route to your destination.

The routing and final destination of each car is usually shown just outside its door as well as in its vestibule. First-class cars are marked with the numeral "1" near the door, and with a yellow stripe above the windows.

Most express trains offer a **food and beverage service** of some sort, as indicated on the schedules. Riding in a regular dining car, bar car, or self-service *Gril-Express* car can be a delightful experience, but beware the pushcarts in other cars that sell well-shaken cans of warm beer. You are much better off stocking up on snacks and refreshments at the station and bringing them along with you, as most Europeans do. Establishments offering take-out food and drinks are usually marked with the word *Emporter*.

RAILPASSES can be a terrific bargain if you intend to do any real amount of train travel. Ask your travel agent about them before going to France, as they are difficult if not impossible to purchase once there. The French National Railroads (**SNCF**) accepts the following passes:

EURAILPASS—The best-known and most popular pass, allows unlimited first-class travel throughout 17 European countries, excluding Great Britain. It is available for periods of 15 or 21 days, or 1, 2, or 3 months. The Eurailpass includes a wide variety of fringe benefits, such as rides on many private railroads including the Provence Railroad (see page 324), some buses, several popular lake and river cruises, and a variety of international ferry steamers.

EURAIL SAVERPASS—An economical version of the Eurailpass that offers the same first-class benefits as outlined above, but for groups of three or more people traveling together. Between October 1st and March 31st the group size can be as small as two persons. This pass is available for a period of 15 days only, and the rail travel must always be done as a group.

EURAIL FLEXIPASS—The latest innovation in railpasses allows unlimited first-class travel on any nine days within a 21-day period. It is valid in the same 17 countries and has the same benefits as the regular Eurailpass. This is a particularly attractive deal if you intend to spend much time exploring your base cities between making day-trips from them.

EURAIL YOUTHPASS—This low-cost version of the Eurailpass is available to anyone under the age of 26 and allows unlimited second-class travel in the same 17 European countries for periods of 1 or 2 months. The fringe benefits are pretty much the same.

FRANCE RAILPASS—Valid for unlimited travel in France only (and to Monaco), this flexible pass is available for use either on any 4 days within a 15-day period, or on any 9 days within one month. It is offered in both first- and second-class versions, for either adults or for children between the ages of 4 to under 12. The substantial extra benefits include free transfers from Charles de Gaulle (Roissy) or Orly airports to Paris and back; a 1-day Métropass for use on the Paris Métro, RER or buses within Paris; and discounts on sightseeing tours, some museums, the Provence Railway, and a host of other attractions. All told, it represents a worthwhile saving over the similar Eurail Flexipass and should certainly be considered if your travels are limited to France.

BRITFRANCE RAILPASS—Allows unlimited rail travel throughout both Britain and France on any 5 days within a 15-day period; or any 10 days in a one-month period. It is offered in both first- and second-class versions, and includes a round-trip crossing of the Channel by Hovercraft.

All railpasses must be **validated** at the information window of a train station on the first day of actual use. The first and last days of validity will be entered on the pass at that time. Be certain that you agree with the dates *before* allowing the agent to write them in.

If you intend to take several of the daytrips in this book, and especially if at least one of them is to a distant location such as Lyon, Dijon or Angers, a railpass will probably wind up saving you a considerable amount of money. Even if the savings are less than that, a pass should still be considered for the convenience it offers in not having to line up for tickets, and for the freedom of just hopping aboard almost any train at whim. Possession of a railpass will also encourage you to become more adventurous, to seek out distant and offbeat destinations. And, should you ever manage to get on the wrong train by mistake, your only cost will be your time.

The various Eurailpasses, the France Railpass, and the BritFrance Railpass are sold by most travel agents in North America, who also have current information and prices, and by mail from the Forsyth Travel Library mentioned on page 12. Alternatively, you could contact the nearest office of their North American agency, FrenchRail Inc.,

A RAIL TRAVELER'S GLOSSARY

Abonnement	Season ticket or pass
Aller	To go one way
Aller et Retour	Round trip
A Partir	From (date) on
Arrêt	Stop, halt
Arrivée	Arrival
Autobus, Autocar	Bus
Autorail	Railcar
Avec Supplément	With surcharge
Banlieue	Suburban (commuter trains)
Billet	Ticket
Billet Simple	Ordinary one-way ticket
Bureau de Change	Currency exchange
Changement	Change (of trains)
Chariot	Luggage cart
Composition des Trains	Train make-up
Composteur	Ticket validating machine
Compostez votre Billet	Validate your ticket
Consigne	Checkroom, left luggage
Consigne Automatique	Luggage locker
Contrôleur	Ticket collector
Correspondence	Connection
Couchette	Inexpensive sleeping car with bunks
Couloir	Aisle (seat)
Dames	Women
Défense de Fumer	No smoking
Demi-Tarif	Half fare
Départ	Departure
Deuxième Classe	Second class
Douane	Customs
Emporter	To take out, as in items from snack bar
Enregistrement	To send baggage ahead
Entrée	Entrance
Entrée Interdite	Do not enter
Étranger	Foreign
Facultatif	Optional, on request (train or bus stop)
Fenêtre	Window (seat)
Fêtes	Holidays
Fiches-Horaires	Free pocket-sized timetables
Fumeurs	Smoking
Gare	Station
Gare Routière	Bus station

Grandes Lignes	Main lines
Grève	Strike of workers
Gril-Express	Cafeteria car
Guichet	Ticket window
Hommes	Men
Horaire	Timetable
Jusqu'au	Until (date)
Libre	Free, available
Libre Service	Self service
Ligne	Line
Location de Voitures	Car rental
Métro	Subway
Messieurs	Men
Monter	To board (the train)
Objects Trouvés	Lost-and-found
Occupé	Occupied
Place	Seat
Plein Tarif	Full fare
Poste-PTT	Post office, telephone service
Première Classe	First class
Prochain	Next (departure)
Quai	Platform
Quotidien	Daily
RATP	Paris Transit Authority
Remboursement	Refund
Renseignements	Information
RER	Paris commuter rail lines
Réseau	Network, system
Réservation	Reservation
Retardé	Delay
Salle d' Attente	Waiting room
Sauf	Except
Sortie	Exit
Sortie de Secours	Emergency exit
SNCF	French National Railroads
Tarif	Fare
Tous les Jours	Every day
Train + Vélo	Bicycle rental at station
Vers	To
Voie	Track
Voiture	Car (of train or otherwise)
Voiture Directe	Through train to indicated destination
Voyage	Trip, travel
Voyager	To travel
Voyageur	Traveler, passenger
Wagon	Railroad car
Wagon-Lit	Sleeping car
Wagon-Restaurant	Dining car

located in Chicago, Coral Gables FL, Dallas, Montreal, New York, San Francisco, Santa Monica CA, Toronto, Vancouver BC, and White Plains NY. Their principal address is:

FrenchRail Inc.
230 Westchester Ave.,
White Plains, NY 10604
Phone (914) 682-2999

Any of their locations will happily supply you with a booklet of current French and European fares, useful in determining whether to buy a railpass, and a catalog of custom travel programs. The French National Railroads (SNCF) also has offices in London and throughout Europe.

Those who have decided against a railpass can purchase **tickets** (*billets*) at ticket windows (*guichets*) in the stations, or from automatic vending machines. There is usually no saving to be had by buying a round-trip ticket. Be sure to **validate** your ticket—*compostez votre billet*—before use by inserting into one of the orange ticket-stamping machines (*composteur*) located near the platforms. Round-trip (*aller et retour*) tickets must also be stamped on the return journey. Failure to validate could result in a fine, since the SNCF operates on an honor system with only a few spot checks made, and unvalidated tickets could be used over and over again or even redeemed for cash.

BY BUS:

A few of the daytrips in this book are to destinations not served by the railroad. To reach them by public transportation, you should first take a train to the nearest town on a rail line and then continue on by connecting bus. Instructions for doing this are given in each case. Railpasses are valid on buses operated by or for the SNCF; others require payment of a fare. Buses, often called *Autobus* or *Autocar,* usually depart from a bus station (*gare routière),* most often located next to or near the train station.

BY CAR:

Many tourists prefer to explore France by car, which may be economical when several people are traveling together. Although slower, cars offer a complete freedom from schedules. All of the daytrips in this book (except those within Paris) can be made this way, with distances and road directions provided for each. In addition to a car you will need a valid driver's license and a good regional road map. Those published by Michelin are excellent and highly detailed.

Driving in France is essentially the same as in the U.S.A. or Canada, but attention should be paid to a few points. Seat belts are compulsory at all times for both the driver and front-seat passenger, with children under 10 confined to the rear seat. Failure to heed this rule could result in a fine. Similarly, the penalties for driving while intoxicated can be quite severe. Be particularly wary of the notorious *priorité à droite* rule, in which vehicles coming from the right have the right-of-way. While there are many exceptions to this, you should always be careful and never try to bluff a French driver—they *know* their rights and take them very seriously.

Roads in France are excellent and well marked. *Autoroutes,* designated by the letter "A" preceding their number, are usually limited-access toll *(péage)* roads with a 130-kph speed limit. This may be lower in some areas, or where there is no toll. Other main roads, known as *Routes Nationales* or "N" roads, are free and most often have a 90-kph limit (60-kph in built-up areas). To get the real flavor of the country, however, you should at least occasionally drive on the *Routes Départementales* (letter "D"), local roads that meander from village to village. The routes suggested in the book for each daytrip are the fastest ones. If you have the time, you might find it more enjoyable to use minor roads instead, following a good local road map.

A brief **glossary** for drivers is provided on page 20. For more comprehensive automotive terms, you may want to use a pocket-size phrase book, such as *French for Travellers* by Berlitz.

CAR RENTALS *(Location de Voitures)* can be arranged in advance through your travel agent or one of the major chains such as Hertz, Avis, National, Dollar, or Budget. There are also many local firms that might charge less, but which may impose severe restrictions on drop-off possibilities and other conveniences. Among the best deals available are the **fly/drive** plans offered by Air France and some other carriers in conjunction with their transatlantic flights. Check with your travel agent about this as arrangements must be made in advance. Those traveling primarily by train may also want to rent a car on occasion. The **Train + Auto** service operated in connection with SNCF is an excellent way to do this, with discounts for holders of the economical France Railpass. If you intend to rent a car for over three weeks it will pay to consider **leasing**—an arrangement that is exempt from the stiff 33% tax on rentals and which saves money on insurance. Finally, in estimating your·expenses, remember that gasoline *(essence)* costs several times as much in France as in North America. Before returning a rental car, be sure to fill up the tank to avoid a high refilling charge.

BY AIR:

You may prefer air travel for the long haul between major base cities in France, particularly from Paris to Nice. Both Air France and Air Inter operate frequent flights on this route. Air Inter also has an

A DRIVER'S GLOSSARY

Accotement non Stabilisé ... Soft shoulder
Allumez vos Phares .... Turn on headlights
Arrêt Interdit .... No stopping
Attention .... Caution
Au Pas .... Slow
Autoroute .... High-speed limited-access highway, usually toll. Indicated by letter "A" preceding route number
Autres Directions .... Through traffic
Bifurcation .... Junction
Carrefour .... Crossroads
Carte Grise .... Car registration papers
Carte Routière .... Road map
Céder le Passage .... Yield
Centre Ville .... To the center of town
Chaussée Déformée .... Bad road surface
Chantier .... Road construction
Chute de Pierres .... Falling rocks
Circuit Touristique .... Scenic route
Circulation Interdite .... No thoroughfare
Descente Dangereuse ...... Steep hill
Déviation .... Detour (Diversion)
Douane .... Customs
Eau .... Water
École .... School
Entrée Interdite .... No entrance
Essence .... Gasoline (Petrol)
Fin d'Interdiction .... End of restriction
Fin de Limitation de Vitesse End of speed restriction
Gravillons .... Gravel road surface
Halte .... Stop
Hauteur Limitée .... Low clearance
Huile .... Oil
Impasse .... Dead-end road (Cul-de-sac)
Interdiction de Doubler ..... No passing
Interdiction de Stationner ... No parking
Itinéraire Bis .... Alternative route
Limitation de Vitesse .... Speed restriction
Location de Voitures .... Car rental (Hire)
Nids de Poule .... Pot holes
Passage à Niveau .... Grade crossing
Passage Interdit .... Entry forbidden, no thoroughfare
Passage Protégé .... Right-of-way at intersection ahead
Péage .... Toll (road)
Pente Dangereuse .... Steep incline
Permis de Conduire .... Driver's license
Piétons .... Pedestrians

Piste Reservée aux
    Transports Publics . . . . Lane reserved for public transport
Pneus . . . . Tires
Poids Lourds . . . . Truck (Lorry) route
Priorité è Droite . . . . Vehicles coming from the right have the right-of-way
Priorité à Gauche . . . . Vehicles coming from the left have the right-of-way
Ralentir . . . . Reduce speed
Rappel . . . . Previous sign still applies
Réservée aux Piétons . . . . Pedestrians only
Réservée aux Transports
    Publics . . . . (Lane) reserved for public transport
Rond Point . . . . Traffic circle
Route Barrée . . . . Road closed
Route Étroite . . . . Narrow road
Route Glissante . . . . Slippery road
Sauf (Seulement) Riverains . . (Private road) for residents only
Sens Interdit . . . . Wrong direction
Sens Unique . . . . One-way street
Serrez à Droite . . . . Keep to the right
Serrez à Gauche . . . . Keep to the left
Sortie . . . . Exit
Sortie de Camions . . . . Truck crossing
Stationnement Autorisé . . . . . Parking allowed
Stationnement Interdit . . . . No parking
Tenez vos Distances . . . . Keep your distance
Toutes Directions . . . . All directions
Travaux . . . . Road work
Verglas . . . . Slippery road
Virages . . . . Curves ahead
Voie de Dégagement . . . . Private entrance
Voie Unique . , ... Single-lane traffic
Voiture . . . . Car, vehicle
Voiture à Louer . . . . Rental car
Zone Bleue . . . . Time-indicator disc required for parking
Zone Rouge . . . . Tow-away zone

APPROXIMATE CONVERSIONS

1 Mile = 1.6 km
1 km = 0.6 miles

1 U.S. Gallon = 3.78 litres
1 Litre = 0.26 U.S. Gallons

extensive network of domestic services between all major cities in France, with competition from several regional carriers.

As to transatlantic services, **Air France** offers direct flights from more North American gateway cities to France than any other carrier. These include New York, Boston, Philadelphia, Chicago, Washington D.C., Miami, Houston, Los Angeles, San Francisco, Anchorage, Montreal, Toronto, and Mexico City. Both the wide-body 747 and the supersonic Concorde are used for transatlantic crossings. Four classes of service are available: **Concorde** (the only class on supersonic flights), **Première** (first class with sleeper seats), **Le Club** (business class), and **Economique** (economy class). Passengers bound for Nice will be happy to know that Air France makes quick and easy connections with through luggage checking from North America. During the summer they have direct flights between New York and Nice.

Paris has two major airports, **Charles de Gaulle** (also called Roissy), north of the city; and **Orly**, to the south. Air France transatlantic flights land at Charles de Gaulle, where the airline has its own terminal with convenient connecting flights to other cities in Europe and throughout the world. The airline operates a frequent bus service to both airports, which can be used by passengers on other airlines as well. Those going to Charles de Gaulle leave from Porte Maillot in Paris, and those to Orly from Invalides (see the map on page 13). In either case the travel time is about 30 minutes or so. They also have buses running directly between the two airports, taking about one hour, which are free for connecting Air France passengers. Taxis are a more convenient way of getting into town and have the advantage of going directly to your destination. Holders of the France Railpass have vouchers for the combination bus/train services called "Roissy Rail" and "Orly Rail," which are convenient if you don't have too much luggage. You can also buy tickets for these, or use the Eurailpass. They leave from Nord and Austerlitz train stations respectively.

On the Riviera, the Nice-Côte d'Azur Airport is so close to downtown Nice that taxis are practical for all but the slimmest budgets. There is also a local bus service.

PACKAGE PLANS:

The cost of your trip to France can be cut substantially by selecting one of the many attractive package plans that combine transatlantic airfares with local hotel accommodations and/or car rentals. **Air France** has the widest selection of these, offering a flexible length of stay to fit the needs of independent travelers. Similar plans are offered by other carriers. Since the details of these programs, as well as the airfares, change frequently you should consult with a reliable travel agent well ahead of time.

HOLIDAYS:

Legal holidays *(Fêtes Légales)* in France are:

January 1	July 14 (Bastille Day)
Easter Monday	August 15 (Assumption Day)
May 1 (Labor Day)	November 1 (All Saints' Day)
May 8 (V-E Day)	November 11 (Armistice Day)
Ascension Day	Christmas
(40 days after Easter)	
Whit Monday (Second Monday	
after Ascension)	

In addition, the Principality of Monaco celebrates:

January 27 (Feast of	November 19 (National Day)
(St.-Dévote)	

Trains operate on holiday schedules on these days, and some attractions may be closed. Banks close at noon on the day preceding a holiday. When any of these falls on a Sunday, the following Monday is taken as a holiday.

FOOD AND DRINK:

Several choice restaurants are listed for each destination in this book. Most of these are long-time favorites of experienced travelers and serve French cuisine. Their approximate price range, based on the least expensive complete meal offered, is indicated as follows:

$ — Inexpensive, but may have fancier dishes available.

$$ — Reasonable. These establishments may also feature daily specials.

$$$ — Luxurious and expensive.

$$$ + — Very expensive.

X: — Days or periods closed.

Those who take their dining *very* seriously should consult an up-to-date restaurant and hotel guide such as the classic red-covered *Michelin France,* issued annually in March.

It is always wise to check the prices posted outside the restaurant before entering. Remember that in France the word **"menu"** refers to a fixed-price *(prix-fixe)* set meal, consisting of several courses, often with a range of choices for each, and possibly including a drink *(boisson comprise).* Ordering from the *menu* is almost invariably the most economical way to dine. Most restaurants offer several *menus* in which

MENU TRANSLATOR

Abricot apricot
Agneau lamb
Aiglefin haddock
Ail garlic
Aîoli garlic mayonnaise
Alsacienne in the style of Alsace, often with sauerkraut, sausages and ham
Amande almond
Ananas pineapple
Anchois anchovies
Andouillette chitterling sausage
Aneth dill
Anguille eel
Anis aniseed
Arachides peanuts
Artichaut artichoke
Asperges asparagus
Assiette assortie mixture of cold hors d'oeuvre
Aubergine eggplant
Avocat avocado
Baguette long loaf of bread
Banane banana
Bar sea bass
Barbue brill
Basilic basil
Baudroie anglerfish
Béarnaise sauce with egg yolks, tarragon, shallots, butter, and white wine
Béchamel white sauce
Beignet fritter
Bercy sauce with white wine, shallots and herbs
Betterave beet
Beurre butter
Bifteck, biftek beefsteak
Bisque shellfish soup, chowder
Blanquette stew with egg and cream sauce
Boeuf beef
Bouef à la mode beef braised in red wine with vegetables
Boeuf Bourguignon beef stew in red wine with vegetables
Bombe fancy ice cream dish

Bordelaise in the style of Bordeaux with red wine, shallots, beef marrow, and mushrooms
Boudin blood sausage
Boudin blanc white sausage of veal, pork or chicken
Bouillabaisse fish and seafood stew
Bouquet shrimp
Bourguignonne in the style of Burgundy with red wine, onions, and bacon
Bourride fish and shellfish soup with aîoli
Brioche soft yeasty roll
Brochette skewered meat or fish
Caille quail
Canard duck
Caneton duckling
Carbonnade flamande beef braised in beer
Carotte carrot
Carpe carp
Carré d'agneau rack of lamb
Cassis blackcurrant
Cassoulet casserole of white beans with pork, goose, duck, and sausage
Céleri celery
Cèpes wild flat mushrooms
Cerises cherries
Cervelles brains
Champignons mushrooms
Chantilly sweet whipped cream
Chapon capon
Charcuterie cold cuts, pâtés, cured meats, and terrines
Chasseur hunter style
Châteaubriand thick fillet of beef
Chèvre goat or goat cheese
Chicorée curly endive
Chou cabbage
Choucroute sauerkraut
Choucroute garnie sauerkraut with pork, sausage, or other meats
Choufleur cauliflower
Ciboulettes chives
Citron lemon

Citron vent lime
Civet de lièvre jugged hare
Clémentine tangerine
Cochon pig
Concombre cucumber
Confit preserved
Confit de canard duck preserved in its own fat
Confiture preserves, jam
Consommé clear broth
Contre-filet sirloin steak
Coq cock, hen, or chicken
Coq au vin stewed chicken in red wine with mushrooms, onions, and bacon
Coquillage shellfish
Coquille St.-Jacques sea scallop
Cornichon small pickle
Côte chop or rib
Côtelette cutlet
Coupe de fruits fruit cup
Courgette zucchini
Crabe crab
Crème cream
Crème caramel custard
Crêpes thin pancakes
Cresson watercress
Crevette shrimp
Croissant flaky crescent-shaped roll
Croque-monsieur grilled ham and cheese sandwich
Cru raw
Crudités raw vegetable salad
Crustacés shellfish
Cuit cooked
Daube meat stew in wine stock
Daurade sea bream
Dijonnaise in the style of Dijon, with mustard
Dinde, dindon, dindonneau turkey
Échalote shallot
Écrevisses crayfish
Émincé thin slice
Endive endive
Entrecôte rib steak
Épices spices
Épinards spinach
Escalope thin slice
Escargots snails
Estragon tarragon
Faisan pheasant
Farci stuffed
Farine flour
Faux-filet sirloin steak

Fenouil fennel
Flageolets small green kidney beans
Flan custard tart
Foie liver
Foie gras goose liver
Fondue melted cheese dish
Forestière with mushrooms
Four oven
Frais, fraîche fresh, chilled
Fraises strawberries
Framboises raspberries
Frappé surrounded by crushed ice
Fricassée stewed or sautéed, braised in wine with cream
Frit fried
Frites French fries
Friture small fried fish
Fromage cheese
Fruits de mer seafood
Fumé smoked
Galantine cold meat, fish, or vegetables in jelly
Galette pancake with stuffing
Gambas large prawns
Garbure thick soup
Garni garnished
Gâteau cake
Gelée aspic
Gibelotte rabbit stewed in wine
Gibier game
Gigot d'agneau leg of lamb
Glace ice cream
Glacée iced or glazed
Graisse fat
Gratin crisp topping of cheese and bread crumbs
Grenouilles frogs (legs)
Grillade grilled meat
Grillée grilled
Groseille red currant
Haché, hachis minced, hashed
Hareng herring
Haricots beans
Haricots verts green beans
Homard lobster
Huile oil
Huîtres oysters
Jambon ham
Jardinière garnished with fresh vegetables
Julienne thin sliced vegetables
Jus juice
Lait milk
Laitue lettuce

Lamproie lamprey eel
Langouste spiny lobster
Langue tongue
Lapereau young rabbit
Lapin rabbit
Lard bacon
Légumes vegetables
Lentilles lentils
Loup sea bass
Macédoine diced mixed fruit or vegetables
Margret de canard duck steak or breast
Maïs sweet corn
Mandarine tangerine
Maquereau mackerel
Marrons chestnuts
Matelote freshwater fish stew
Menthe mint
Miel honey
Mirabelle yellow plum
Mornay cheese sauce
Morue salt cod
Moules mussels
Moutarde mustard
Mouton mutton
Myrtille blueberry
Navet turnip
Noisette hazelnut, or round piece of boneless meat
Noix nuts, walnuts
Nouilles noodles
Oeufs eggs
Oie goose
Oignons onions
Oseille sorrel
Oursins sea urchins
Paillard slice of veal or chicken breast
Pain bread
Palombe pigeon
Palourdes clams
Pamplemousse grapefruit
Panaché mixture of foods
Papillote cooked in parchment or foil
Parfum flavor
Paramentier dish with potatoes
Pastèque watermelon
Pâté cold minced meat or fish spread
Pâtes pasta
Pâtisserie pastry
Pêche peach
Perche perch
Perdrix partridge

Persil parsley
Petits-pois little green peas
Pied de porc pig's foot
Pigeonneau squab
Pignons pine nuts
Piments pimentos
Pintade guinea fowl
Pipérade omelette with peppers, onions, tomatoes, and ham
Piquante spicy
Pistache pistachio
Pistou purée of basil, garlic, and olive oil
Plateau de fromages cheese board
Poché poached
Poire pear
Poireau leek
Pois peas
Poisson fish
Poivre pepper
Poivron sweet bell pepper
Pomme apple
Pommes de terre potatoes
Pommes Frites French fries
Porc pork
Porcelet young suckling pig
Potage soup
Pot-au-feu boiled beef and vegetable stew
Potée boiled pork and vegetables
Poularde capon
Poulet chicken
Poulpe octopus
Praire clam
Profiterole cream puff filled with chocolate
Provençale in the style of Provence, with garlic, tomatoes, and olive oil
Prune plum
Pruneau prune
Quenelles dumplings of fish or poultry
Quiche open pie with egg and cream plus filling
Raclette melted cheese dish
Radis radish
Ragoût stew
Raie skate
Raisins grapes
Ratatouille vegetable casserole
Rémoulade sauce of mayonnaise, capers, mustard, anchovies, and herbs
Rillettes potted meat

Ris de veau   veal sweetbreads
Riz   rice
Rognons   kidneys
Rosbif   roast beef
Rôti   roast
Rouget   red mullet
Roulade   meat or fish, rolled and stuffed
Safran   saffron
Salade composée   mixed salad
Salade Niçoise   salad with tuna, olives, tomatoes, potatoes, and beans
Salade verte   green salad
Salé   salted
Saucisses   fresh sausages
Saucisson   dried sausage
Sauge   sage
Saumon   salmon
Sauté   browned in fat
Sauvage   wild
Scarole   escarole
Sel   salt
Sorbet   sherbet
Soupe   soup
Steak au poivre   steak with crushed peppercorns
Steak haché   chopped steak

Steak tartare   minced raw beef
Sucre   sugar
Suprême de volaille   fillet of chicken breast in cream sauce
Tarte   pie
Terrine   cold baked minced meat or fish
Tête de veau   calf's head
Thon   tuna
Thym   thyme
Tomate   tomato
Tournedos   center cut beef fillet
Tranche   slice
Truffes   truffles
Truite   trout
Vapeur   steamed
Veau   veal
Venaison   venison
Viande   meat
Vichyssoise   cold potato and leek soup
Vinaigre   vinegar
Vinaigrette   oil and vinegar dressing
Volaille   poultry
Vol-au-vent   puff pastry case with stuffing
Yaourt   yogurt

DAYS OF THE WEEK:

Lundi . . . . Monday
Mardi . . . . Tuesday
Mercredi . . . . Wednesday
Jeudi . . . . Thursday
Vendredi . . . . Friday
Samedi . . . . Saturday
Dimanche . . . . Sunday
Aujourd'hui . . . . Today
Demain . . . . Tomorrow

SEASONS:

Saison . . . . Season
Printemps . . . . Spring
Été . . . . Summer
Automne . . . . Autumn
Hiver . . . . Winter

complexity increases with price. The cheapest of these is often called the *menu touristique* and the most expensive the *menu gastronomique* or the *menu dégustation,* which is a sampling of small portions of the chef's best dishes. **A la carte**, on the other hand, means that each item is individually priced, affording a greater choice but usually costing quite a bit more. These items are listed on the *carte.*

The word **entrée** does not have the same meaning as in North America, rather it designates a course served between the appetizer *(hors d'oeuvre)* and the main course. **Meats** in France are not cooked as thoroughly as most Americans are accustomed to. If you want a steak well done *(bien cuit),* be sure to tell the waiter. **Coffee** is never consumed during a meal and its cost is not included in the *prix-fixe.* Wait until after the dessert, then enjoy a small cup of *café express,* a black brew as delicious as it is strong. **Water** may be drunk during the meal, with or without wine. You can order a mineral water *(eau minérale),* either sparkling *(gazeuse)* or still *(non-gazeuse)* for a small cost; or just plain tap water *(eau fraîche, une carafe d'eau),* which is free. A **salad**—frequently just lettuce with a dressing—is generally served after the main course, unless it is an appetizer such as *crudités.* A selection of **cheeses** *(plateau de fromage)* is almost always offered just before the dessert or as the dessert.

Menus and **cartes** are usually written in French only. While the waiter can often be of help, it is much better if you understand the names of various dishes. The simplified **Menu Translator** beginning on page 24 and the **Glossary of Dining Terms** on page 29 cover the most basic names and terms, while the more adventurous may want to use a pocket-sized translator book such as the *Marling Menu Master for France,* which will help you to try unfamiliar dishes without anxiety.

Tips are often included in the price of the meal *(service compris, s.c.,* or *prix net).* If not *(service non compris,* or *s.n.c.),* an amount—usually 15%—will be added to the bill *(l'addition).* The policy of the restaurant is noted on the *menu* or *carte,* although sometimes cryptically. Asking about this is perfectly proper and will offend no one. Leaving a small additional tip is an accepted way of saying "thank you" for good service.

One of the secrets to keeping your restaurant bills within reason is to order the **house wine** *(vin de maison)* rather than the more expensive choices. In any good restaurant the chef is proud of his cooking and selects the house wine as a complement to it, so you really can't go wrong. These wines, often served in an open pitcher *(carafe* or *pichet),* half-bottle *(demi-bouteille)* or whole bottle *(bouteille)* are usually available in red *(rouge),* white *(blanc),* or *rosé.*

Unless you are familiar with French vintages, it is best to consult

A GLOSSARY OF DINING TERMS

Meal   repas
Breakfast   petit déjeuner
Lunch   déjeuner
Dinner   dîner

Headwaiter   maître d'hôtel
Waiter   monsieur
Waitress   mademoiselle, madame
The menu, please   la carte, s'il vous plaît
Set meal menu   menu prix-fixe
Ordering items individually   à la carte
Today's special   plat du jour
Sampling of dishes or wines   dégustation
The wine list   la carte des vins
Another serving of . . . , please   encore un . . . , s'il vous plaît
The check, please   l'addition, s'il vous plaît
Drink included in price   boisson comprise
Cover charge   couvert
Tip included   service compris, s.c., prix net
Tip not included   service non compris, s.n.c.
Gratuity   pourboire

Plate   assiette
Knife   couteau
Fork   fourchette
Spoon   cuillère
Glass   verre
Cup   tasse
Napkin   serviette

Drink   boisson
Pre-dinner drink   apéritif
After-dinner drink   digestif

White wine   vin blanc
Red wine   vin rouge
Rosé wine   vin rosé
Half-bottle   demi-bouteille
Beer   bière
Draft beer   bière à la pression
Mineral water   eau minérale
Carbonated   gazeuse
Still   non-gazeuse
Tap water   eau fraîche, une carafe d'eau

Hot   chaud
Cold   froid
Very rare   bleu
Rare   saignant
Medium   à point
Well done   bien cuit
Sweet   doux
Dry   sec

Bread   pain
Butter   beurre
Salt   sel
Pepper   poivre
Mustard   moutarde
Oil   huile
Vinegar   vinaigre

Coffee   café
Small black coffee   café express
Coffee with cream   café crème
Breakfast coffee with milk   café au lait
Tea   thé
Lemon   citron
Chocolate   chocolat
Milk   lait
Sugar   sucre
Orange or tomato juice   jus d'orange / de tomate

the waiter before choosing a more complex wine. He has the experience to suggest the right wine for the meal you ordered. Nearly every
corner of France has its own type of wine, and most of these go very
well with the local cuisine. French **beers** can be quite good, especially
those from Alsace. Beers imported from nearby Germany, Belgium,
and Holland are also very popular.

Those in a hurry to get on with their sightseeing will find that there
are many low-cost alternatives to restaurant dining. These range from
the traditional *pique-nique* lunch made from ingredients purchased
at nearby markets to having a *croque-monsieur* or other sandwich at
a café; or whatever catches your eye in a self-service cafeteria (the
nation-wide *Flunch* chain is quite good) or even a French hamburger
and *crudités* at one of those ubiquitous fast-food outlets such as *Quick*
or *Free Time.*

If you are not completely famished but would still like a traditional
French meal, why not stop in at a *crêperie?* The specialties there include *galettes* (pancakes stuffed with meat, cheese, vegetables, or fish),
dessert *crêpes* and hard cider. These places are often quite atmospheric and very inexpensive. Pizzerias are also extremely popular with
the French.

SUGGESTED TOURS:

The do-it-yourself walking tours in this book are relatively short
and easy to follow. Walking is almost always the best way to explore
the old towns of France, and certainly the healthiest, although you
may want to use local transportation for the occasional steep hill or
long stretch. Details about this are mentioned whenever they might
apply. On the assumption that most readers will be arriving by public
transportation, the tours always begin at the local train station, bus or
Métro stop. Those going by car can make a simple adjustment. Suggested routes are shown by heavy broken lines on the maps, while
the circled numbers refer to major attractions or points of reference
along the way, with corresponding numbers in the text.

Trying to see everything in any given town could easily become an
exhausting marathon. You will certainly enjoy yourself more by being
selective and passing by anything that doesn't catch your fancy in favor of a friendly sidewalk café. God will forgive you if you don't visit
every church.

Practical information, such as the opening times of various attractions, is as accurate as was possible at the time of writing. Everything
is, of course, subject to change. You should always check with the
local tourist office if seeing a particular sight is crucially important to
you.

As a way of estimating the time any segment of the walking tour will take, you can look at the scale on the map and figure that the average person covers about 100 yards in one minute. The maps, by the way, were drawn to best fit the page size. North does not necessarily point to the top, but is always indicated by an arrow.

TOURIST INFORMATION:

Virtually every French town of any tourist interest has its own information office, usually called a *Syndicat d'Initiative* or *Office de Tourisme,* which can help you with specific questions, furnish maps and brochures, or book local accommodations. They almost invariably have at least one person on staff who speaks English. Sometimes these offices are closed on Sundays, holidays, or over the noon meal period.

The location of the offices is shown on the town maps in this book by the word "**info.**," and repeated along with the phone number under the "Tourist Information" section for each trip. To phone ahead from **Paris** to somewhere else in France, first dial 16, wait for a tone, then continue on with the complete 8-digit number. To phone from anywhere else in France to anywhere *except* Paris, just dial the 8-digit number. Phone calls to Paris from the rest of France are made by dialing 16, waiting for a tone, then continuing with the prefix 1 and the complete 8-digit Paris number. Calling ahead is useful if the whole reason for your daytrip hinges on seeing a particular sight that might possibly be closed, or perhaps to check the weather.

Many pay phones in France still use coins—just load up the slot with small denominations and any that are not used will be returned. The newer type of pilfer-proof pay phones accept no coins but are operated by inserting a *"Telecarte"* card, available in various denominations at any post office or from most *"Tabac"* shops. The cost of each call is electronically subtracted from the value of the card as it is used.

ADVANCE PLANNING INFORMATION:

The **French Government Tourist Office** has branches throughout the world that will gladly help you in planning your trip. In North America these are located at:

610 Fifth Ave. *(mail requests only)*

—or—

628 Fifth Ave. *(personal callers)*
New York, NY 10020
Phone (212) 757-1125

645 North Michigan Ave.,
Chicago, IL 60611
Phone (312) 337-6301

9454 Wilshire Blvd.,
Beverly Hills, CA 90212
Phone (213) 272-2661

1 Hallidie Plaza, Suite 250
San Francisco, CA 94102
Phone (415) 986-4161

103 World Trade Center
2050 Stemmons Freeway
P.O. Box 58610
Dallas, TX 75258
Phone (214) 742-7011

1981 Ave. McGill College, Suite 490
Montreal, P.Q. H3A 2W9
Phone (514) 288-4264

1 Dundas Street West
Suite 2405, Box 8
Toronto, Ont. M5G 1Z3
Phone (416) 593-4723

In England, they are at 178 Piccadilly, **London** WIV OAL, phone (01) 493-65-94.

COMMENTS:
We are always grateful for comments from readers, which are extremely helpful in preparing future editions of this or other books in the series. Please write directly to the author, Earl Steinbicker, c/o Hastings House, 141 Halstead Avenue, Mamaroneck, NY 10543

Paris

Paris is quite simply the most beautiful city on earth, and exploring it in depth could easily become a lifelong passion. Like most visitors, you probably don't have that much time available, but still want to see some of its best and most famous sights within a period of a few days. The five walking tours in this section are efficiently organized to provide a good overall impression of the city at a fairly leisurely pace by connecting the major attractions with routes that lead along some of the most interesting streets. Each tour is intended to last the better part of one day, depending on the amount of time you spend at stops along the way, having lunch, and just sitting at outdoor cafés or in parks. There is no need to rush—the actual walking time should never be much more than one hour.

Each tour begins where the previous one left off, which is always at a Métro (subway) station. Truly ambitious walkers could continue on and do part or all of the next tour. After completing the five routes you will have seen most of the main sights of Paris, but only begun to nibble at the visual feast it offers. To experience the best of what remains you should refer to the "Additional Attractions" chapter beginning on page 88.

GETTING AROUND:

The **Métro** (subway) is by far the fastest, easiest, and cheapest way of getting around Paris. For convenience, all of the walking tours described in the next five chapters begin and end at a Métro station. Wherever you are in Paris, you're never more than a few minutes from one of the 360 stations spread along 120 miles of tracks. The trains run frequently between about 5:30 a.m. and 12:30 the following morning. They are cleaner than you might expect in a large city, and plagued with very little actual crime other than occasional pickpockets. Hang onto your wallet.

Despite its complexity, the Métro is amazingly simple to use once you master a few basic rules. First, you must determine the name of the station closest to your destination, then trace a route on the subway map to it. Continue your tracing in the same direction to the end of the line *(ligne),* where you will see the name of its last station. This is the *direction* in which you should travel. The *lignes* also have numbers, but these are seldom referred to. It may be necessary to make a change *(correspondence)* of trains en route, in which case you should note the *direction* of the first line, the name of the station at which the change is made, and the *direction* of the second line. In a very few cases a second change may be needed.

All Métro stations have system-wide maps on their walls. In addition, major stations have electric maps where you press a button for your final destination and the best route automatically lights up. Some stations now have SITU computer terminals that give you a printout of the quickest route to your destination. A pocket-size map *(Plan de Métro)* of the system is available free at major stations.

Fares are the same regardless of the distance traveled, with a few exceptions for stations well out of town. You can save quite a bit of money by purchasing a pack of ten tickets, called a *carnet.* It is also possible to buy a **"Paris-Sésame" pass** valid for unlimited travel on the Métro, some RER lines, or city buses for 2, 4, or 7 consecutive days. These are sold upon presentation of your passport at major stations and RATP service booths. **RATP,** by the way, is the Paris Transit Authority. Tickets are available for both first- and second-class travel. The first *(première)*-class cars are in the center of the trains but are otherwise exactly the same as second-class cars. Between 6 p.m. and 9 a.m. the first-class cars may be used with second-class tickets. Other than being slightly less crowded between 9 a.m. and 6 p.m., there is no particular advantage to traveling first class.

The magnetically-encoded tickets operate electric turnstiles and are then returned to you. Be sure to retain them until the end of the trip as occasional spot checks are made. Once in the station, follow the *direction* signs to the proper platform. Changes of trains are made by following the orange *correspondence* signs, while the blue *sortie* signs lead to the exits.

The **RER** is a commuter rail service that runs as an express subway within Paris and continues on the surface to outlying towns such as Versailles, St. Germain-en-Laye, and both airports. Some of its lines are operated by the RATP and others by the SNCF (National Railroads). Métro tickets may be used for travel on RATP lines within the city limits of Paris, but otherwise a special ticket to your particular destination is needed, or you can use the Paris-Sésame pass. The SNCF lines accept regular railpasses, but you must get a free magnetized

The Eiffel Tower

ticket to operate the turnstile by showing your pass at the information counter. All RER trains carry both first- and second-class cars. Most of its stations have a direct connection to Métro stations.

Buses are a slow but picturesque way to get around Paris. They are operated by the RATP and use regular second-class Métro tickets—one for short distances and two for longer ones. If you're not sure about this just ask the driver. In either case they must be punched in the canceling machine near the entrance. Do not punch the ticket that comes with the *Paris-Sésame* pass as this invalidates it. Be sure to keep your ticket as you may have to show it to an inspector. A system map *(Plan d'Autobus)* is available free at major Métro station information booths, and a route diagram posted at each bus stop. In general, city buses operate between about 7 a.m. and 8:30 p.m., while some run later and a few continue all night long.

Taxis are a reasonable way of getting around Paris, especially if two or three people are traveling together. They usually do not cruise looking for passengers, but can be found parked at taxi ranks marked *Tête de Station* or *Arrêt Taxis*. Be aware that there are day (6:30 a.m. to 10 p.m.) and night fares plus additional charges for stopping at train stations or airports, and for excess luggage. For your own safety use metered cabs only. A tip of 15% is expected.

By car, in a word—don't. Driving (and parking!) in Paris is at best an experience to avoid.

WHEN TO GO:

Any time is a good time to visit Paris, but the city is probably at its best in late spring and early fall. Many Parisians take their lengthy vacations in July and August, leaving the streets to the tourists. Quite a few of the attractions are closed on Tuesdays, and others on Mondays. These are noted in the "When to Go" section for each walking tour.

FOOD AND DRINK:

A selection of good restaurants and cafés in different price categories has been included for each of the five Paris walking tours. All of these are on or near the suggested route. For a more comprehensive list covering more of Paris you should refer to one of the many published dining guides to the city.

TOURIST INFORMATION:

The main Paris tourist office is located at 127 Avenue des Champs-Élysées, phone 47-23-61-72. There are also branches at the Nord, Est, Lyon, and Austerlitz train stations. All of these offices can make last-minute hotel reservations for you if necessary, as well as provide information.

MONEY SAVER:

A new museum pass called **La Carte** is available at major museums and Métro stations. It allows unlimited visits with free admission to more than 60 museums and monuments in and around Paris, including the Louvre, the Orsay Museum, Versailles, and many others. One great advantage to this pass, besides saving money, is that you can usually avoid having to stand in line for admission. La Carte is available for periods of one, three, or five consecutive days.

Paris
The Left Bank

Nothing is more symbolic of Paris than the Eiffel Tower, so it seems appropriate to begin your walks with the classic view of it, perhaps ascending to the top for a sweeping panoramic survey of the city. The suggested tour described in this chapter continues on through the most interesting neighborhoods *(quartiers)* of the Left Bank *(Rive Gauche)* but stops short of the Latin Quarter, which is covered in the next chapter. Along the way you will be able to visit some of the greatest sights in Paris, including the Invalides, the Rodin and Orsay museums, the picturesque quays along the Seine, and the colorful St.-Germain-des-Prés district. The walk ends in a delightful area that is especially rich in outdoor cafés, where you can relax in the traditional Parisian fashion.

GETTING THERE:

The quickest way to get to the starting point of this walk from most parts of Paris is to take the **Métro** to Trocadéro. You can also reach it via **bus** routes 22, 30, 32, or 63. Buses 72 and 82 stop at the foot of the bridge opposite the Eiffel Tower. By **taxi**, ask the driver for Place du Trocadéro.

WHEN TO GO:

This walking tour can be taken on any day, but note that the popular new Orsay Museum is closed on Mondays, and the Rodin and Delacroix museums are closed on Tuesdays.

FOOD AND DRINK:

There is no shortage of restaurants and cafés along or near the suggested route, while you find a particularly good selection around Place St.-Germain-des-Prés. Some outstanding choices in all price categories are:

> **Bistrot de Paris** (33 Rue de Lille, behind the Orsay Museum) A very popular place with exceptional food and wines. X: Sat. lunch, Sun. $$$

Allard (41 Rue St.-André-des-Arts, 3 blocks west of Place St.-Michel) A longtime favorite of Parisians. Reservations needed, phone 43-26-48-23. X: Sat., Sun., Aug. $$$

Thoumieux (79 Rue St.-Dominique, 3 blocks northwest of the Invalides) Fine traditional cuisine in a turn-of-the-century atmosphere. $$

Brasserie Lipp (151 Blvd. St.-Germain, 1 block west of the Church of St.-Germain-des-Prés) A famous old café with an intellectual clientele. Alsatian specialties. X: early Aug. $$

Vagenende (142 Blvd. St.-Germain, 2 blocks east of Church of St.-Germain-des-Prés) Serving traditional cuisine in a Belle Époque setting since 1898. $$

Le Muniche (27 Rue de Buci, 2 blocks east of the Church of St.-Germain-des-Prés) Hearty eating in a bustling atmosphere. $$

Le Petit Zinc (25 Rue de Buci, 2 blocks east of the Church of St.-Germain-des-Prés) Old-fashioned home cooking. $$

Le Procope (13 Rue de l'Ancienne-Comédie, 5 blocks east of the Church of St.-Germain-des-Prés) A café since 1686, now a restaurant. X: Nov. $$

Restaurant des Beaux-Arts (11 Rue Bonaparte, by the Beaux-Arts school) Good food and very crowded. A great value. $

L'Assiette au Boeuf (22 Rue Guillaume-Apollinaire, 1 block northwest of the Church of St.-Germain-des-Prés) Steaks, salads, and the like. $

Le Petit Saint-Benoît (4 Rue Saint-Benoît, 2 blocks northwest of the Church of St.-Germain-des-Prés) A simple neighborhood bistro with low prices. X: Sat., Sun., Aug. $

Aux Charpentiers (10 Rue Mabillon, 2 blocks south of the Church of St.-Germain-des-Prés) This is what Left Bank bistros were like decades ago. X: Sun., holidays. $

SUGGESTED TOUR:

Begin your walking tour at the **Trocadéro Métro Station** (1). Next to this stands the massive **Palais de Chaillot**, a Neo-Classical structure left over from the Paris Exposition of 1937. Built in two symmetrically-curved wings, it now houses a theater and four museums that you might want to visit on another day. These are the **Naval Museum** *(Musée de la Marine)*, the **Museum of Mankind** *(Musée de l'Homme)*, the **Museum of French Monuments**, and the **Museum of the Cinema**.

Step out onto its central terrace for the most spectacular view of the Eiffel Tower possible, then continue straight ahead, going down steps past he gardens and fountains. The Pont d'Iéna, built by Napoleon in 1814 to commemorate a victory over the Prussians, spans the Seine and leads to the Left Bank.

Rising dramatically in front of you is the **Eiffel Tower** *(Tour Eiffel)* (2), all 1,051 feet of it. It may be hard to imagine Paris without its beloved symbol, but at first many leading Parisians didn't think so. In fact, there was a strong movement to have it torn down, and the tower was saved only after the French Army discovered its strategic use as a radio antenna, a function it still serves. When it was built for the World's Fair of 1889 it was the tallest structure on earth, and it retained that record for decades. The tower is named after its designer, Gustave Eiffel, a structural engineer who also built the inner framework of the Statue of Liberty in New York.

You can **ascend** the tower on any day between about 10 a.m. and 11 p.m. for a birds-eye view of Paris and the surrounding countryside, but expect long lines for the elevator during the tourist season. The truly energetic can save a few francs by climbing on foot as far as the second platform, and taking the elevator up from there. Actually, the view is better around sunset when the lights of Paris come on, so you might want to return here later in the day.

From the base of the tower a large open park called the **Champ-de-Mars**, originally a military parade ground, spreads southeast to the imposing **École Militaire**. Built in the 18th century, this famous military academy had among its graduates a young artillery lieutenant named Napoleon Bonaparte, who it predicted would "go far under favorable circumstances."

Napoleon, of course, did go far, but today he rests just around the corner at **Les Invalides** (3). Built by Louis XIV in the late 17th century as a retirement home for wounded war veterans, this monumental complex now houses several attractions. Along its southern end stands the **Church of the Dome**, an outstanding structure in the French Classical style designed by the most important architect of the time, Jules Hardouin-Mansart. Inside, in an open circular crypt, is a red porphyry sarcophagus containing the mortal remains of Napoleon. The great emperor is still deeply revered by the French people. Other notable soldiers buried here include Vauban and Marshal Foch. The Church of the Dome is open daily from 10 a.m. to 6 p.m., closing at 5 p.m. in winter, and the same ticket admits you to the two museums within the Invalides on this or the following day.

The most interesting of these is the **Museum of the Army**, one of the greatest military museums on earth. Part of it is on the east side of the inner courtyard and is devoted to the history of the French Army, while the section on the west side has a fine collection of medieval armor, weapons, and intriguing exhibits dealing with the two world wars of this century. The Museum of the Army is open daily from 10 a.m. to 6 p.m., closing at 5 p.m. from October through March. Connecting with it is the **Museum of Relief Maps**, which features superb

Paris
The Left Bank

M = Métro Station

1,000 Yards

scale models of French strongholds from 1668 to 1870.

Continue on through the complex and follow the map to one of the most enchanting sights in Paris, the **Rodin Museum** (4). Housed in a small 18th-century mansion called the Hôtel Biron and surrounded by delightful private gardens, the museum is devoted to the works of the renowned sculptor Auguste Rodin who worked here from 1908 until his death in 1917. Even if you don't care for museums, you'll probably love this place. The house contains his own works, personal collection, and furnishings; while scattered around the gardens are casts of such masterpieces as *The Thinker, Balzac,* the *Burghers of Calais,* and the fabulous *Gates of Hell.* Their strength and vitality is astonishing, especially in so marvelous a setting. Visits may be made on Wednesdays through Mondays, from 10 a.m. to 5:45 p.m., closing at 4:30 p.m. from October through June. It is closed on Tuesdays, and there is a café on the premises.

The route now leads through the elegant **Faubourg-Saint-Germain**, a district of gracious mansions presently occupied by government ministries and foreign embassies. Next to the river is the **Palais-Bourbon**, an 18th-century palace built by a daughter of Louis XIV and later embellished by Napoleon. Since 1827 it has housed the National Assembly (formerly called the Chamber of Deputies), the lower house of the French Parliament.

A right turn on Quai Anatole-France takes you along the Seine, passing the rather unusual *Piscine Deligny,* a floating swimming pool that has been here since 1842. Its water is advertised as being independent of the polluted river.

Just beyond the next bridge is the **Gare d'Orsay** (5), a former railroad station built around 1900. Alas, its platforms proved to be too short for express trains and after 1939 it fell into virtual disuse. There were plans to demolish the noble structure, but reason prevailed and it was recently converted into a museum.

Opened at the end of 1986 as the **Orsay Museum**, this is certainly one of the most popular attractions in Paris, despite a storm of controversy raised by critics. Covering the entire scope of art from 1848 to 1914, it bridges the immense gap between the Classical collections of the Louvre and the modern works in the Pompidou Center. Many of its Impressionist paintings are from the old Jeu de Paume Museum, but there is a great deal more than this. In addition to painting and sculpture, you will find sections on the decorative arts, photography, cinema, architecture, and town planning. Everything is linked chronologically with counterpart movements in literature, music, sociology, politics, and economics. This utterly fascinating museum is a must-see for any visitor to Paris, although you may prefer to return here when you can spend the amount of time it deserves. The Orsay Mu-

View from the Pont des Arts

seum is open on Tuesdays through Saturdays, from 10:30 a.m. to 6 p.m.; and on Sundays from 9 a.m. to 6 p.m. On Thursdays it remains open until 9:45 p.m. It is closed on Mondays. Expect crowds during the tourist season.

Continue along the quay, which becomes even more colorful as you approach the **Pont des Arts**, a charming iron footbridge across the Seine that was opened in 1803. It offers some of the best river views in the city. Just beyond it is the **Institut de France**, home of the venerable *Académie Française*, a prestigious body charged with protecting the purity of the French language. This is surely a hopeless task in the land of *le week-end* and *le hamburger*. Four other learned societies also meet beneath its majestic dome. Adjacent to it is the former Royal Mint, the **Hôtel des Monnaies** (6). This now houses the small **Museum of Coins and Medals**, which you can visit on Tuesdays through Saturdays, from 1–6 p.m.

From here the route gets a bit tricky, so you will have to follow the map carefully. It leads through some very old and colorful streets to the **School of Fine Arts** (*École des Beaux-Arts*) (7), founded in the early 19th century on the site of a former monastery. Although not generally open to the public, there are occasional exhibitions of works by the students that you might be able to see.

Turn left on Rue Bonaparte and left again on Rue Jacob, continuing on to the tiny **Place de Fürstemberg** . This is easily among the most charming and romantic small squares in Paris, with an atmosphere right out of the 17th century. On its west side is the house where the artist Eugène Delacroix lived and worked until his death in 1863. It has been preserved as he left it, and is now the **Delacroix Museum** (8), which may be visited on any day except Tuesdays and some holidays, from 9:45 a.m. to 12:30 p.m. and 2–5:15 p.m. Don't miss seeing this little gem.

A right turn into the quiet Rue de l'Abbaye brings you to **Place St.-Germain-des-Prés**, one of the main centers of activity on the Left Bank. This is a great place to sit down at an outdoor café and just watch the world go by, perhaps at the famous **Deux Magots** or the **Flore**. Facing the square is the 11th-century **Church of St.-Germain-des-Prés** (9), whose origins go back to the 6th century and which ranks as the oldest church in Paris. Originally this was part of an enormous Benedictine abbey whose 42,000 acres of land were surrounded by a defensive moat and extended all the way to the Seine. During the French Revolution the abbey was broken up and much of its church was vandalized. An unsatisfactory restoration in the 19th century didn't help matters, but the interior is still worth visiting for its interesting mixture of Romanesque, Gothic, and later styles.

Continue down the lively Boulevard St.-Germain. Many of the narrow streets leading off this thoroughfare in either direction are worth exploring if you have the time. When you get to the Odéon Métro stop, turn left into the well-hidden **Cour du Commerce St.-André**, a tiny alleyway lined with old shops. At number 9 there was a workshop where, it is said, in 1790 an inventor named Dr. Guillotin first tested his new beheading machine on some luckless sheep.

There is so much to see around here by just poking into the little passageways and following your instincts. When you tire of this, turn down the delightful Rue St.-André-des-Arts to its eastern end, where some nice outdoor cafés provide the perfect spot to relax at the end of this walk. From here it is only a few steps to the **St.-Michel Métro Station** (10), where you can get a subway or RER train back to your hotel. If you happen to be still bursting with energy, you might want to begin the next walk, described in the following chapter.

The Church of St.-Germain-des-Prés and the Deux-Magots Café

Paris

The Latin Quarter and the Cité

This walking tour takes you through the very oldest sections of Paris. The Latin Quarter, first settled by the Romans around the time of Christ, is on the Left Bank while the still more ancient Ile de la Cité, an island in the Seine, has been inhabited for well over 2,000 years. Although many changes have occurred during their long histories, the neighborhoods covered in this walk are still charged with a romantic atmosphere that is quite different from that of the rest of Paris. This is mostly due to the presence of the Sorbonne and other colleges, whose students bring a youthful vitality to a venerable district.

Some of the highlights passed along the suggested walking route include the Cluny Museum, the Luxembourg Gardens, the Panthéon, the Concieregerie, the Sainte-Chapelle, Notre-Dame Cathedral, and the Ile St.-Louis. Seeing all of them could take the better part of a day, but by skipping by a few you might be able to continue on and do part of the next tour, or at least have more time for relaxing at an outdoor café or in one of the gardens.

GETTING THERE:

The start of this walking tour may be easily reached by taking the **Métro** to Saint-Michel. It is also served by **bus** routes 21, 27, 38, 85, and 96. By **taxi**, ask the driver for Place St.-Michel.

WHEN TO GO:

This walk can be made on any day in good weather, although you should note that the Cluny Museum is closed on Tuesdays, and the Sainte-Chapelle on some holidays.

FOOD AND DRINK:

There is a wide choice of restaurants and cafés along the entire walking route, including:

In the Latin Quarter:

Dodin Bouffant (25 Rue Frédéric-Saoton, on the Left Bank, 2 blocks south of Notre-Dame) Renowned for its seafood. X: Sun., Aug. $$$

Auberge des Deux Signes (46 Rue Galande, by the Church of St.-Julien-le-Pauvre) Regional cuisine from the Auvergne with a light touch, in a medieval setting. X: Sun., Aug. $$$

Au Pactole (44 Blvd. St.-Germain, on the Left Bank, 3 blocks south of Notre-Dame) Known for its inventive cuisine. X: Sat. lunch, Sun. $$$

Polidor (41 Rue Monsieur-le-Prince, 1 block east of the Odéon Theater) Very famous for its old-fashioned cooking and Left Bank atmosphere. X: Sun., Mon., Aug. $$

Le Mange Tout (30 Rue Lacépède, 2 blocks east of Place de la Contrescarpe) Traditional country fare in a contemporary setting. X: Sun., Mon. lunch, Aug. $$

Le Jardin de la Mouffe (75 Rue Mouffetard, south of Place de la Contrescarpe) A country-style restaurant with a garden view. X: Sun., Mon. lunch. $$

Le Balzar (49 Rue des Ecoles, 4 blocks north of the Panthéon) A traditional Latin Quarter brasserie. X: Aug. $$

Chez Toutoune (5 Rue de Pontoise, on the Left Bank, 3 blocks southeast of Notre-Dame) Specializes in sophisticated Provençal cuisine. X: Sun., mid-Aug. to mid-Sept. $$

Auberge "In" (3 Rue des Ecoles, 5 blocks northeast of the Panthéon) Vegetarian food in a rustic setting. X: Sat. eve., Sun., Aug. $

Around the Cité:

Paul (15 Place Dauphine, near Square du Vert-Galant) An old-fashioned bistro on the Ile de la Cité. X: Mon., Tues., Aug. $$

Au Gourmet-de-l'Isle (42 Rue St.-Louis-en-l'Ile, on the Ile St.-Louis) Country cooking in a traditional ambiance. X: Mon., Tues., $$

Le Trumilou (84 Quai de l'Hôtel-de-Ville, on the Right Bank, 4 blocks northeast of Notre-Dame) An unpretentious bistro with huge servings of home cooking. X: Mon. $

For a special treat, don't miss the **Berthillon** ice cream shop at 31 Rue St.-Louis-en-l'Ile on the Ile St.-Louis.

SUGGESTED TOUR:

This walking tour begins where the previous one left off, at **Place St.-Michel** (1). Carved out of a medieval warren of tiny alleyways in the 19th century, the large and highly animated square is embellished with a huge fountain at its southern end. From here, the **Boulevard St.-Michel**, popularly known as the *Boul' Mich,* leads into the heart of the Latin Quarter. That term derives from the language spoken by early scholars, not from the fact that this was once the Roman town of *Lutetia.*

Very little remains of the Roman era, but some sections of its 2nd-century baths can be seen within the **Cluny Museum** (2), which incorporates parts of the ancient ruins. Actually, bits of this are visible from the street, but a visit to the museum is highly worthwhile for its stunning collection of medieval art and treasures. The present structure was built in the 15th century as a town mansion, or *hôtel,* for the abbots of Cluny, who frequently traveled to Paris to visit their college. Today it is regarded as one of the finest examples of late medieval domestic architecture in France. Parts of the museum spill over into the adjacent **Roman Baths** *(Thermes),* some of which is still in good condition. Among the many treasures on display is a remarkable series of 15th-century **tapestries** called the *Lady and the Unicorn,* thought to symbolize the five senses and mastery of them. Also not to be missed is the **Chapel** with its superb Gothic decorations. The Cluny Museum is open daily except on Tuesdays, from 9:45 a.m. to 12:30 p.m. and 2–5:15 p.m. Enter through a small courtyard on the side street.

Now cross Boulevard St.-Michel and stroll down Rue Racine to the **National Theater of the Odéon** (3), built in 1782 as a suitable home for the French Comedians. After the Revolution this theatrical group moved to the Right Bank and the present theater, rebuilt after a fire in 1807, was used for drama—a role it continues today.

Continue on, following the map, to the **Church of St.-Sulpice** (4). Begun in 1646 on the site of earlier churches, it acquired its present monumental façade in 1766. The church is famous for its organ concerts, and its interior has some noted murals by Delacroix in the first chapel on the right. A metal strip embedded in the floor of the transept runs due north and south, marking the equinoxes and solstices as the sun strikes different points. The Lady Chapel has an excellent statue of the *Virgin and Child* by Jean-Baptiste Pigalle, and there are two rather enormous holy-water stoups from Venice.

Exit into the attractive Place St.-Sulpice and follow around to the **Luxembourg Gardens** (5), an utterly delightful park where children sail toy boats on the pond and watch puppet shows in a little theater near the southwest corner. All over the park are scattered countless statues of prominent French men and women, while the **Medici Foun-**

In the Luxembourg Gardens

tain near the northeast corner attracts lovers and stollers alike. The **Luxembourg Palace** at the north end was built in the early 17th century for Marie de Medici, widow of Henri IV. She disliked living in the Louvre and had this grandiose mansion designed in the style of the Pitti Palace in Florence to remind her of home. Used as a prison during the Revolution, it is now the seat of the Senate, the upper house of the French parliament.

Leave the park and follow Rue Soufflot to the **Panthéon** (6), where many of France's heroes are entombed. Begun as a church by Louis XV in fulfillment of a vow, the monumental structure alternated back and forth between religious and secular uses, but in 1885 it was permanently taken over by the State as a final resting place for the remains of Victor Hugo. Other notables interred in its crypt include Emile Zola, Voltaire, and Rousseau. You can visit them on a guided tour and also examine the marvelous 19th-century frescoes depicting mythical scenes from the early history of Paris, these on the main floor. Be warned in advance, however, that all-in-all, it's a pretty gloomy experience. The Panthéon is open daily from 10 a.m. to noon and 2–5 p.m. Just north of it is the **Sorbonne**, one of the oldest and most famous universities in Europe.

Continue on past the fascinating **Church of St.-Étienne-du-Mont** (7), a 16th-century structure in a wild variety of styles whose interior is enlivened with a strange rood screen, the only one left in Paris; and

Paris
The Latin Quarter
and the Cité

M = Métro Station

500 Yards

with some exquisite stained-glass windows in the apse. A right turn on Rue Descartes leads to **Place de la Contrescarpe** (8). This pleasantly seedy little square was famous in the Middle Ages for its rowdy character, and still preserves the somewhat rustic ambiance of the old Latin Quarter in years gone by. The Rue Mouffetard, leading south from it, is a lively place noted for its eclectic selection of good cheap restaurants.

From here you might want to make a short side trip to one of Paris' lesser-known sights, the **Arènes de Lutéce** (9). Located in a tranquil public park, this partially-restored Gallo-Roman amphitheater probably dates from about A.D. 200 and once provided some 15,000 spectators with typical Roman entertainments. It was destroyed by the Barbarians around 280 and lay buried until being rediscovered in 1869 during construction of the adjacent Rue Monge. Now used mostly by local residents for quiet games of *boules,* it makes a lovely resting place away from the hubbub of the city.

The route now leads downhill towards the Seine, passing through the attractive Place Maubert before continuing down the narrow Rue de Bièvre to the river. Stroll partly across the bridge for the classic rear view of Notre-Dame Cathedral, then follow the map to the **Church of St.-Julien-le-Pauvre** (10). The aura of medieval Paris hangs heavy in this utterly delightful neighborhood, and the simple church seems transplanted from a distant time and place. The present structure dates from the 12th century although there were previous churches on the site as far back as the 6th century. Since 1889 it has belonged to the Melchite (Greek Catholic) faith. Step inside for a look at the unusual choir screen with its icons, and the beautifully carved pillar capitals. The garden next to the church, Square René Viviani, offers a remarkable view of Notre-Dame.

In just a few steps you will come to another great medieval church, that of **St.-Séverin** (11). Built in the 13th century and later enlarged, it has an unusual interior layout featuring a double ambulatory filled with a veritable thicket of elegant columns. The stained-glass windows, some from the 15th century, are particularly fine and make a wonderful setting for the musical concerts that are frequently given here.

Return to nearby **Place St.-Michel** (1), the starting point of this walk, where you might want to take a break at one of the many attractive outdoor cafés. Now cross the bridge over the Seine to the **Ile de la Cité**, an island where Paris began in the 3rd century B.C. as a settlement of the Parisii tribe—a defensive place well protected against marauding tribes. During the Middle Ages it was a densely packed warren of little alleyways holding a population of some 25,000 along with the Royal Palace and the Cathedral of Notre-Dame. A massive rebuild-

Notre-Dame Cathedral from the Seine

ing program in the late 19th century has left it what it is today; primarily the home of several government agencies spread between broad streets and open squares.

Turn left along the Quai des Orfèvres to the **Pont Neuf** which, despite its name (meaning "new"), is the oldest existing bridge in Paris. Completely spanning both arms of the Seine, it was opened in 1607 and appears today much as it did then. Although the colorful vendors, entertainers, and pickpockets who once lined its sidewalks are gone, it is still one of the most interesting and possibly the most beautiful of the 33 bridges that span the Seine within Paris.

A flight of steps behind the equestrian statue of Henri IV descends to the delightful **Square du Vert-Galant** (12), a green spit of land jutting out into the river. Named in honor of France's most beloved king, Henri IV, it is among the nicest places in Paris for relaxing and taking in the riverside view. Don't miss this special treat.

Return to the bridge level and amble into Place Dauphine, which still retains a touch of its quiet 17th-century charm. Continue around on the Quai de l'Horloge to the dreaded **Conciergerie** (13), where thousands of unlucky souls spent their last hours before going to the guillotine during the Revolution. Dating in part from the early 14th century and originally a section of the former royal palace, it is now incorporated into the massive Palais de Justice (Law Courts) complex. You can visit the impressive Salle des Gens d'Armes, the dungeons, the cell of Queen Marie Antoinette (who lost her head on October 16, 1793), and the Girondin's Chapel—now a small museum displaying a rather unsharp guillotine blade and similar Revolutionary memorabilia. All of this can be seen daily from 9:30 a.m. to 7 p.m.; closing at 5 p.m. from October through March. What is perhaps best about this chilling place is that you can emerge from it a free person.

Turn right on Boulevard du Palais and right again into the courtyard of the **Palais du Justice.** This labyrinth of buildings evolved from the former medieval royal palace and still includes quite a few parts of it. While it is perfectly possible to visit the courts on weekdays from 9 a.m. to 6 p.m. and perhaps sit in on a public trial, the main attraction of the complex is the **Sainte-Chapelle** (14), reached through a passageway to the left. Built in the mid-13th century by the Crusader King Louis IX (popularly known as St. Louis), this exquisite church is one of the most sparkling gems of Paris and should not be missed. Its Lower Chapel, used by commoners, is impressive enough, but the nobility's Upper Chapel is the supreme embodiment of what Gothic was all about. It was here that the supposed Crown of Thorns and relics of the True Cross, purchased by St. Louis from the rulers of the East, were kept in a setting that seems to consist solely of gorgeous stained glass, glowing like the inside of a fine jewel. The precious relics are now in Notre-Dame Cathedral as the brilliantly restored Sainte-Chapelle is seldom used for religious ceremonies. Visits may be made daily from 10 a.m. to 6 p.m.; closing at 5 p.m. from October through March, and closed on major holidays.

Little of the island's former charm seems to have escaped the urban renewal schemes of the last century, but one spot that is still a joy for the eye is **Place Louis Lépine** (15), where the picturesque **Flower Market** is held daily all year round, except that on Sundays the posies are replaced with a chirping bird market.

Stroll over to the nearby **Place du Parvis** (16), a large open area in front of Notre-Dame Cathedral. Until the mid-19th century this neighborhood was crowded with small buildings and narrow lanes, leaving only a tiny square in front of the cathedral—an entirely different view than the one you have today. Much of ancient and medieval Paris still lies buried beneath this, and was rediscovered during construction of an underground parking garage. Since 1980 the subterranean ruins have been open to the public as the **Crypte Archéologique**, entered from the west end of the square. You can walk among the Gallo-Roman remains, ancient ramparts, and cellars from the Middle Ages, all dramatically lit and explained in English. This superb and imaginative trip into the forgotten past can be made on Mondays through Saturdays, from 10 a.m. to 6 p.m.; and on Sundays from 2–6 p.m. A bronze plaque on the square above it marks the "kilomètre zéro," the point from which all distances in France are measured.

Man has worshipped on the site of **Notre-Dame Cathedral** (17) since pagan times, with Celtic gods followed by Roman deities, then by a succession of Christian churches. The present Gothic structure was begun in 1163 and not really completed until the mid-14th century. It is the most important church in France, long used as the setting for many of the major ceremonies that have punctuated the nation's history. Tourists flock here by the thousands, but their presence does not seriously detract from the splendor of the building or its setting.

Notre-Dame was not always held in such high regard. During the Renaissance the Gothic style had fallen out of favor and disastrous alterations were made to "improve" the cathedral. With the Revolution of the late 18th century it was thoroughly ransacked and turned first into a "Temple of Reason," with a resident goddess, and then allowed to decay. When Napoleon crowned himself emperor here in 1804 the walls had to be covered with tapestries to disguise their dilapidated condition. Ironically, Notre-Dame's salvation came principally from the writings of a professed atheist, the author Victor Hugo, whose novel *The Hunchback of Notre Dame* focused public attention on the glory that was fast falling into ruin. Feeling compelled to act, the government in 1841 entrusted a complete restoration to the noted architect Viollet-le-Duc, who spent the next 23 years directing a splendid rehabilitation. He has often been criticized for going too far, but the cathedral today looks very much as it did in medieval drawings.

Notre-Dame's front **façade** is a triumph of the early Gothic style, despite the two somewhat squat towers. It must be remembered that the cathedral was intended to be seen from the small square then in front of it, not from the vast open area of today—which gives a very different perspective. A better view will be had from the rear or from across the Seine, where the majestic **flying buttresses**—those slender supports that transfer weight away from the walls, thus allowing greater window space—add so much to the cathedral's beauty.

Three elegant **doorways** grace the front façade. From left to right, these are known as the portals of the Virgin, of the Last Judgement, and of St. Anne. They are elaborately decorated with appropriate carvings, which were once painted in brilliant colors against a gilt background. Some of these are modern replacements as many of the originals were mutilated during the Revolution. Above them is the **Kings' Gallery**, a row of 28 statues of the kings of Judea, destroyed in 1793 when a mob mistook them for the hated kings of France. They were reconstructed later in the 19th century. The **Rose Window**, over 30 feet in diameter, is centered between this and the **Great Gallery**, richly festooned with fantastic gargoyles of various demons.

The **interior** of Notre-Dame is enormous, easily accommodating a crowd of 9,000, and served as the prototype for all of the major Gothic cathedrals. Most of the stained-glass windows are modern replacements, executed according to medieval techniques, although there is original 13th-century glass in the rose window of the north transept, said to be a gift from St. Louis. To the right of the center of the transept, just before the chancel, is a marvelous 14th-century statue of the *Virgin and Child,* which fortunately was in another church when the revolutionary mobs attacked. More violence occurred on August 26, 1944 during the Liberation *Te Deum* service, when the Germans opened fire on a congregation that included General De Gaulle, who refused to duck and remained unhurt.

A doorway along the south ambulatory leads to the **Treasury**, whose precious objects including what is believed to be a fragment of the True Cross are on display on Mondays through Saturdays, from 9 a.m. to 6 p.m.; and on Sundays from 2–6 p.m.

You may want to round out your visit to Notre-Dame by climbing the **Towers** for a close look at the gargoyles and for a splendid low-level view of medieval Paris. Ascents—on foot—begin from the outside of the north tower and continue across the open west gallery, then climb the south tower to see the great 13-ton bell reserved for solemn occasions. Along the way there is a small museum of the cathedral's history. Climbs may usually be made daily, from 10 a.m. to 5 p.m.

If Notre-Dame has whetted your appetite for French Gothic cathedrals, there are several others that can be seen on the daytrips described in other sections of this book. Those generally regarded as being the most beautiful in the country are at Chartres, Amiens, Reims, and Bourges.

Walk around to Square Jean XXIII, a lovely garden with an unsurpassed view of the east end of Notre-Dame. Just behind this, at the tip of the island, steps lead down to the touching **Deportation Memorial** (18), an underground crypt built in remembrance of the 200,000 French victims of Nazi concentration camps.

You have now seen all of the major sights along this walking tour. By continuing on to the Métro station at Sully-Morland, however, you will discover one of the most delightful areas in Paris, the **Ile St.-Louis** (19). Happily, there are several attractive outdoor cafés and restaurants there, along with the best ice cream shop in France (Berthillon, at 31 Rue St.-Louis-en-l'Ile).

Trailing right behind the Ile de la Cité, the Ile St.-Louis has a completely different atmosphere. Created in the mid-17th century by joining together two smaller islands, it has always been a residential area where many of France's leading citizens such as Voltaire, Jean-Jacques Rousseau, Baudelaire, Cézanne and, more recently, Georges Pompi-

On the Ile St.-Louis

dou, lived in quiet understated elegance. A number of foreigners, especially writers, continue to call it home.

Cross over to the island via the Pont St. Louis, a pedestrian span that has recently been reconstructed, and follow the lovely Quai d'Orléans along the river's edge. There are no particular sights to see, but the route on the map takes you through some of the most interesting streets. When you reach the park at its eastern end, turn left onto the Pont de Sully and cross it to the **Sully-Morland Métro Station** (20). This is the end of this walking tour and the beginning of the next—which you will probably want to save for another day.

Paris

From the Bastille to the Opéra

You'll find an exceptionally broad range of fascinating sights along the route of this walking tour, which covers the oldest and most historically interesting *quartiers* of the Right Bank *(River Droite)*. Beginning near the site of the Bastille, it meanders through the marvelously picturesque Marais district, then follows colorful old streets to the stunningly modern Pompidou Center and the up-to-the minute Forum des Halles. It then continues on past the Louvre, the Palais Royal, the delightful Tuileries Gardens, the fashionable streets around Place Vendôme, and ends up at the Opéra, in the center of a smart shopping area.

Along the way you will have to chance to see some of the most exciting museums in Paris, most of which are located in historic buildings. Which of these you actually stop at will depend on your particular interests and the amount of time available, although you should really save the Louvre for later as even a cursory visit there requires the better part of a day.

GETTING THERE:

Those continuing on from the previous walking tour will begin at the Sully-Morland Métro Station, from which a short stroll up the Boulevard Henri IV leads to the real start of this route, Place de la Bastille. If you're coming from another part of town, just take the **Métro** directly to Bastille. This is also served by **bus** routes 20, 29, 65, 69, 76, 86, 87, and 91. By **taxi**, ask the driver for Place de la Bastille.

WHEN TO GO:

This walk can be enjoyed on any fine day, but note that the Victor Hugo and Carnavalet museums are closed on Mondays and some holidays, while the Picasso Museum, Pompidou Center, the Louvre, and some of the smaller museums are closed on Tuesdays and a few holidays.

FOOD AND DRINK:

You will pass a very broad selection of restaurants and cafés along nearly all of this walking route, including:

In the Marais:

    L'Ambroisie (9 Place des Vosges) Superb dining in quiet elegance, reservations needed, phone 42-78-51-45. X: Sun., Mon. lunch, Aug. $$$+

    Bofinger (5 Rue de la Bastille, 1 block west of Place de la Bastille) A beautiful turn-of-the-century brasserie with Alsatian specialties. $$

    Jo Goldenberg's (7 Rue des Rosiers, 3 blocks southeast of the Carnavalet Museum) A favorite place for Jewish deli food since 1920. $$

From Pompidou Center to Forum des Halles:

    Ambassade d'Auvergne (22 Rue du Grenier St.-Lazare, 2 blocks north of Pompidou Center) Hearty dishes from the Auvergne in rustic surroundings. $$$

    Monsieur Boeuf (31 Rue St.-Denis, between Pompidou Center and Forum des Halles) Renowned for its beef. $$

    Au Pied de Cochon (6 Rue Coquillière, just west of St.-Eustache church) A landmark restaurant from the glory days of Les Halles. $$

    Pavillon Baltard (9 Rue Coquillère, just west of St.-Eustache church) Traditional Alsatian and other hearty dishes. $$

From the Louvre to the Opéra:

    Pierre Traiteur (10 Rue de Richelieu, just west of the Palais Royal) Excellent home cooking of the Auvergne. X: Sat., Sun., holidays, Aug. $$$

    Hubert (25 Rue de Richelieu, 2 blocks west of the Palais Royal) Sophisticated nouvelle cuisine. X: Sat. lunch, Sun. $$$

    La Barrière Poquelin (17 Rue Moliere, 2 blocks west of the Palais Royal) Nouvelle cuisine in a bistro setting. X: Sat. lunch, Sun., early Aug. $$

    Le Soufflé (36 Rue du Mont-Thabor, 2 blocks south of Place Vendôme) Featuring a wide variety of soufflés. X: Sun., holidays. $$

    Le Grand Café (4 Blvd. des Capucines, 1 block southeast of the Opéra) Classic French cuisine in a grand old brasserie. $$

    André Faure (40 Rue du Mont-Thabor, 2 blocks south of Place Vendôme) Country-style cooking at bargain prices. X: Sun. $

    L'Incroyable (26 Rue de Richelieu, 1 block west of the Palais Royal) A tiny old-fashioned restaurant hidden in a narrow passageway, great value. X: Sat. eve., Sun., Mon. eve. $

Those in a hurry to get on with the walk may want to refuel at one of the many familiar fast-food outlets around Pompidou Center and Forum des Halles.

SUGGESTED TOUR:

If you are continuing on from the previous tour you should take a short walk up Boulevard Henri IV to the start of this walk, **Place de la Bastille** (1). Otherwise, you can get there directly by Métro, bus or taxi. Virtually nothing remains of the former **Bastille**, a 14th-century fortification that was long used as a royal prison, reserved principally for high-ranking citizens who had incurred the king's displeasure. These included such notables as Mirabeau, Voltaire (who was twice a guest), the mysterious "Man in the Iron Mask," and the notorious Marquis de Sade. The name "Bastille" gained its place in history on July 14, 1789, when a rioting mob stormed it in the mistaken belief that weapons were stored there. Finding none, they freed the seven remaining prisoners and created a political symbol that fueled the French Revolution.

Actually, if the king's bureaucracy had not been so slow there would have been no Bastille to storm, as Louis XVI had already approved plans to tear it down as an economy measure. Just a few months after the attack it was completely demolished to prevent it from falling into the hands of Revolutionary splinter groups. Today, its ground plan is marked out by paving stones in the square, which continues to be a rallying point for political demonstrations. The **July Column** in its center commemorates not the French Revolution, but the Parisians killed in the riots of July, 1830.

The area around the Bastille has long been a rough neighborhood, succumbing recently to gradual gentrification with a boating marina at the south end of the Canal St.-Martin and a controversial new opera house, the **Opéra de la Bastille**, recently opened to a storm of criticism.

From here the route leads into the enchanting **Marais** district, once a marsh (hence the name), then an elegant residential zone, eventually nearly a slum, and now a restored—and very fashionable—bit of old Paris. In the 13th century the swamp was drained and members of the wealthier classes began building their impressive town houses (hôtels) there as a way of escaping the crowded conditions on the Ile de la Cité. Reaching a climax of urban civilization during the 17th century, it gradually declined as society moved into the new suburbs to the west. The Revolution brought the final blow and the once-lovely houses fell into a state of dilapidation. Threatened by bulldozer redevelopment after World War II, the historical neighborhood of ancient houses and narrow streets was saved by preservation laws in the

The Place des Vosges

1960s and is now among the most desirable residential areas in Paris, with an interesting and highly varied population.

Continue down Rue St.-Antoine and turn right into Rue de Birague, which opens through a passage into the incomparable **Place des Vosges** (2). Begun in 1605 by Henri IV as a set of town houses for himself and his aristocracy, it is the oldest intact square in Paris, and arguably the most beautiful. Alas, he was assassinated before its completion in 1612 and, in fact, no king ever lived there. Despite this, its original name was Place Royale, which was changed in 1800 in honor of the first *département* of France to pay its Revolutionary taxes.

All of the houses have street-level arcades, behind which lurk shops, restaurants, cafés and the like. Victor Hugo lived upstairs at number 6 from 1833 to 1848, and his apartment is now the **Victor Hugo Museum**, where you can examine his numerous drawings, homemade furniture, and various memorabilia of the great author. It is open on Tuesdays through Sundays, from 10 a.m. to 5:40 p.m.

Leave the square via Rue des Francs-Bourgeois and turn right on Rue de Sévigné. The **Carnavalet Museum** (3) is housed in a much-altered 16th-century *hôtel* that was the home of the witty hostess Madame de Sévigné from 1677 to 1696. The magnificent displays here cover the entire history of Paris from the Renaissance to the early 20th century. Far from being stuffy, the museum is alive with fascinating

mementos of everyday life in a bygone age, including shop and tavern signs, models of the Bastille and the guillotine, Revolutionary propaganda, period furniture and room settings, and enough other items to keep you entranced for at least an hour. Don't miss it. The museum is open daily except on Mondays and major holidays, from 10 a.m. to 5:30 p.m.

Now follow the map to the 17th-century **Hôtel Salé** (4), which since 1985 has been home to the extremely popular **Picasso Museum** . When Pablo Picasso died in 1973 he left behind an enormous collection of paintings, sculptures, ceramics, drawings, graphics and the like covering all of the periods of his extraordinary career. A large selection of these were given to the French government in lieu of estate taxes, along with his private collection of works by other modern artists such as Cézanne, Renoir, Rousseau, Matisse, Braque and so on. All of these can be seen in a magnificent setting with explanations in English and an audio-visual introductory show. There is also a good, inexpensive cafeteria. The museum is open on Wednesdays through Mondays, from 9:45 a.m. to 5:30 p.m.; remaining open until 10 p.m. on Wednesday evenings. It is closed on Tuesdays.

There are two rather specialized museums nearby that might be of interest to you. One of these, the **National Archives** (5), with its entrance at 60 Rue des Francs-Bourgeois, contains the **Historical Museum of France**. Among the documents on display here are such treasures as the Edict of Nantes, the wills of Louis XIV and Napoleon, and a letter from Joan of Arc. They can be seen on Wednesdays through Mondays, from 2–5 p.m.; but not on holidays. Close to this, at 60 Rue des Archives, is the splendid 17th-century **Hôtel Guénégaud** (6), home of the **Museum of Hunting** (Musée de la Chasse et de la Nature). This well-restored mansion is worth a visit in itself, and as a bonus you get to see a superb collection of hunting weapons, paintings of the hunt by famous artists, stuffed animals, and much more. It is open daily except on Tuesdays and holidays, from 10 a.m. to 12:30 p.m. and 1:30–5:30 p.m.

The route now leads through an increasingly modernized area and turns south to the incredible **Pompidou Center** (Centre National d'Art et de Culture Georges Pompidou) (7), often referred to as **Beaubourg** after the neighborhood it dominates. And dominate it certainly does. As a cultural institution this is pure theater, aimed at the widest possible audience. Everyone in Paris comes here to gawk at the immense structure of dazzling colors that looks more like an oil refinery than anything else, what with its inside-out construction of steel rods, ventilator shafts, pipes, and a huge plastic tube carrying escalators. Opened in 1977 to a storm of controversy, it has become one of the most popular attractions in Paris. The wide sloping piazza in front of the center

Pompidou Center

is at least as much fun as the building itself, and is filled with pedestrians enjoying the antics of street musicians, mimes, jugglers, fire-eaters, acrobats and other struggling entertainers—along with the usual pickpockets.

Pompidou Center contains a variety of cultural institutions, the most important of which is the **National Museum of Modern Art**, installed on the third and fourth floors and reached by the external escalator. By putting all of the building's functional parts on the outside, an enormous clutter-free internal environment has been created, one that is ideal for the needs of changing art exhibitions. The museum's collections, frequently rearranged, cover the entire scope of modern art right up to the present day. Nearly all of the famous names are represented including a great many foreigners, especially Americans. All in all, a visit here is a delightful experience even if you have little interest in art.

Other parts of Pompidou Center are devoted to the **Public Information Library** with its more than one million books, photos, records, video tapes, periodicals and other documents; the **Industrial Creation Center** with exhibitions on contemporary design; and the **Cinémathèque**, which shows interesting films. Just outside the main building is the **Atelier Brancusi**, where works by the Romanian sculptor Constantin Brancusi are displayed in a reconstruction of his Paris stu-

Place Igor Stravinsky

dio. **IRCAM**, an organization for contemporary music, is located underground and is open for concerts only. Be sure to ride the escalator to the top of Pompidou Center for a stunning **view of Paris** and perhaps a drink or a bite to eat at the cafeteria. The center is open daily except on Tuesdays and a few major holidays, from noon until 10 p.m. On Saturdays and Sundays the hours are from 10 a.m. to 10 p.m.

Opening off the south end of Pompidou Center is a marvelous little square called **Place Igor Stravinsky**, where amusing mobile fountains by Jean Tinguely and Niki de St.-Phalle dance out the composer's creations. Getting too close to these can result in an unexpected shower, but you can always dry off at one of the outdoor cafés under the adjacent trees. Facing the south end of this is the 16th-century **Church of St.-Merri** (8), curiously built in the Flamboyant Gothic style at a time when the Renaissance was all the rage. Its interior, opening on Rue St.-Martin, is especially attractive with its 17th-century organ loft, 16th-century stained-glass windows, and a bell dating from 1331.

Now follow the map to the **Forum des Halles** (9), a neat solution to an unwanted hole in the ground. As the name suggests, this was the site of the late, lamented Les Halles—fondly remembered by all who knew Paris prior to 1969. The "Belly of Paris," as the area was then called, once throbbed with late-night activity as a wholesale food market, where fashionable people came for a bowl of onion soup after a night on the town. Alas, the markets are now located near Orly Airport and the charming 19th-century iron-and-glass pavilions are long gone. In their place a gigantic, deeply underground transportation center for RER commuter trains and the Métro was built, above which was The Hole *(Le Trou)*. Instead of filling this in, an amazing shopping center descends in levels around a sunken courtyard, bringing light, air, and outdoor cafés to the lower depths. Hundreds of shops, theaters, and restaurants operate in a futuristic environment, providing a delightful ambiance for commercial activities.

While there, you might want to visit the **Holographic Museum**, where strange three-dimensional moving images are created by lasers. Located on Level *(niveau)* -1, it is open on Mondays through Saturdays from 10 a.m. to 7 p.m.; and on Sundays from 1–7 p.m. On the same level is a branch of the famous **Grévin Waxworks Museum**, the Madame Tussaud's of France, which re-creates street scenes in Paris at the turn of the century.

Take only a few steps from the Forum and you are back in the past at the **Church of St.-Eustache** (10). Second in size only to Notre-Dame Cathedral among the churches of Paris, it was built between the 16th and 17th centuries and has a curious combination of Gothic form overlaid with Classical detailing. This was the parish church of the rich food merchants of *Les Halles,* whose immense wealth is evident throughout the entire majestic structure and particularly in its luxurious decoration. The proximity of St.-Eustache to the Louvre made it a favorite among the aristocracy. Louis XIV took his first communion here while still a child; Richelieu, Molière, and Madame de Pompador were baptized here; and this was the setting for the funerals of Mirabeau, Rameau, and La Fontaine. Among the outstanding works of art is an early Rubens painting of the *Pilgrims at Emmaus,* a sculpture of the *Virgin* by Pigalle, and the tomb of Colbert by Le Brun—all near the northeast end. Note also the marvelous 17th-century stained-glass windows in the choir.

Amble through the gardens behind the Forum des Halles and follow Rue du Pont-Neuf down to the Seine. A short walk along the river brings you to the Louvre, whose enormous bulk totally dominates the neighborhood. Before examining it in more detail, however, it is best to continue on to the nearby **Palais Royal** (11). Built in 1634 by Cardinal Richelieu as his own palace, it was willed to Louis XIII, whose widow and young son, the future Louis XIV, lived there for a few years after the king's death in 1643, thus making it a royal palace. After that it was given to Louis XIV's brother and passed into the Orléans family, who added the apartment houses and shopping arcades around its park.

In the late 18th century the entire complex became notorious as a center for Revolutionary activities and later as a den for gambling and prostitution. Cleaned up after the Restoration, the palace itself is now used as government offices and cannot be visited, but its often-overlooked **gardens** are a delightful little corner of Paris that should not be missed. Enter via a passageway on Rue de Valois and take a stroll through this enclave of tranquillity, then exit through more passageways onto Rue de Richelieu and turn left. At the intersection of Avenue de l'Opéra and Rue St.-Honoré stands the famous **Comédie-Française**, a 19th-century theater where French classical plays are still performed along with modern works.

Continue straight ahead and enter into the Louvre complex on Rue de Rivoli. Most of this former royal palace—the largest in Europe—is occupied by the world-renowned **Louvre Museum** *(Musée du Louvre)* (12), established in 1793. Although they may appear to have a certain sense of unity, the various sections of the palace actually evolved over many centuries, beginning in 1202 as a fortress inside what is now the Square Court *(Cour Carrée)* at the eastern end. Parts of this have been recently excavated and form a new underground archaeological display on the history of the Louvre. The defensive bastion was converted into a palace during the 14th century by Charles V, the first king to reside in the Louvre. His successors disliked the place and avoided it (and Paris!), until François I began a reconstruction in the 16th century. Since then it has continued to grow as various kings and emperors added their own wings, while changing the look of the older ones.

The latest—and most controversial—appendage was begun on the initiative of President Mitterand and opened in 1989 as the new **main entrance**. Externally, this is in the form of a giant **glass pyramid** designed by the American architect I.M. Pei, while its functional parts are decently buried beneath the central courtyard.

A **visit** to the Louvre Museum can be a formidable experience, best saved for another day. Even then, you will be able to see only a tiny fraction of the hundreds of thousands of works of art on display along the miles of corridors and galleries. **Guided tours** of the highlights are conducted in English throughout the day, or you can get a printed layout plan at the entrance and explore on your own. The arrangement of the galleries is currently being reorganized as new space in the north wing—previously occupied by the Ministry of Finance—becomes available. Three of the most popular attractions are Leonardo da Vinci's **Mona Lisa** *(La Joconde)*, the **Venus de Milo**, and the **Winged Victory of Samothrace**. You may expect to find huge mobs of tourists around these, but many of the other treasures are practically ignored and may be appreciated in peace. The Louvre Museum is open daily except on Tuesdays, from 9 a.m. to 6 p.m. Some of the minor galleries close at 5:15 p.m. and all day on certain days, but are always open on Mondays and Wednesdays. The greatest crowds appear on Sundays, when admission is free. Enter via the new glass pyramid. If you plan on making a day of it, you will be happy to know that there are cafeterias and restaurants on the premises.

From the glass pyramid you can look straight ahead for a fabulous **view** past Napoleon's Carrousel Triumphal Arch, the Egyptian Obelisk in the Place de la Concorde, the Champs-Élysées, and the distant Arc de Triomphe—all of which are in a perfectly straight line.

If you've sensibly put off visiting the Louvre Museum for another day, you might be interested in two other small museums in the northwest corner of the Louvre Palace. These are the **Museum of Decorative Arts** *(Musée des Arts Décoratifs)* (13) and the adjacent **Museum of Fashion** *(Musée des Arts de la Mode)*. Recently refurbished, the first has marvelous room settings, furniture, household objects and the like from the Middle Ages right up to the present time, with an emphasis on contemporary styles, Art Deco, and Art Nouveau. The second, opened in 1985, concerns itself with the evolution of costume and present-day trends in fashion. Both are open Wednesdays through Saturdays, from 12:30–6 p.m.; and on Sundays from 11 a.m. to 6 p.m.

Now continue past the small **Arc de Triomphe du Carrousel**, which celebrates Napoleon's victories in 1805, and enter the **Tuileries** (14). These formal gardens, extending over half a mile along the Seine as far as the Place de la Concorde, are a favorite spot for Parisians and visitors alike. They were first laid out in the mid-16th century as part of the royal palace, but their present appearance dates from 1664, when the noted landscape gardener André Le Nôtre—who also created the magnificent gardens at Versailles—was commissioned to redesign them.

About midway between the two ponds, on either side of the central avenue, there are small outdoor cafés under the trees where you can stop for a drink or a snack. Turn right here and leave the park via steps leading to Rue de Castiglione. Continue straight ahead to **Place Vendôme** (15), a dignified square that speaks quietly of opulence and wealth. Designed by the renowned architect Jules Hardouin-Mansart in the late 17th century, it is home to such symbols of luxury as the Ritz Hotel, Cartiers, Boucheron, and Van Cleef & Arpels. In its center once stood a statute of Louis XIV that was destroyed during the Revolution, only to be replaced with a column commemorating Napoleon's victory at Austerlitz. As the political winds shifted, the emperor was knocked off his perch and Henri IV put in his place, followed by a gigantic fleur-de-lys. Napoleon, now in military uniform, regained the position and was again pulled down by an angry mob. The present statue of Napoleon dressed as Caesar dates from the late 19th century.

The Opéra

A short stroll up the Rue de la Paix brings you to the bustling intersection known as Place de l'Opéra, where you can meet your friends at the famed Café de la Paix. Everyone in the world seems to wind up here sooner or later.

The grandiose structure filling the north side of the square is the **Opéra** (16), built by the young architect Charles Garnier between 1861 and 1875 in a suitably theatrical style. Construction took so long because of the existence of an underground stream, whose grottoes gave birth to the legendary *Phantom of the Opera*. Yes, a chandelier did fall, in 1896, thus adding credence to that wonderfully spooky tale.

Inside, the Opéra is every bit as lavish as its exterior promises. The spectacular Grand Foyer, the Great Staircase, and the auditorium itself are about as richly decorated as is conceivably possible. Although the best way to see them is to attend a performance, visitors are usually admitted—subject to rehearsals—daily from 11 a.m. to 4 p.m. There is also a small **Opéra Museum** in the west wing.

You have now reached the end of this walking tour, with convenient Métro stations located both in front of and behind the theater. In case you are continuing on, the next tour begins at the Chaussée d'Antin Métro Station, one block to the northeast.

Paris

North to Montmartre

After probing the historical sections of Paris on the previous three walking tours, you might want to try something a bit different. There are no important cultural sights along this amble through picturesque Montmartre, but there's a lot of fun to be had exploring what was once a great artists' quarter and what remains today a well-preserved remainder of Bohemian life in the *Belle Époque*.

Occupying the highest hill in Paris, Montmartre was only a simple country village when it was joined to the capital in 1860. The steepness of its narrow, twisted streets and the porous nature of its soil—riddled with countless tunnels of abandoned gypsum mines—have prevented any large-scale development, so its character remains refreshingly simple and down-to-earth. In contrast to this, the bawdy entertainment quarter at its base is a sea of neon signs, sleazy porno shops and dubious revues, attracting bus loads of tourists intent on having a naughty time.

Locals call the hill *La Butte Montmartre* or, more simply, just *La Butte* (The Mound). The name *Montmartre* probably derives from the Roman god Mercury, who might have had a temple there in ancient times. A more colorful explanation, originating in the 8th century, attributes it to the three martyrs who were beheaded there around A.D. 250. One of these, St.-Denis (Dionysius), the first Bishop of Paris, is said to have picked up his head and carried it to the northern suburb where his basilica stands today, expiring there no doubt from exhaustion.

Montmartre is still haunted by memories of the great artists who lived there between the 1880s and the end of World War I. Toulouse-Lautrec, Renoir, Van Gogh, Braque, Picasso, Utrillo—these are just some of the famous names. The present-day painters, although not nearly as talented, add a touch of color to the delightful Place du Tertre, while other sights along the tour include the notorious Pigalle district, the spectacular Sacré-Coeur Basilica, the only vineyards in Paris, and a few tiny but engrossing museums.

GETTING THERE:

If you are continuing on from the previous tour, you should take **bus** number 68 from the northeast corner of Rue de la Chaussée-d'Antin and Boulevard Haussmann, just beyond the Opéra. Get off at Place Blanche and begin the tour. You could also walk there, a slightly uphill distance of nearly one mile.

Those coming from another part of town can take the **Métro** directly to the Blanche stop. The area is also served by **bus** routes 30, 54, 68, and 74. By **taxi**, ask the driver for Place Blanche.

WHEN TO GO:

Anytime is a good time to make this walk as there are no really important cultural attractions that might be closed. Montmartre is quite hilly, so wear comfortable shoes.

FOOD AND DRINK:

The numerous restaurants on and around Place du Tertre are oriented to the tourist trade, serving acceptable food at somewhat inflated prices. While many of the cafés are nice for a drink, you will be better off dining at:

Up to Place du Tertre:

Au Clair de la Lune (9 Rue Poulbot, just south of Place du Tertre) A genuine atmosphere in a touristy area. X: Sun., Mon. lunch. $$$

La Crémaillère 1900 (15 Place du Tertre) Excellent meals in a romantic turn-of-the century bistro with outdoor garden dining. $$

Relais Normand (32 bis Rue d'Orsel, one block south of the funicular) An excellent value for traditional cuisine. X: Mon. except in July and Aug. $

Le Bon Bock (2 Rue Dancourt, 3 blocks east of Place Pigalle) French and Italian food in an unpretentious old-fashioned setting. $

Beyond Place du Tertre:

Beauvilliers (52 Rue Lamarck, 3 blocks northwest of the Sacré-Coeur) Celebrated cuisine in lovely surroundings. Proper dress expected, for reservations phone 42-54-54-42. X: Sun., Mon. lunch, early Sept. $$$ +

Le Clodenis (57 Rue Caulaincourt, 4 blocks northeast of the Montmartre cemetery) Light, imaginative dishes in an attractive atmosphere. X: Sun., Mon. $$$

Poulbot Gourmet (39 Rue Lamarck, 2 blocks north of the Sacré-Coeur) A favorite with a loyal clientele. X: Sun. $$

Le Maquis (69 Rue Caulaincourt, 4 blocks northeast of the Montmartre cemetery) Good food at reasonable prices. X: Sun., Mon. $$

The Sacré-Coeur Basilica

Grandgousier (17 Ave. Rachel, just south of the Montmartre cemetery) A delightful little place with excellent dishes. X: Sat. lunch, Sun., Aug. $$

Le Wepler (14 Place de Clichy) A big, bustling restaurant famous for its seafood. X: Aug. $$

SUGGESTED TOUR:

Begin your tour at **Place Blanche** (1), which can be reached directly by Métro to the Blanche stop. Those continuing on from the previous tour can take bus number 68 or walk up Rue de la Chaussée-d'Antin and Ruc Blanche. This is the heart of Montmartre's entertainment district, at the foot of the hill. On the north side of the square is the famous **Moulin Rouge**, immortalized around the turn of the century by Toulouse-Lautrec's renderings of its can-can dancers. The cabaret is still going strong after a century of operation, still drawing bus loads of tourists beneath the turning vanes of its fake windmill.

A stroll down Boulevard de Clichy takes you past a number of seedy bars, porno shops and assorted peep shows, all promoted by peculiar hustlers on the lookout for customers. You can avoid being pestered and still see all the sights by walking along the tree-lined strip in the center of the street. **Place Pigalle** (2), the infamous "Pig Alley" of the 1940s, is named for a famous 19th-century sculptor who specialized in religious art. It is somewhat ironic that this area has long been the

Steps to the Sacré-Coeur

raunchiest center of commercialized sex in Paris; ever since the last genuine artists fled to Montparnasse.

Things begin to look better after you turn left on Rue Houdon. Another left at the top of the street brings you into **Place des Abbesses**, whose rather quaint Métro stop is the one closest to the top of the hill. Continue on to **Place Émile-Goudeau** (3), often regarded as the birthplace of modern art. Several renowned painters, including Picasso, Juan Gris, Van Dongen, and Modigliani lived and worked in a house at number 13 known as the *Bateau-Lavoir,* which burned down in 1970 and was replaced with new artists' studios.

The route now leads to the base of the famous **Funicular** (4) where, for the price of one Métro ticket, you can ride up the steep hill instead of making the long climb on foot.

Crowning the top—and visible from all over Paris—is the monumental **Sacré-Coeur Basilica** (5), a neo-Romanesque-Byzantine monstrosity that has become almost as much a symbol of Paris as the Eiffel Tower. Begun in 1876 as an act of contrition for the disastrous Franco-Prussian War and the bloody Commune uprisings of 1871, the church was not completed until 1910 and only consecrated in 1919. Prayers have been said here day and night, perpetually since 1885, without a break for even the wars. The enormous weight of its gleaming white stones, much too heavy for the hill to bear, is supported by underground columns to a depth of 100 feet. One of the largest bells in the

Place du Tertre

world hangs in its north tower. Step inside for a look at the ornate mosaics, to visit the rather gloomy crypt, or perhaps to ascend the dome for a spectacular **panorama** of Paris extending some 30 miles. Actually, there is an excellent view from the terrace in front of the church, a popular gathering spot for tourists from all over the world.

A short stroll around the rear of the basilica leads to the ancient **Church of St.-Pierre-de-Montmartre** (6), all that remains of a 12th-century Benedictine abbey. Although much altered over the years, the interior of this modest church—the third-oldest in Paris—has some interesting columns once believed to be from a Roman temple dedicated to Mercury but which are more likely remnants of the 7th-century Merovingian church that previously occupied the site. There are also some attractive modern plaques depicting scenes of old Montmartre.

No visitor to Paris should miss seeing the adjacent **Place du Tertre** (7), truly a scene right out of *La Bohème,* or a painting by Utrillo. The artists whose easels surround the old village square may not be terribly talented, but their presence does stir memories of Montmartre during the *Belle Époque.* This effect is heightened by the period restaurants and cafés, with outdoor tables under the trees—a delicious place to linger over a drink.

Just a few steps to the south and you are on the tiny Rue Poulbot, home to the intriguing **Historial** (8). This noted waxworks museum

(*Musée de Cire*) may look small, but inside it is a warren on unexpected tunnels and passages filled with re-creations of Montmartre's glory days, complete with artists' studios and cafés. It is open daily from 10:30 a.m. to 12:30 p.m. and 2–6 p.m.

Now continue around and follow Rue des Saules to Rue Cortot, where you will find the **Montmartre Museum** (9) in a delightful 17th-century house inhabited at different times by Renoir, Utrillo, Dufy and others. The displays here recall the Montmartre of old with mementos of the Bohemian life, all of which may be seen on Tuesdays through Saturdays, from 2:30–5:30 p.m.; and on Sundays from 11 a.m. to 5:30 p.m. Directly aside of the museum are the only remaining **vineyards** in Paris, whose white wines may not be very distinguished but are certainly a novelty. Their early-October harvest is always celebrated with great festivities.

Across the street from the bottom of the vineyards is another survivor from old Montmartre, the rustic **Lapin Agile Cabaret** (10). Still functioning after all those years, it was at one time the haunt of impoverished artists and now features folk music in a wonderfully crude atmosphere, open every night except Mondays.

From here the route snakes its way through colorful neighborhoods and turns down the winding Rue Lepic. The Montmartre hill was once dotted with dozens of windmills, of which only the remnants of a few remain. One of these, often painted by Renoir, Van Gogh and others, is the famous **Moulin de la Galette**, stuck on a slope between Rue Lepic and Avenue Junot. A bit farther down, at number 54 Rue Lepic, is the house where Van Gogh shared lodging with his brother Theo before going south to Arles.

Turn right on Rue Joseph-de-Maistre and left on the busy Rue Caulaincourt. To the right is the **Montmartre Cemetery** (11), the final resting place of many famous painters, writers, composers, and actors. Among them are Emile Zola, Hector Berlioz, Alexandre Dumas, Edgar Degas, Jacques Offenbach, and the German poet Heinrich Heine. The main entrance is on the short Avenue Rachel, just north of Boulevard de Clichy.

The walk ends at the bustling intersection of **Place de Clichy** (12), where there is a Métro stop. If you would like to continue on to the next tour, you can take a bus back to the Opéra or walk there by following Rue de Clichy and Rue de la Chaussaée-d'Antin, a slightly downhill distance of just under one mile.

Paris

From the Opéra to the Arc de Triomphe

With a few notable exceptions, the four previous walking tours have focused on the classical Paris of the past. Now it is time to explore today's busy international city of commerce and fashion. From the bustling shopping precincts near the Opéra to that grandest of promenades, the Champs-Élysées, this is the part of Paris that developed since the time of Napoleon.

By getting off to an early start, energetic walkers should be able to combine this tour with the previous one as there are few time-consuming attractions along the way. If you choose to do this, it will be better to start with the Montmartre tour first.

GETTING THERE:

The walking tour begins at the **Chaussée-d'Antin Métro Station**, only one block northeast of the Opéra and easily reached by Métro from anywhere in Paris. It is also served by **bus** routes 22, 26, 42, 52, 53, 66, 68, and 81. By **taxi**, just ask the driver for the Galeries Lafayette—Opéra.

WHEN TO GO:

You can enjoy this walk at any time in good weather, but note that nearly all of the shops are closed on Sundays and that the museums in the Petit Palais and Grand Palais—both relatively minor sights—are closed on Mondays and holidays except for special exhibitions.

FOOD AND DRINK:

The neighborhoods covered on this tour are exceptionally rich in restaurants, although prices may be a bit steeper than in other parts of town. Advance reservations and a thick wallet are nearly always necessary for the renowned temples of gastronomy near the Champs-Élysées, making them impractical choices for the purposes of this walk. You will be better off saving these treats for another day, and considering some of the following for an excellent lunch:

To the Place de la Concorde:

Cartouche Édouard VII (18 Rue de Caumartin, 2 blocks west of the Opéra) Hearty cuisine from southwestern France. X: Sat., Sun., early Aug. $$$

Bar Romain (6 Rue de Caumartin, 4 blocks northeast of the Madeleine) Famous for its steaks. $$$

Mövenpick (12 Bd. de la Madeleine, 2 blocks east of the Madeleine) Part of a Swiss chain renowned for its superb food. $$$

Le Roi du Pot-au-Feu (34 Rue Vignon, 2 blocks northeast of the Madeleine) Hearty peasant dishes in an old-fashioned bistro. X: Sun., holidays, July. $$

Fauchon (26 Place de la Madeleine, behind the church) The fanciest food shop in Paris also offers gourmet specialties to be eaten standing up at the counter. A unique experience. $$

Lescure (7 Rue de Mondovi, 2 blocks northeast of Place de la Concorde) A rustic country restaurant with traditional home cooking. X: Sat. eve., Sun., July. $

Near the Champs-Élysées:

Au Petit Montmorency (5 Rue Rabelais, 2 blocks northeast of Rond-Point) Inventive cuisine in a chic setting. For reservations phone 42-25-11-19. X: Sat., Sun., Aug. $$$

Tong Yen (1 bis Rue Jean-Mermoz, at the Rond-Point) Renowned for its Chinese specialties and gracious service. X: Aug. $$$

Le Boeuf sur le Toit (34 Rue du Colisée, 2 blocks north of Rond-Point) Known for its fresh seafood in a charming atmosphere with a piano bar. X: Sun., Mon., July. $$ and $$$

Chez Edgard (4 Rue Marbeuf, 4 blocks southwest of Rond-Point) A local favorite with a broad range of dishes and prices. X: Sun. $$

Boulangerie St.-Phillippe (73 Av. Franklin-D.-Roosevelt, 3 blocks north of Rond-Point) A lunch-only restaurant in the rear of a bakery, with superb food. X: Sat., Aug. $$

Le Drugstorien (1 Av. Matignon, at the Rond-Point) Snacks downstairs, full restaurant upstairs. Nice views in smart surroundings. $ and $$

La Boutique à Sandwiches (12 Rue du Colisée, 2 blocks northwest of Rond-Point) Wonderful sandwiches downstairs, while an attractive dining room upstairs features Alsatian and Swiss dishes. X: Sun. $ and $$

Bistro de la Gare (73 Av. des Champs-Élysées, 4 blocks northwest of Rond-Point) A chain restaurant specializing in meat dishes. $ and $$

L'Assiette au Boeuf (123 Av. des Champs-Élysées, 2 blocks southeast of the Arc de Triomphe) One of a popular chain of restaurants, features steak and salad. $

Le Dante (4 Rue Balzac, 3 blocks southeast of the Arc de Triomphe) A simple bistro near the Champs-Élysées. X: Sun. $

Drugstore Champs-Élysées (133 Av. des Champs-Élysées, 1 block southeast of the Arc de Triomphe) Light meals featuring salads, burgers, chili and the like. $

There are a number of attractive outdoor cafés around Place de la Madeleine. Those along the Champs-Élysées are invariably overpriced but the view might be worth the extra francs.

SUGGESTED TOUR:

Directly facing the **Chausee-d'Antin Métro Station** (1) is the world-famous **Galeries Lafayette** department store, spread over three adjacent buildings. Go into the central (and largest) of these to marvel at the incredible glassed-in courtyard, and ride the escalators all the way up to the roof for a superb close-up view of Paris. An equally great store, just down the street, is **Au Printemps**, again located in three adjoining buildings. It, too, has a roof garden, in the "Havre Magasin." Both stores are usually open on Mondays through Saturdays, from 10 a.m. to 7 p.m., and both offer tax rebates *(détaxe)* for purchases taken out of the country. The details on this service change occasionally, so ask about the current procedures and minimums. Their English-speaking "welcome" personnel can also aid you in making purchases as well as provide general information.

Continue down Boulevard Haussmann and turn left on Rue Tronchet. This leads directly to the rear of the **Madeleine** (2), a church with both an extraordinary appearance and an amazing history. Begun in 1764 in the baroque style, it was quickly altered to resemble the Panthéon, but never finished. Napoleon started to rebuild it as an imitation Greek temple dedicated to the glory of his Grand Army, then lost interest in the project. Following his downfall, the Parisians had no idea of what to do with this unfinished white elephant in their midst. Among the uses considered were a bank, a stock exchange, a parliament, a library, and a theater. In 1837 it almost became the first railway station in Paris, but it was really not large enough for that. Finally, all other ideas having failed, it was consecrated as the Church of St.-Mary Magdalen in 1842. It still looks like a bank. The richly decorated interior, although rather dark, is well worth a quick visit.

A number of luxury shops surround the Madeleine, notably that most sophisticated of delicatessens, Fauchon, where you can sample gourmet specialties on the spot at modest prices. Near the southeast

Paris

From the Opéra to
the Arc de Triomphe

M = Métro Station

500 Yards

The Madeleine

corner of the square stands Aux Trois Quartiers, the most exclusive department store in Paris.

Stroll down the elegant **Rue Royale**, passing the Rue du Faubourg St.-Honoré—one of the world's most glamorous shopping streets—and the renowned *Belle Époque* restaurant, Maxims, where you can dine rather well for exorbitant sums. Opening in front of you is the largest and most impressive square in Paris, the **Place de la Concorde** (3). This was laid out during the reign of Louis XV to accommodate an equestrian statue of the king. With the Revolution, the statue was destroyed and a guillotine erected as the new center of attraction. The "Nation's Razor," as it was called, shaved off well over a thousand heads at this spot alone, including those of Louis XVI, Marie-Antoinette, Madame du Barry, Danton, and in the end Robespierre himself.

With the end of the Reign of Terror, the blood-soaked square was re-named Concorde and decorated with statues. In its center stands the **Egyptian Obelisk** from the 13th century B.C., a gift from the Viceroy of Egypt in 1829. You might want to brave the constant car traffic to reach this for what is probably the most sweeping panoramic **view** in all Paris.

The east side of the square is bordered by the gardens of the **Tuileries**, visited on one of the previous walking tours. Near the southwestern corner of this is the **Orangerie** (4), a small art museum specializing in paintings from the late Impressionists to the 1930s. Included in its collection are works by Monet, Renoir, Cézanne, Picasso and others. It is open daily except Tuesdays, from 9:30 a.m. to 5:30 p.m. To the north of it stands the **Jeu de Paume**, formerly the home of a great Impressionist museum (recently moved across the river to the Orsay) and now used for temporary exhibitions.

Stroll around to the west side of Place de la Concorde, where the **Champs-Élysées** begins its stately procession to the Arc de Triomphe. The entrance to what is arguably the most renowned avenue on earth is flanked by the **Marly Horses**, two marvelous statuary groups of rearing horses transplanted from Louis XIV's château at Marly. From here to the Rond-Point the Champs-Élysées (meaning Elysian Fields) retains its 19th-century character, with English-style gardens on either side. Once a marshland, this area was drained and planted with rows of trees according to the designs of Le Nôtre. In the 18th century an avenue was formed and extended to the top of the hill, but it remained un-developed until well into the 19th century.

Turn left on a path past Ledoyen, once a country inn and for the last century a luxury restaurant known for its classic cuisine. A right on the Cours La Reine brings you to Avenue Winston Churchill and the **Pont Alexandre III** (5). This wildly flamboyant bridge, built in 1900 for the World Exhibition and named for a Russian czar, spans the Seine in a single leaping arch of cast steel. Every square inch of it is covered with exuberant decorations that speak volumes about turn-of-the-century optimism.

Another symbol of that age, and erected for the same exhibition, is the **Petit Palais** (6). Although architectural purists may quibble over its mixture of styles, it is indeed a handsome building and now houses the **Museum of Fine Arts of the City of Paris** (*Musée des Beaux-Arts de la Ville de Paris*). All too often overlooked by visitors, the collections here range all the way from classical antiquity to early 20th-century art and include works by Delacroix, Corot, Monet, Cézanne, Redon, Bonnard, and many others. It is open daily except on Mondays and some holidays, from 10 a.m. to 5:30 p.m. The museum is also noted for its temporary·exhibitions, which may have different opening times.

Just across the street stands the much larger **Grand Palais** (7), again dating from the World Exhibition of 1900. Built of stone, glass, and steel, this immense structure is used primarily for temporary exhibitions and shows. Its west wing, opening on Avenue Franklin-D.-Roosevelt, houses the interesting **Palace of Discovery** (*Palais de la Découverte*), a hands-on science museum where you can have lots of fun pushing buttons to make things work. There is also a planetarium with several heavenly shows a day. The museum is open daily except on Mondays and holidays, from 10 a.m. to 6 p.m.

On the Champs-Élysées

Continue up Avenue Winston Churchill, cross the Champs-Élys-ées, and follow Avenue de Marigny. An outdoor **stamp market** *(Marché aux Timbres)* is held on Thursdays, Saturdays, and Sundays, from 10 a.m. until evening, at the intersection of Avenue Gabriel. Beyond this, to the right, is the **Élysée Palace** (8), which you cannot visit as it is the official home of the French president and the multitude of heavily-armed guards just won't let you in. You can however, usually catch a glimpse through the gateway. Built in 1718, it was later home to Ma-dame de Pompadour and then used by both Napoleon I, who signed his final abdication here, and his nephew, Napoleon III, who plotted his 1851 *coup d'état* within its walls. Recent presidents have often pre-ferred to use it as an office only and to actually live elsewhere.

Turn left on that most elegant of shopping streets, the **Rue du Faubourg St.-Honoré**, where top designer names embellish the many boutiques. Another left on Avenue Franklin-D.-Roosevelt—one of six streets in Paris named for American presidents—brings you to the **Rond-Point** (9). From here on the **Champs-Élysées** completely changes its character from a shady green belt to a broad, bustling avenue of of-fices, shops, theaters, and sidewalk cafés as it gently climbs to the Arc de Triomphe. This is the great promenade of Paris, where everyone—native and tourist alike—wanders about to see and be seen. It is also where the massive parades are held, like the annual celebration on Bastille Day, July 14.

Some of the **shopping arcades** along the north side of the Champs-Élysées are well worth exploring, especially the Galerie Élysée Rond-

The Arc de Triomphe

Point, the Arcades du Lido, and the Galerie des Champs. In them you will find a colorful variety of boutiques and cafés where you can window shop or have a drink. The most fashionable outdoor café, on the southeast corner at the intersection of Avenue George V, is **Fouquet's**—a bit expensive but worth it for the experience. The main tourist information office for Paris is at number 127, on the south side between the Air France ticket office and the top of the hill.

The summit is crowned by the magnificent **Arc de Triomphe** (10), located in the center of Place Charles-de-Gaulle, an enormous circular hub still known to Parisians by its former name, *Place de l'Étoile*. From here, eleven other great avenues besides the Champs-Élysées radiate outwards to all points in Paris. The Arc de Triomphe was begun by Napoleon in 1806 to commemorate French military victories, but political changes and cost overruns delayed its completion until 1836. It is the largest triumphal arch in the world, and since 1920 has sheltered the **Tomb of the Unknown Soldier**, whose memory is rekindled each evening at 6:30 by an eternal flame.

You can safely reach the arch by using the underpass from the north side of the Champs-Élysées or the Avenue de la Grande-Armée, rather than risk your life in the ferocious traffic. Visits to its top platform may be made by elevator or steps, from 10 a.m. to 5 to 6 p.m. The **sweeping panoramic view** from it is absolutely spectacular, and makes the perfect climax to end your walking tours of Paris.

Paris

Additional Attractions in and around the City

This chapter has absolutely nothing to do with daytrips, but gives a brief description of the more outstanding attractions in and around Paris that were not covered on the five previous one-day walking tours. They are listed alphabetically and include the address, the *arrondissement* (district) number, the name of the nearest Métro or RER station(s), and the times of opening when appropriate.

WITHIN PARIS:

Advertising Museum *(Musée de la Publicité)*—A truly remarkable collection of advertising posters from their beginning until the present, along with contemporary television commercials and audio-visual techniques. Works by Toulouse-Lautrec, Mucha, Erté and others are featured; and there are temporary exhibitions as well. Located at 18 Rue de Paradis, 10ᵉ, reached by Métro to Gare de l'Est or Château-d'Eau. The museum is open daily except Tuesdays, from noon until 6 p.m.

African and Oceanic Arts Museum *(Musée des Arts Africains et Océaniens)*—Situated at the edge of the Bois de Vincennes, this museum houses superb collections of native art, weapons, masks, pottery, jewelry, and similar artifacts from Africa, Oceania, and Australia. There is also a tropical aquarium with crocodiles. 293 Avenue Daumesnil, 12ᵉ, served by Métro to Porte Dorée. Visits may be made on any day except Tuesdays, from 9:45 a.m. to noon and 1:30–5:15 p.m.

Balzac Museum *(Maison de Balzac)*—The great author Honoré de Balzac lived in this charming country house from 1840 to 1847, escaping his creditors. It is filled with mementos of his life, manuscripts, and personal effects. 47 Rue Raynouard, 16ᵉ, reached by Métro to Passy. The door is open daily except Mondays, from 10 a.m. to 5:40 p.m.

Bois de Boulogne—Once a royal hunting preserve, this 2,224-acre park is a favorite recreational area for Parisians. Among its many attractions are the **Lower Lake** *(Lac Inférieur)* where rowboats and bicycles can be rented, the **Upper Lake** *(Lac Supérieur)*, the **Pré Catelan**

(a park-within-a-park with its famous Shakespeare Garden), the **Bagatelle** (a former estate with lovely gardens), and the **Jardin d'Acclimatation** (primarily a childrens' amusement park with a zoo and a miniature railway). In addition, there are two racetracks, waterfalls, the Municipal Flower Gardens, several restaurants, and enough other sights to keep you busy all day. Located in the 16ᵉ *arrondissement,* it is best reached by Métro to Porte Maillot, Sablons, Porte Dauphine, or Porte d'Auteuil.

Botanical Gardens *(Jardin des Plantes)*—Much more than its name suggests, the Botanical Gardens also encompass a zoo, hothouses, and the **Natural History Museum**. Located in the 5ᵉ *arrondissement* close to the Seine and Gare d'Austerlitz train station, it can be reached by Métro to Gare d'Austerlitz, Jussieu, or Monge. The park is open daily from 7 a.m. until 8 p.m., the zoo daily from 9 a.m. to 5 or 6 p.m., and the museum daily except Tuesdays and holidays, from 10:30 a.m. to 5 p.m.

Buttes-Chaumont Park—This is the most unusual and possibly the most romantic parks in Paris. Laid out over a former quarry, it has steep wooded paths and a lake with a rocky island whose summit is crowned with a temple. Set in the 19ᵉ *arrondissement,* its most convenient Métro stop is Buttes-Chaumont. The park is open daily, until 11 p.m. in summer or 9 p.m. in winter.

Catacombs—As Paris expanded in the 18th and 19th centuries, some of its cemeteries had to be emptied to make room for buildings. All of those generations of bones from millions of bodies were ghoulishly stacked in these abandoned underground quarries, where they have been on public view since 1874. During World War II the Catacombs served as a headquarters of the Resistance. A flashlight will be helpful for this macabre experience. 1 Place Denfert-Rochereau, 14ᵉ, served by Métro to Denfert-Rochereau. Visits may be made on Tuesdays through Fridays, from 2–4 p.m.; and on Saturdays and Sundays from 9–11 a.m. and 2–4 p.m.

Cernuschi Museum—Chinese art from prehistoric times all the way up to the present is the focus of this delightful little museum just east of the Monceau Park. 7 Avenue Vélasquez, 8ᵉ, reached by Métro to Villiers or Monceau. The museum is open on Tuesdays through Sundays, 10 a.m. to 5:40 p.m.

City Museum of Modern Art *(Musée d'Art Moderne de la Ville de Paris)*—An outstanding museum for art of the 20th century, this *avant-garde* institution specializes in Cubist, Fauve, and School of Paris paintings along with temporary exhibitions. 11 Avenue du Président-Wilson, 16ᵉ, close to the Métro stops Iéna and Alma-Marceau. It is open daily except on Mondays, from 10 a.m. to 5:30 p.m.; remaining open until 8:30 p.m. on Wednesdays.

Cognacq-Jay Museum—Both the fine and decorative arts of 18th-century Europe are well displayed in this elegant and intimate museum, the epitome of refined French taste. 25 Boulevard des Capucines, 2e, served by Métro to Opéra or Madeleine. Visits may be made any day except Mondays, from 10 a.m. to 5:40 p.m.

Flea Market *(Marché aux Puces)*—The largest flea market in Paris is held at Saint-Ouen, on the northern city limits. Walk under the elevated highway and turn left into an area filled with several thousand stalls selling all kinds of junk, some of which might actually be of value. You'll need to bargain, and you're up against expert dealers. Of course, you can come here just for the fun and not buy anything at all. Located on the edge of 18e *arrondissement,* it is easily reached by taking the Métro to Porte de Clignancourt·and strolling north. The markets are open on Saturdays, Sundays, and Mondays only; from about 9 a.m. to perhaps 7 p.m.

Gobelins Tapestry Factory *(Manufacture Nationale des Gobelins)*—Craftsmanship of the highest level can be witnessed in these government-owned workshops where works of art are woven with intricate care. The results, each taking years to finish, are for state use only and are never sold. 42 Avenue des Gobelins, 13e, served by Métro to Gobelins. Guided tours are conducted on Tuesdays, Wednesdays, and Thursdays; at 2:15 and 2:45 p.m.

Grévin Museum—A waxworks fantasy world where contemporary personalities compete with historical tableaux for your entertainment. Distorting mirrors, magic tricks, and strange environments add to the fun. 10 Boulevard Montmartre, 9e, reached by Métro to Richelieu-Drouot or Rue Montmarte. It can all be enjoyed on any day from 1–7 p.m.

Guimet Museum—Oriental art from all over the Far East is gathered together here to form one of the most outstanding museums of its kind in the world. 6 Place d'Iéna 16e, served by Métro to Iéna. The museum is open daily except Tuesdays, from 9:45 a.m. to noon and 1:30–5:15 p.m.

Gustave Moreau Museum—The strange paintings of the great 19th-century symbolist artist are displayed in his former studio and home. 14 Rue de la Rochefoucault, 9e, take the Métro to Trinité. The small museum is open daily except Tuesdays, from 10 a.m. to 12:30 p.m. and 2–5 p.m.

Jacquemart-André Museum—A magnificent private collection of European art from the Italian Renaissance through the 18th century is handsomely displayed in a late 19th-century mansion with exquisite furnishings. 158 Boulevard Haussmann, 8e, reached by Métro to St.-Philippe-du-Roule or Miromesnil. Visits can be made on Wednesdays through Sundays, from 1:30–5:30 p.m.

Marmottan Museum—Famous throughout the art world for its marvelous collection of Impressionist paintings, this museum is especially noted for its major works by Monet. There are also objects, pictures, and furniture from many other periods in this grand 19th-century mansion. 2 Rue Louis-Boilly, 16e, served by Métro to La Muette. The museum is open daily except Mondays, from 10 a.m. to 5:30 p.m.

Monceau Park—A wonderful oasis of greenery in the fashionable 8e *arrondissement,* this delightful park is adjacent to the Cernuschi and Nissim de Camondo museums. Its small lake is embellished with a Roman colonnade, and curious follies are scattered among the trees, all legacies of the time when this was the private garden of the Duke of Orléans. Its main entrance is on Boulevard de Courcelles, opposite the Métro stop Monceau.

Montparnasse—The Montmartre of the Left Bank, Montparnasse has changed greatly since the days of Hemingway, Picasso, Cocteau, Stravinsky, Chagall, Modigliani, Lenin, Trotsky, and other famous personalities who lived and worked here in the early 20th century. Some of the atmosphere survives in the La Coupole and Le Sélect cafés on Boulevard du Montparnasse, and around the nearby Montparnasse Cemetery, but the area is noted today mostly for its modern office buildings and shopping centers. You can ascend the sleek 59-story **Tour Montparnasse** for a spectacular view of the city. Located at the

Montparnasse

500 Yards

junction of the 6e, 14e, and 15e *arrondissements,* the district is best served by the massive Métro stop Montparnasse-Bienvenüe.

Mosque of Paris—A 130-foot-high minaret towers over one of the most impressive mosques in the world, a corner right out of the Middle East or North Africa. Take your shoes off and join a guided tour, then relax at the traditional Arab café. Place du Puits-de-l'Ermite, 5e, reached by Métro to Monge. Visitors are welcome daily except on Fridays or Moslem holidays; from 10 a.m. to noon and 2–5:30 p.m.

National Technical Museum *(Musée National des Techniques)*— Admirers of mechanical devices will enjoy this vast collection of technology, ranging from the 16th century right up to the present. 292 Rue St.-Martin, 3e, served by Métro to Réamur-Sébastopol or Arts-et-Métiers. The museum is open on Tuesdays through Saturdays, from 1–5:30 p.m.; and on Sundays from 10 a.m. to 5:15 p.m.

Nissim de Camondo Museum—A sumptuous mansion decorated with priceless objects in the 18th-century manner, this was one of the most luxurious homes in Paris. In 1936 it was presented to the nation by the Count de Camondo in honor of his son Nissim, killed in World War I. 62 Rue de Monceau, 8e, reached by Métro to Villiers or Monceau. Visits may be made on Wednesdays through Sundays, from 10 a.m. to noon and 2–5 p.m.

Père-Lachaise Cemetery—An enormous number of famous personalities, from the tragic 12th-century lovers Héloise and Abélard to recent rock stars, are buried in what is probably the most famous cemetery in the world. You can get a map of their graves at the entrance and explore some of the most interesting tombs anywhere. Be sure to see the Federalists' Wall in the southeast corner, where in 1871 the last 147 insurgents of the Paris Commune were lined up and shot, then interred on the spot. It still has strong political overtones. Located in the 20e *arrondissement,* the main entrance is on Boulevard de Ménilmontant, and the closest Métro stop is Père-Lachaise. The gates are open daily from 7:30 or 8:30 a.m. to 5 or 6 p.m., depending on the season.

Popular Arts and Traditions Museum—Everyday life in rural France before the Industrial Revolution is explored in this exceptionally interesting museum near the northern end of the Bois de Boulogne. 6 Route de Mahatma-Gandhi, 16e, reached by Métro to Sablons. The museum is open daily except on Tuesdays, from 9:45 a.m. to 5 p.m.

St.-Martin Canal—Dug in the early 19th century, this commercial waterway with six locks links the Seine with a northern canal system and other rivers. It runs underground from the Place de la Bastille for about one mile to the north, then continues on the surface through strangely atmospheric and oddly romantic neighborhoods to La Villette, where it joins the St.-Denis and Ourcq canals. Boat rides are available from the Quai Anatole-France on the Seine near the Orsay Museum in the 7e *arrondissement,* reached by Métro to Solférino. These depart around 9 a.m. and take three hours to reach La Villette. There is a return ride around 2 p.m., or you can save time and money by taking the Métro back. The service operates daily except on holidays, from May to November. Reservations are essential, phone "Quiztour-Paris Canal" at 48-74-75-30. Ask the tourist office about other similar boat rides on the canal.

Sewers of Paris *(Les Égouts de Paris)*—Explore a sample section of the over 1,300 miles of sewer tunnels under Paris on these smelly but nevertheless popular tours that begin with an audio-visual presentation. This is an experience you will never forget. The tours depart from the corner of Quai d'Orsay and the Pont de l'Alma, 7e, reached by Métro to Alma-Marceau. They are held on Wednesdays through Sundays, from 3–8 p.m. Naturally, there are no tours during periods of heavy rain or flooding.

La Villette—Slaughterhouses once occupied this vast site in the northeast corner of Paris, bisected by industrial canals and bordered by an elevated highway. It has now been transformed into the pride of French technology with the opening of the **City of Science and**

Industry, a gigantic high-tech, space-age, hands-on museum that celebrates the very latest in technological progress. Next to it is the **Géode**, an enormous sphere of stainless steel surrounded by water and containing a spectacular Omnimax projection theater. The rest of the 125-acre site is laid out as a futuristic park dotted with exhibition halls, modernistic follies, and a huge space for rock concerts. The main entrance is on Avenue Corentin-Cariou, 19e, served by Métro to Porte de la Villette. The science museum is open on Tuesdays, Thursdays and Fridays, from 10 a.m. to 6 p.m.; on Wednesdays from noon to 9 p.m.; and on Saturdays and Sundays from noon to 8 p.m. It is closed on Mondays.

Vincennes—Located in the 12e *arrondissement* near the southeast corner of Paris, the Bois de Vincennes park is similar to the Bois de Boulogne, although not as fashionable. Its two main features are the **Château de Vincennes**, a medieval castle, and the **Zoo de Paris**, the largest zoo in France. There are also several lakes, lovely floral gardens, and a Buddhist temple. The château and floral gardens are best reached by Métro to Château de Vincennes, while the zoo and the temple are served by Métro to Porte Dorée. The château is open daily except on holidays, from 10 a.m. to 6 p.m.; and the zoo daily from 9 a.m. to 5 p.m.

JUST BEYOND PARIS:

In addition to the six attractions outlined below, there are several major daytrip destinations within the immediate area surrounding Paris. These are described in full detail in Section III, *The Ile-de-France*, beginning on page 99.

Air and Space Museum (*Musée de l'Air et de l'Espace*)—Over 150 historic aircraft are displayed in six exhibition halls at Le Bourget Airport just north of Paris, covering the history of aviation from its beginnings until the present. Audio-visual presentations describe the conquest of space, while you can inspect the first Concorde and an Ariane rocket on display outdoors. The museum may be reached by taking bus number 152 from the Porte de la Villette or bus number 350 from the Gare de l'Est or Gare du Nord. Get off a Musée de l'Air. By car, take the A-1 highway northeast to the Le Bourget exit. The museum is open daily except on Mondays, from 10 a.m. to 6 p.m.; closing at 5 p.m. in winter.

La Défense—The city of the future is here today, at least in part. Whether you like it is another matter. Begun in the 1960s and still incomplete, La Défense embodies the fondest aspirations of architects and city planners in a mixed commercial and residential center built on a gigantic elevated concrete platform, with streets below and pedestrians above. Walking along its open terraces provides a fabu-

La Défense

lous view of Paris, and there are shopping centers and a magnificent exhibition hall to keep you busy for a few hours. This "Manhattan-on-the-Seine" is best reached by taking the RER line A to the La Défense stop. The RER connects with the Métro at several points, including Charles-de-Gaulle-Étoile.

Malmaison—Napoleon and Josephine lived in this lovely château and, after their divorce, the empress continued to occupy it until her death in 1814. Still furnished as it was in those days, it makes for an interesting and very pleasant little excursion. To get there, take the RER line A to La Défense, then change to bus number 158A. The château is open on Wednesdays through Mondays, from 10 a.m. to noon and 1:30–5 p.m.

St.-Denis Basilica—The first major structure in the Gothic style, the Basilica of St.-Denis was the prototype for the great cathedrals of France. Begun in 1136 on the site of a 5th-century church, it served as the royal necropolis for nearly all of the kings of France, from Dagobert I in the 7th century until Louis XVIII in the 19th. During the Revolution the mausoleums were plundered and the bones thrown into a common grave beneath the crypt, but the tombs themselves had previously been removed for safekeeping and are now back in place, albeit empty. The historic basilica is located in the town of St.-Denis, just north of Paris. You can get to it by taking the Métro to St.-Denis-Basilique. Visits may be made on Mondays and Wednesdays through

St.-Germain-en-Laye

Saturdays, from 10 a.m. to 5:30 p.m.; and on Sundays from 2–6:30 p.m.

St.-Germain-en-Laye—This attractive old suburb is famous for its château—the birthplace of Louis XIV and other kings—and for its unusual Priory Museum. Set atop a hill overlooking Paris, the town also has a long terrace with magnificent views, and some beautiful English gardens. The **Château**, long a royal residence, was once home to the young Mary, Queen of Scots, and to the deposed King James II of England. It now houses the **National Antiquities Museum**, where artifacts from prehistoric times to the 8th century are exquisitely displayed. It is open daily except on Tuesdays, from 9:45 a.m. to noon and 1:30–5:15 p.m. A short walk through the town leads to the **Priory Museum** (Musée du Prieuré). Located in the former home of the symbolist painter Maurice Denis, it displays his works along with those of Gaugin, Bonnard, Vuillard, and others. It is open daily except on Mondays, Tuesdays, and holidays; from 10:30 a.m. to 5:30 p.m. The easiest way to get there is by RER line A to St.-Germain-en-Laye.

Vaux-le-Vicomte—This fabulous château was in a way responsible for the building of Versailles. When young Louis XIV was entertained there by his finance minister, Fouquet, in 1661, he became enraged at the thought of a public servant living better than the king. Suspecting embezzlement, he had Fouquet thrown in jail and then employed the same architects to build an even greater palace for himself at Versailles. Restored to its original splendor, Vaux-le-Vicomte is located just east of Melun, on the way to Fontainebleau. There is fairly frequent train service from the Gare de Lyon in Paris to Melun, after which you will have to take a taxi to Vaux-le-Vicomte. By car, follow the N-6 to Melun, 34 miles southeast of Paris, then local roads. The château is open daily from April through October, from 10 a.m. to 6 p.m.; with shorter hours the rest of the year. You can phone them at 60-66-97-09. There is a cafeteria on the grounds.

The Ile-de-France

To explore the Ile-de-France is to see the story of a great civilization unfold before your eyes, an experience no visitor to Paris should miss. This central region, without defined borders and existing in the mind almost as much as in reality, is the very heart and soul of France—the royal island from which a remarkable nation emerged.

Roughly speaking, the Ile-de-France is the area within about a fifty-mile radius of Paris. A dense network of rail lines and highways provides easy access to its many attractions. The seven daytrip destinations that follow were chosen for both their high quality and for the broad variety of adventures they offer. Once having sampled these delights, you may want to try other places in the same region—such as St.-Denis, Compiègne, Vaux-le-Vicomte, Barbizon, Rambouillet, St.-Germain-en-Laye, Malmaison, or Beauvais. Some of these were briefly described in the previous chapter.

Paris is by far the most convenient base for one-day excursions into the Ile-de-France, but those wishing to stay outside the city might consider nearby towns with both hotels and fast commuter service. Two excellent choices for this are Versailles and St.-Germain-en-Laye.

Because of the short distances involved, it is sometimes possible to visit two destinations in the same day, albeit at a rather hectic pace. Such pairings that work well in this region are: Versailles with Chartres, Fountainbleau with Moret-sur-Loing, and Chantilly with Senlis.

Those traveling by rail will note that several different train stations in Paris are used for the various trips. The map on page 13 shows the general location of these.

Versailles

By far the most popular daytrip destination in France, Versailles embodies in stone the awesome will of Louis XIV, the "Sun King." A visit to this enormous place will tell you a great deal about the Age of Absolutism, for Louis XIV did not merely rule a country, he *was* the State.

Versailles was built, in effect, as the seat of government—a place where the king could keep his eye on the treacherous nobility. Begun in 1661, it took over fifty years to complete. Few structures on earth can begin to match its splendor, with so much to see that attempting to do it all could lead to the visual equivalent of indigestion. A more sensible plan is to hit only the highlights of the château, the gardens, and the Trianons on the first visit; then plan on returning at some later date. The tour outlined here is limited to the most important features and—with a bit of rushing—could be done in half a day.

Energetic travelers making an early start will find it possible to combine this trip with one to Chartres, the subject of the next chapter.

GETTING THERE:

Trains on the SNCF-RER commuter line C-5 leave very frequently from the underground Invalides Station in Paris, located on the left bank of the Seine just across the Alexandre III bridge. These take you to Versailles' Rive Gauche Station, a short stroll from the château, in under 30 minutes. Railpasses are valid, but ask at the information office for a free ticket to operate the turnstiles. There are also regular trains from Montparnasse and St.-Lazare stations in Paris that go to other stations in Versailles, farther from the château.

By car, Versailles is about 13 miles southwest of Paris via the A-13 Autoroute or the N-10 road.

WHEN TO GO:

Good weather is necessary to appreciate the marvelous gardens at Versailles. Avoid coming on a Monday or major holiday, when the château is closed. Thursdays and Fridays are the least crowded.

The Hall of Mirrors

FOOD AND DRINK:

Versailles has a number of fine restaurants, including:

Les Trois Marches (3 Rue Colbert, by the château) Celebrated cuisine with excellent wines. Proper dress expected, for reservations phone 39-50-13-21. X: Sun., Mon $$$ +

Rescatore (27 Av. de St.-Cloud, 2 blocks northeast of the château) Noted for its seafood. X: Sat. lunch, Sun. $$$

Boule d'Or (25 Rue du Mar.-Foch, near Notre-Dame church) Classic cuisine in the town's oldest inn. Proper dress expected, for reservations phone 39-50-22-97. X: Sun. eve., Mon. $$

Potager du Roy (1 Rue Mar.-Joffre, near St.-Louis cathedral) Excellent cuisine in simple surroundings. Very popular—for reservations call 39-50-35-34. X: Sun., Mon. $$

Le Boeuf a la Mode (4 Rue au Pain, on Place du Marché, near Notre-Dame church) An elegant brasserie with homestyle cooking. $$

In addition, there is an inexpensive cafeteria in the château itself.

TOURIST INFORMATION:

The tourist information office is located at 7 Rue des Réservoirs, near the château. You can phone them at 39-50-36-22.

SUGGESTED TOUR:

Leave the **Rive Gauche Train Station** (1) and follow the map to nearby Place d'Armes. The **Palace of Versailles** *(Château)* (2), open-

Rue du Roi
Blvd. du Roi
Rue d'Angiviller
Rive Droite Station
TO PARIS-ST.-LAZARE
Blvd. de la Reine
Rue du Maréchal Foch
Museum
9
Rue de la
Notre-Dame Paroisse
8
Rue des Réservoirs
CHÂTEAU
Info.
Rue Carnot
Rue Hoche
PARIS A-13 ➔
R. Cotte
Ave. de St.-Cloud
Rue de l'Europe
Rue G. Clemenceau
Rue de Montbauron
2
Place d'Armes
3
Ave. de Paris
Rue Indép.-Américaine
Rue de la Chancellerie
Ave. de Paris
N-10
Ave. Gén. de Gaulle
PARIS N-10 ➔
Rue de Satory
1
Rive Gauche Station
Rue des États-Généraux
TO PARIS-INVALIDES
Rue de l'Orangerie
Potager du Roi
Rue Royale
Ave. de Sceaux
Rue de Noailles
Rue du Mar. Joffre
St.-Louis Cathedral
Carrés St.-Louis
Rue d'Anjou
Chantiers Station
10
Rue E. Charton
Versailles
Town

See other map for Château detail

300 Yards

TO PARIS-MONTPARNASSE
TO CHARTRES

N

N

Allée du Rendez-Vous

N-186

Blvd. St-Antoine

Allée des Hai Hai

Allée de Bailly

LE HAMEAU

⑥

Temple of Love

GRAND TRIANON

PETIT TRIANON

⑤

⑦

Allée St-Antoine

Allée de Trianon

Blvd. de la Reine

GRAND CANAL

Allée d'Apollo

Neptune Basin

Rue des Réservoirs

PETIT CANAL

④

Latona Basin

CHÂTEAU

Info.

⑧

Tapis Vert

Rue de l'Orangerie

②

Versailles
Palace and Gardens

See other map for town detail

⑨

③

N-10 TO CHARTRES

Orangerie

500 Yards

The Palace of Versailles

ing before you, was originally a hunting lodge of Louis XIII. His son, Louis XIV, greatly expanded this to create a sumptuous new palace where the court could be consolidated under one roof, far from the intrigues of Paris. The most noted architects of the time, Louis Le Vau and, later, Jules Hardouin-Mansart, were engaged along with the celebrated landscape gardener André Le Nôtre and the great decorator Charles Le Brun. Together they directed a vast army of workers who drained the marshes, leveled hills and moved forests. A full half-century of monumental labor went into the Versailles you see today. After the death of Louis XIV in 1715, the château continued to be used by his successors until the French Revolution, during which it was ransacked and nearly fell to ruin. Since then, much of it has been magnificently restored, with work continuing to this day.

Enter the château and visit the **State Apartments**, which include the famous **Hall of Mirrors**, the Chapel, the King's Suite and the Queen's Suite. An illustrated guide booklet in English is available at the entrance, which is quite useful since you'll be wandering through on your own. Other parts of the palace, including the **Private Apartments** and the **Royal Opera**, may be seen on guided tours only. The château is open from 9:45 a.m. to 5 p.m. every day except Mondays and some holidays. The great garden fountains are operated between 3:30 and 5 p.m. on certain Sundays from May to October, while spectacular night festivals are held occasionally during the summer. Ask at the tourist office for current schedules.

A Corner of Le Hameau

No visit to Versailles is complete without a stroll through the fabulous gardens. Begin with the **Parterres du Midi** (3), overlooking the **Orangerie**. Walk over to the Latona Basin and follow the Tapis Vert, a long green avenue between some enchanting hidden groves, to the **Grand Canal** (4), where boats may be hired.

Continue on to the **Grand Trianon** (5), a smaller château built in 1687 to avoid the formalities of court life. After the Revolution it was used by Napoleon and is furnished in the Empire style. It may be visited daily except on Mondays and holidays, from 9:45 a.m. to noon and 2–5 p.m.

Now follow the map to **Le Hameau** (6), a thoroughly delightful little hamlet where the unfortunate Marie-Antoinette played at being a peasant. Paths from here lead past the Temple of Love to the **Petit Trianon** (7), an elegant small château erected by Louis XV and later used by Marie-Antoinette. It is open from 2–5 p.m., except on Mondays and some holidays. Return to the main palace by way of the **Neptune Basin** (8).

Before heading back to Paris, you may want to explore a bit of the town of Versailles. An interesting short walk can be made by following the map past the Church of Notre-Dame to the pleasant **Lambinet Museum** (9), which specializes in 18th-century art and is open daily except Mondays and holidays, from 2–6 p.m. Those intrepid souls intent on continuing on to Chartres by rail should depart from Versailles' **Chantiers Station** (10).

Chartres

Rising majestically above the Beauce Plain, the Cathedral of Chartres is one of the great legacies of the Middle Ages and the quintessential Gothic cathedral. Pilgrims and tourists from all over the world are drawn to it by the thousands, yet most overlook the charms of the town itself. And that's a pity—for Chartres is one of those rare French *villes* that kept its essentially medieval character intact.

It may seem surprising that a town as small as Chartres should possess one of the largest cathedrals on earth. The place, however, appears to have a long history of religious significance. Ancient Druids probably worshiped at the well under the cathedral crypt. Later the capital of the Gallic Carnutes, it was called *Autricum* by the Romans, who built a temple on the same site. Early Christians replaced this with a basilica, saving the statue of the Roman goddess whom they took to be the Virgin. Five subsequent churches were built on the spot, culminating in the present 13th-century masterpiece. A precious relic believed to be a garment worn by the Virgin Mary, which has been in the cathedral since 876, is responsible for Chartres being a place of pilgrimage for over a thousand years.

Indefatigable travelers may want to combine a daytrip to Chartres with one to Versailles (see previous chapter), which is entirely possible by train or car but not especially recommended.

GETTING THERE:

Trains leave Montparnasse Station in Paris fairly frequently for the 50-minute trip to Chartres. Return service operates until late evening. These trains also stop at Versailles.

By car, the fastest route is via the A-10 and A-11 Autoroutes, a distance of 55 miles southwest of Paris. A slower but more interesting route is to take the N-10 through Versailles and Rambouillet.

WHEN TO GO:

Try to visit Chartres in good weather, when sunshine illuminates the incredible stained-glass windows to best effect. The art museum is closed on Tuesdays and major holidays.

Chartres Cathedral

FOOD AND DRINK:

Chartres has many restaurants that cater primarily to tourists. Among the better choices are:

Henri IV (31 Rue du Soleil-d'Or, one block south of the cathedral) Inspired classic cuisine, provincial ambiance. X: Mon. eve., Tues., Feb. $$$

La Vieille Maison (5 Rue au Lait, near the cathedral) Modern cuisine in an attractive old house. X: Sun. eve., Mon., Jan. $$$

Normand (24 Place des Épars, on the N-10, a few minutes southwest of the cathedral) The good cooking of Normandy in a country setting. X: Mon. $$

Café Serpente (2 Cloître Notre-Dame, facing the cathedral) An old-fashioned bistro. X: Tues. eve., Wed. $$

Le Minou (4 Rue Mar.-de-Lattre-de-Tassigny, 3 blocks south of the cathedral) An exceptional value. X: Sun. eve., Mon., July. $

Le Biniou (7 Rue Serpente, one block south of the cathedral) Crêpes in a Breton atmosphere. X: Tues., Wed. $

TOURIST INFORMATION:

Make inquiries at the Office de Tourisme, facing the cathedral. The phone number is 37-21-54-03. They also rent cassettes in English with a player and map for walking tours.

SUGGESTED TOUR:

From the **train station** (1) you will have a clear view of the cathedral. Follow the map to its fascinating **West Front** (2), much of which survives from an earlier 12th-century structure largely destroyed by fire in 1194. The two asymmetrical towers make a dramatic study in architectural evolution. On the right is the Old Tower, representing the fullest development of the Romanesque style. The New Tower, to the left, is capped with a 16th-century spire, a masterpiece of the Flamboyant Gothic. Between them stands the Royal Portal, three arched doorways from the 12th century. Look carefully at the stunning *Christ in Majesty* carving above the center door. The figures over the right portal depict the Nativity, while those on the left are of the Ascension.

Step inside to witness the true glory of **Chartres Cathedral**—its miraculous **stained-glass windows**. Almost all of these are original, mostly 13th-century with some dating from the 12th. Replacements account for less than six percent of the total 26,000 square feet, making this the largest collection of medieval glass in the world.

Guided tours of the interior are available—those in English being particularly good—or you can pick up a printed guide and explore on

Chartres

300 Yards

TO PARIS

N

Rue du Pélican

Blvd. Charles Péguy

Rue Muret

Rue de la Brèche

Rue du Massacre

Station

1

Ave. Jehan de Beauce

Rue des Lisses

Rue Chantault

Rue St.-André

8

EURE

10

Rue du Cardinal Pie

Museum

Tert.

St.-Nicolas

9

Place Châtelet

Rue du Cheval Blanc

3

Gardens

Rue de la Corroierie

Rue de la Tannerie

Blvd. de la Résistance

Rue Collin d'Harleville

Info.

2

4

Rue Fulbert

Rue au Lait

Rue Serpente

Rue des Changes

5

Rue Famin

Rue du Soleil d'Or

Rue des Écuyers

Rue Eux Juifs

EURE

Rue de la Foulerie

7

Rue Noël Ballay

Place des Épars

Rue Marceau

Rue de la Pie

Rue des Greniers

Rue St.-Pierre

Rue de la

Blvd. Chasles

Rue des Bouchers

Rue du Petit Change

Place des Halles

Rue St.-Michel

Rue Petion

6

your own. Binoculars can be a great help for studying the biblical stories depicted in the windows. Be sure to visit the **Treasury**, behind the choir, which displays the venerated garment thought to have been worn by the Virgin Mary.

A climb to the top of the **North Tower** will reward you with spectacular views. The entrance to this is by the door in the **North Transept** (3). Another sight not to be missed is the ancient **Crypt** of the original church, which can be visited on special guided tours only. These depart, oddly enough, from a souvenir shop called *La Crypte* in front of the **South Porch** (4).

Leave the cathedral and follow the map to the Rue des Écuyers. On the right, at number 35, you will find a curious old house with a 16th-century turret staircase of carved oak known as the **Escalier de la Reine Berthe** (5). Continue on to the **Church of St.-Pierre** (6). If its great cathedral did not exist, Chartres would still be noted for this magnificent medieval structure, whose flying buttresses and original stained glass are truly impressive.

Stroll over to the Eure River and cross it. There is a nice view of the cathedral from here. Turn left on Rue de la Foulerie and follow along to **Porte Guillaume** (7) to see what little remains of the old town walls. Return to the stream and walk along Rue de la Tannerie, passing several delightful old waterside buildings. Across the Eure stands the 12th-century **Church of St.-André** (8), a Romanesque structure whose choir once spanned the water on a daring arch, long since destroyed.

Continue by following the map to the **Beaux-Arts Museum** (9), reached via the steep Tertre Saint-Nicolas steps which open into lovely gardens. The museum, housed in the former Bishop's Place, contains a superb collection of paintings (particularly those by Vlaminck), enamels, tapestries, furniture, and artifacts of regional history. It is open from 10 a.m. to noon and 2–6 p.m. (5 p.m. in winter), every day except Tuesdays and holidays.

Another attraction you may want to visit is the **Cellier de Loëns** (10) at number 5 Rue du Cardinal Pie. This 13th-century cellar once stored tithes and is now the **International Stained-Glass Center**, offering rotating exhibits of the art that made Chartres famous. It is open daily except on Mondays, from 10 a.m. to 12:30 p.m. and 1:30–6 p.m.

Fontainebleau

Haunted by memories of François I and Napoleon Bonaparte, the Château of Fontainebleau beguiles with its marvelously haphazard layout and intimate atmosphere. Many prefer it to Versailles. This was a real home for the rulers of France, from the 12th century right down to Napoleon III in the 19th.

The palace as it stands today is mostly the result of an extensive construction carried out in the 16th century by François I, the king most credited with bringing the Renaissance to France. Only the keep *(donjon)* in the Oval Court survives from the Middle Ages. Later kings, including Louis XIV, made frequent use of the château, drawn primarily by the sporting opportunities of the surrounding forest. Fontainebleau became the favorite residence of Napoleon I, who had it thoroughly redecorated. It was also the scene, in 1814, of his abdication and departure for Elba.

The Forest of Fontainebleau is exceptionally lovely with its wide variety of wild, natural beauty. Those with cars may want to pick up a map at the tourist office and go exploring, particularly to the charming village of Barbizon. This trip can easily be combined in the same day with one to Moret-sur-Loing, which is only six miles away on the same rail line, and which is described in the next chapter.

GETTING THERE:

Trains depart Gare de Lyon station in Paris frequently for Fontainebleau-Avon, less than 45 minutes away. These are met by a bus marked "Château," which goes to the palace. Return trains run until mid-evening.

By car, the fastest way is via the A-6 Autoroute, followed by the N-37 and N-7 roads. Fontainebleau is 40 miles southeast of Paris.

WHEN TO GO:

Avoid coming on a Tuesday, when the château is closed. Pleasant weather will make a walk in the gardens more enjoyable.

TO PARIS

TO MORET-SUR-LOING

① Station
Bus

Ave. Franklin Roosevelt

Rue Bernard Palissy

Rue des Déportés

Rue Gambetta

N

Rue Rémy Dumoncel

Rue de la Charité

Blvd. Orloff

Rue de la Treille

Blvd. Gén. Leclerc

Allée d'Avon

Allée Napoléon

GRAND CANAL

Rue Aristide Briand

Rue Grande

Route des Cascades

④

Blvd. du Mar. Joffre

Rue des Bois

Rue Béranger

Rue de la Cloche

Rue Grande

Rue du Château

Cirque du Parc

⑥ ⑦

⑤

Rue de la Paroisse

Bus

⑧

Info.

②

③

Bus

Blvd. Magenta

Rue St.-Merry

Rue de France

Rue St.-Honoré

Rue Royale

N-7 TO PARIS

Fontainebleau

Route from Station

*See other map for
detail of Château*

500 Yards

Fontainebleau

Château and Town

*SEE OTHER MAP FOR
ROUTE TO STATION*

300 Yards

FOOD AND DRINK:

The town of Fontainebleau has a great many restaurants and cafés in all price ranges, particularly on and near Rue Grande and Place Général-de-Gaulle. Among the better choices are:

Aigle Noir (27 Place Napoléon Bonaparte, near the tourist office) Excellent cuisine in the renowned hotel's Le Beauharnais restaurant. $$$

Le Filet de Sole (5 Rue du Coq-Gris, near the tourist office) Good food in an ancient house. X: Tues., Wed., July. $$

Chez Arrighi (53 Rue de France, 2 blocks northwest of the château) A local favorite. X: Mon. $$

Le Dauphin (24 Rue Grande, near the tourist office) An exceptional value. X: Tues. eve., Wed., Feb. $

Le Grillardin (12 Rue des Pins, 4 blocks northeast of the tourist office) Good-value dining in a rustic atmosphere. X: Sun. eve., Mon. $

TOURIST INFORMATION:

The tourist office, phone 64-22-25-68, is located at 31 Place Napoléon Bonaparte, near the château.

SUGGESTED TOUR:

The **Fontainebleau-Avon Train Station** (1) is nearly two miles from the palace. Get there by one of the frequent buses marked "Château," or on foot through the park.

Enter the **Château** (2) via the White Horse Courtyard, also known as the **Cour des Adieux**, where Napoleon I bid a tearful farewell to his troops in 1814 as he went into exile. You may stroll through the **Grand Apartments** at your own leisure, following a well-marked route. In order to understand what you're seeing, however, it will help to purchase an illustrated guide in English, available at the entrance. The most outstanding sights are the 16th-century **Galerie François I**, the **King's Staircase**, the **Ballroom**, the **Royal Apartments**, and **Napoleon's Apartments**. To see the more intimate **Petit Apartments** requires taking a guided tour. The château is open every day except Tuesdays, from 9 a.m. to 12:30 p.m. and again from 2–5 p.m., but closed on Sunday afternoons from September through June. In either case, the last admission is 45 minutes before the closing time.

Leave the château and follow the map through a passage in the south wing to an intriguing 16th-century grotto. This opens into the informal **English Gardens** (*Jardin Anglais*) (3) laid out by Napoleon. Continue on past the original spring, the **Fontaine Bliaud**, from which the name of the palace and town derives. Next to this is the **Carp Pond** with its delightful little island pavilion.

The Château of Fontainebleau

You are now in the formal gardens, the Parterre designed for Louis XIV by the architect Le Vau, which offers marvelous views of the château. Stroll down to the **Cascades** (4) and look out over the Grand Canal, a center of pageantry in the time of the Sun King, then return to the palace. Horse carriage rides are usually available along here.

The **Cour de la Fontaine** (5) is a beautiful courtyard overlooking the carp pond. Take an admiring glance, then follow around past the ancient **Oval Court** (6) with its 12th-century keep—used by François I as his bedroom. This is usually locked, but you can peek in through the grill. Continue on past the 17th-century Cour des Offices and visit the **Jardin de Diane** (7), a wonderfully romantic garden noted for its elegant fountain dating from 1603.

Those who would like to see some of the town should exit onto Rue Grande and turn right. A left on Rue Paroisse leads past a market place to the interesting **Napoleonic Museum of Art and Military History** (8) on Rue St.-Honoré. Noted for its fine collection of swords, it is open on Tuesdays through Saturdays, from 2–5:30 p.m.

Return to Place Général-de-Gaulle, facing the entrance of the château. From here you can get a bus back to the train station.

Moret-sur-Loing

Although it has long been a favorite weekend retreat for Parisians, Moret-sur-Loing has yet to be discovered by foreign visitors. This deliciously picturesque old town on the meandering Loing River looks like a scene from an Impressionist painting, and in fact is one. The noted artist Alfred Sisley spent the latter years of his life here, immortalizing for all time its narrow streets, quaint church, delightful bridge, and charming watermills.

Moret was a strategically important border fortress as early as the 12th century, when it protected the Ile-de-France from the counts of Champagne. Many of its original structures still exist, preserved amid a medieval atmosphere virtually unmatched elsewhere in the region.

A daytrip to Moret can be combined quite easily with one to Fontainebleau, just six miles away on the same rail line. If you are driving, you could visit Vaux-le-Vicomte, a fabulous château just outside Melun, instead. This is briefly described on page 98. Those going to Moret only will find that it makes a good afternoon trip.

GETTING THERE:

Trains leave Gare de Lyon station in Paris fairly frequently for Moret-Véneux-les-Sablons Station, usually stopping at Fontainebleau en route. The trip takes less than one hour. Return service operates until mid-evening. Although Moret is a very small town, it is also an important rail junction, with trains to and from Paris using different, widely spaced platforms. Be careful to note the correct one on the departure board.

By car, the quickest route is to follow the directions to Fontainebleau on page 111, then take the N-6 into Moret, which is about 48 miles southeast of Paris.

WHEN TO GO:

Moret can be enjoyed at any time in good weather, particularly on weekends. *Son et Lumière* spectacles are held on Saturday nights in summer—check the tourist office for details.

Porte de Bourgogne Gate and the Bridge

FOOD AND DRINK:

There are a number of charming restaurants, mostly located near the bridge. Some choices are:

> **Auberge de la Palette** (Av. Jean-Jaurès, on way to station) A well recommended inn. X: Tues. eve., Wed., late Apr., late Aug. $$

> **Bon Abri** (90 Av. de Fontainebleau, in nearby Véneux-les-Sablons, not far from the train station) An excellent value. X: Sun. eve., Mon. $

TOURIST INFORMATION:

The tourist office is located on Place de Samois, next to the Porte de Samois. You can call them at 60-70-41-66.

SUGGESTED TOUR:

The **Moret-Véneux-les-Sablons Train Station** (1) is nearly a mile from the town proper. You could call for a taxi, although the walk is rather pleasant. Enter the Old Town through the 12th-century **Porte de Samois** gate (2), next to the tourist office. Continue down Rue Grande where, at number 24, opposite the war memorial park, you will pass the house where Napoleon spent the last night on his return from Elba. Turn right into a passageway leading to a courtyard behind the town hall. Here stands the so-called **Maison François I** (3), a splendid Renaissance façade built in 1527 and later moved, stone by stone, to Paris, where it remained until 1956. It was then returned to Moret. Back on the Rue Grande there are two fine Renaissance houses at numbers 28 and 30.

Stroll straight ahead through the venerable 12th-century **Porte de Bourgogne** gate (4). From here a famous bridge spans the Loing River. Midstream, on either side, are two striking old mills, now private residences. Once across, make a left into the **park** (5) on the river's edge where you can enjoy the romantic view captured in Sisley's renowned painting *The Bridge at Moret,* displayed in the new Orsay Museum in Paris.

Follow the map past a set of locks on the Burgundy Canal to the **Georges Clemenceau Museum** *(La Grange Batelière)* (6). Designed as a retirement place by the eminent French premier shortly before his death, this intimate, very personal and extremely charming small house was occupied by his son until 1964. It is now open to the public for escorted visits daily from Easter through November, from 2:30–6 p.m. Try to see this special treat if you can.

Return across the bridge and follow Rue de la Tannerie to the ancient **Castle Keep** *(Donjon)* (7) on Rue du Donjon. Built in 1128, it was used for several months as a prison for Nicolas Fouquet, Louis XIV's finance minister who amassed a great fortune at the State's expense.

At number 9 Rue du Donjon is the **house** (8), where the artist Alfred Sisley spent the last years of his life. One of the pioneers of Impressionism, he showed little aptitude in promoting his work and died in poverty. Ironically, his paintings now hang in the world's greatest museums.

Stroll through the evocative narrow alleyways in the immediate area, then continue on to the magnificent Gothic **Church of Notre-Dame** (9). Begun in 1166 on a site consecrated by Thomas à Becket, the Archbishop of Canterbury, construction continued until the 15th century, when its Flamboyant porch was added. The church is quite interesting to visit—its flying buttresses dramatic in their upward surge. To the right of the church, in an old timbered house, nuns once sold their famous *Sucres d'Orge,* the barley-sugar specialty of Moret. The nuns are gone, but the candy is still available at several shops in town.

Follow the map via Rue Grande and make the first possible turn through an old building to the river's edge. Wander along to some **old fortifications** (10) which are now parts of houses, then return to Rue Grande and the station.

N

BURGUNDY CANAL

Locks

⑥

Quai du Canal

R. de la Saussaie

Rue du Peintre Sisley

Route de St.-Mammes

⑤

LOING

Rue Edmond Dupray

⑩

④

⑦

Rue Lemasson-Henrion

Rue Grande

⑨

⑧

Rue de Madame

Rue

de la Pierre Morin

Info.

③

②

Ave. Jean Jaurès

Rue Eugene Moussor

Rue de la République

Ave. Georges Clemenceau

Rue du Viaduc

Rue de la Liberté

Rue des Chapelles Morin

Rue Montrichard

Rue du Pont National

Rue des Jarsines

Avenue de la Gare

TO PARIS

Ave. de Fontainebleau

Station

R. Victor Hugo

Rue de la Fleur

Rue Pasteur

①

Moret-sur-Loing

⊢ 300 Yards ⊣

Provins

Another one of those intriguing medieval towns that somehow get overlooked by tourists, Provins can be a real charmer. Once the third-largest city in France (after Paris and Rouen), it is now a pleasant backwater with distant echoes of a long-ago past. This is a place for quiet contemplation far from the madding crowds, where vestiges of the early Middle Ages have survived intact.

The town's decline began as early as the 13th century. Before that, Provins was the capital of Brie, seat of the counts of Champagne and the site of major fairs famed throughout Europe. It has a curious connection with English history. During the 13th century it was ruled by Edmund, duke of Lancaster, who adopted as his own the famous red rose of Provins—later to become a symbol in the War of the Roses. Both the plague and the Hundred Years War took their toll, but it was perhaps the growing importance of nearby Paris that contributed most to the downfall of this once-great city.

Provins is built on two levels. The lower town *(Ville Basse)* is reawakening with renewed prosperity, while the upper town *(Ville Haute)*, perched high on a promontory overlooking the Brie plain, slumbers on amid ruined memories. Both have their fascinations, and both are covered on the suggested walking tour.

GETTING THERE:

Trains depart Gare de l'Est station in Paris in the morning and again around noon for Longueville, where you change to a connecting local for the short ride to Provins. The total journey takes a bit over one hour. Return service operates until early evening. Study the schedules carefully to avoid a wait at Longueville, not exactly the most scintillating place in France.

By car, it's the N-19 all the way to Provins, 53 miles southeast of Paris. A more complex but probably faster route is to leave Paris on the A-4, switching quickly to the N-4, then finally the D-231 into Provins.

The Tour de César

WHEN TO GO:

Good weather is essential for this largely outdoor trip. The famous Tour de César is open every day except Christmas and New Year's, but some other attractions tend to operate only on Sundays and holidays.

FOOD AND DRINK:

Provins offers a nice variety of restaurants along the walking route. Some suggestions are:

Aux Vieux Remparts (3 Rue Couverte, in the upper town, near the Tour de César) Real country cooking in a charming environment. X: Tues. eve. $$

La Croix d'Or (1 Rue des Capucins, in the lower town near the Durteint stream) Dining in a small and very ancient hotel. X: Sun. eve., Mon. $$

La Fontaine (10 Rue Victor Arnoul, in the lower town near St.-Ayoul) Light Burgundian specialties in a rustic setting. X: Thurs. $$

Le Chalet (3 Place Honoré-de-Balzac, 1 block east of the Durteint stream) Local cooking in a small hotel. $

Le Berri (17 Rue Hugues-le-Grand, in the lower town near St.-Ayoul) A good value in regional cuisine. X: Mon., July. $

TOURIST INFORMATION:

The local tourist office, phone 64-00-16-65, is at the Tour de César in the upper town.

SUGGESTED TOUR:

Leave the **train station** (1) and follow the map past several streams in the colorful lower town. The climb to the upper town is rather steep, but manageable and highly worthwhile. Once there, step into the **Jardin des Brébans** park for a nice view, then stroll over to the **Tour de César** (2). Dating from the 12th century, this massive octagonal tower was erected on the site of a Roman fortress and is still in magnificent condition. Its circular base was built by the English during the Hundred Years War as a platform for their artillery. Enter the tower and climb its narrow staircases, which get somewhat spooky as you ascend to the very top for a fantastic panorama of the entire region. The tower is open on Mondays through Saturdays from 9:30 a.m. to noon and 2–6 p.m.; and on Sundays from 2–6 p.m.; closing at 5 p.m. in winter. At its base is the tourist information office.

The **Church of St.-Quiriace** (3), equally ancient, is just a few steps away. Originally planned to be much larger, its choir, apse and transepts were the only parts completed before the days of prosperity ran out for Provins. Its interior, however, is quite impressive and should not be missed. The church is open on weekends and holidays; otherwise see the tourist office for entry.

Stroll over to the **Maison Romane** (4) on Rue du Palais. This partly 10th-century house now contains an interesting museum of local archaeology, usually open in the afternoons on Sundays and holidays during the season. Return to the Tour de César and continue along the footpath at its base to Rue de l'Ormerie, following that to Place du Châtel.

The **Grange aux Dîmes** (5), a curious 12th-century tithe barn now housing a museum of medieval artifacts, can be visited daily except on some major holidays, from 10 a.m. to noon and 2:30–5 p.m., closing earlier in winter. In the basement there is an entrance to a large network of underground passageways.

Now follow Rue de Jouy to the **Porte de Jouy** (6), a medieval gate in the still-extant town walls. Turn right and follow the inside of the ramparts for a short distance, then return and go through the gate. A left of a delightful country lane leads along the massive fortifications.

Re-enter the town through the 12th-century **Porte St.-Jean** (7), another fortified gate, and return on Rue St.-Jean to Place du Châtel. From here, walk downhill on Rue St.-Thibault to the **Hôtel Dieu** (8). Once the palace of the countess of Champagne, this heavily reconstructed medieval building has an entrance to the mysterious, enig-

A Corner of the Ramparts

matic subterranean passages *(Souterrains)* of Provins, some of which may date from the time of the Franks. These can be seen on guided tours—ask at the tourist office for details.

You have now returned to the lower town. Stroll along Rue du Val and Rue de la Cordonnerie to the **Church of St.-Ayoul** (9), once the center of a cult around which the *Ville Basse* developed. Destroyed by fire in the 12th century, the church was soon rebuilt and features some truly outstanding sculptures along with other works of art. From here it is a short walk back to the station.

Chantilly

The Ile-de-France region is justly renowned for its many splendid châteaux. Some of these, especially Versailles, are monumental in scope while others, such as Fontainebleau, leave the visitor endowed with an immensely satisfying sense of history. For sheer beauty, however, the dream-like Château of Chantilly is by far the most outstanding. Many even consider it to be the loveliest in all France. This is surely reason enough to make the easy daytrip, but Chantilly gilds the lily with yet more sumptuous attractions. There are enchanted gardens, a magnificent forest, one of the nation's best art museums, stables that resemble a palace, a world-famous racetrack, a great horse training center and—of course—the delicious whipped cream and black lace for which the town is noted.

Chantilly has an illustrious history going back to a Roman named Cantilius. The present château—actually two separate châteaux joined by a common entrance—is the fifth on the same site. Its larger part, the impossibly romantic Grand Château, is a late-19th-century pastiche while the older Petit Château dates from the 16th century. It was here that a well-known event (or story?) occurred in 1671, when Louis XIV came calling for a three-day visit—along with five thousand of his retainers. The greatest chef in France at the time, François Vatel, was employed at the château and had to feed all those hungry mouths on virtually no notice. Things went wrong and finally, when the promised fish failed to arrive in time, the overwrought Vatel ended it all with a sword thrust through his body.

By getting off to an early start, a trip to Chantilly could easily be combined in the same day with one to Senlis (see page 130), just five miles away by bus from the train station, or by car. Alternatively, you could visit Compiègne instead.

GETTING THERE:

Trains leave Nord Station in Paris almost hourly for the 30-minute ride to Chantilly. Return service operates until early evening.

By car, leave Paris on the A-1 Autoroute, switching to the N-1 near St.-Denis and then to the N-16. Chantilly is about 25 miles north of Paris.

WHEN TO GO:

Good weather is essential for a visit to Chantilly. Avoid coming on a Tuesday, when nearly everything is closed.

FOOD AND DRINK:

There are a few good restaurants between the train station and the château. Some choices are:

> **Le Relais Condé** (42 Av. du Mar.-Joffre, near the station) Classic cuisine with good wines in an elegant restaurant. X: Mon. $$$
>
> **Les Quatres Saisons** (9 Av. du Général-Leclerc, south of the station) Both French and Scandinavian specialties. X: Mon., Feb. $$
>
> **Tipperary** (6 Av. du Mar.-Joffre, on the way to town.) A pleasant place for regional specialties. $$
>
> **Château** (22 Rue du Connétable, near the Grandes Ecuries) Good dining on the garden terrace or indoors. X: Mon. eve., Tues., late Aug. $$
>
> **Capitainerie** (in the Château) A self-serve cafeteria for light lunches. X: Tues. $

TOURIST INFORMATION:

The local tourist office is located on Avenue Maréchal-Joffre, one block from the train station. You may want to call them first to avoid coming on a crowded race day, usually held on certain Sundays in June. The number is 44-57-08-58.

SUGGESTED TOUR:

Leave the **train station** (1) and follow the map past the tourist office to the **Racetrack** (2), where the prestigious *Prix de Diane* and *Prix du Jockey Club* races are run each June. This beautifully situated course has been attracting Paris society since 1836.

Continue on to the **Château** (3), rising from the middle of a tiny lake like a fantastic scene from a fairytale. One single admission covers both the castle and its grounds. Cross the bridge and enter the **Condé Museum**, which occupies the entire château. The sumptuous collection of art, along with the estate, was bequeathed to the *Institut de France* in 1897 by its last owner, the Duke of Aumale, fifth son of Louis-Philippe, the last king of France. A small guide brochure in English is available at the entrance.

The rooms to your right, in the **Grand Château**, contain the picture galleries and may be seen at your own leisure. Laid out in a charming 19th-century style, the walls are covered from top to bottom with an amazingly good collection of canvases. To see the rest of the château

Chantilly

500 Yards

Le Hameau

N

TO SENLIS

RACETRACK

Route de l'Aigle

R. de la Faisanderie

Rue des Cascades

Rue du Connétable

Rue d'Aumale

Blvd. de la Libération

Ave. du Mar. Joffre

N-16

Rue de Gouvieux

Info.

Ave. de Sylvie

TO PARIS

Ave. Gén. Leclerc

N-16 TO PARIS

Bus to Senlis

Station

The Château of Chantilly

you will have to take a guided tour, included in the admission price. Don't miss the private apartments in the **Petit Château**, especially the Chapel and the Library, whose greatest treasure is the *Très Riches Heures du Duc de Berry*, one of the great masterpieces of the Middle Ages. Because of its fragile condition this is rarely exhibited, but copies are on display. The château is open every day except Tuesdays, from 10:30 a.m. to 6 p.m., with shorter hours in winter.

Leave the castle and walk straight ahead into the park. Once in the woods, turn right and follow the map past the tiny Chapel of St.-Paul to the **Maison de Sylvie** (4), a house with a long history of romantic affairs. The paths now lead through an enchanted forest, complete with statuary in little clearings, to **Le Hameau** (5), a rustic hamlet where the nobility played at being peasants. This was the prototype for Marie-Antoinette's famous *hameau* at Versailles. Continue around to the formal **gardens** and **waterways** (6) designed by that great landscape artist, André Le Nôtre, who was also largely responsible for the gardens at Versailles.

The picturesque **English Gardens** (7) come as a great contrast. Stroll through them to the **Ile d'Amour** (8), an idyllic little island, then continue on to the **Jeu de Paume** (9), which is sometimes open.

In the Forest

One last sight remains at Chantilly, just outside the palace precincts. This is the **Grandes Écuries** (10), a stable built like a fabulous palace. The story is told about the Duke of Bourbon, owner of the château during the early 18th century, having this luxurious barn erected because he expected to be reincarnated as a horse and wanted to assure his future comfort. Whether this event actually occurred is not known, but the posh interiors are open to visitors as the **Living Museum of the Horse** *(Musée Vivant du Cheval)*. Demonstrations of dressage, a great treat, are given several times daily. The stables are open from April through October, daily except Tuesdays, from 10:30 a.m. to 6 p.m.; and from November through March on weekdays from 2–4:30 p.m. and on Saturdays, Sundays and holidays from 10:30 a.m. to 5:30 p.m. From May through August they are also open on Tuesdays.

Senlis

Permeated with a distinctly medieval atmosphere, Senlis has almost totally escaped the turmoils of history. Its ancient, twisting lanes remain largely as they were during the Middle Ages, when the long line of French royalty began there in 987 with the election of Hugues Capet as the first true king of France. Senlis was old even then, having been built on the foundations of a Gallo-Roman settlement.

The town continued as a seat of kings, at least on a part-time basis, until the reign of Henri IV in the 16th century. After that, royalty no longer came and Senlis entered a peaceful period, interrupted only now and then by a few wars, the French Revolution, and a close brush with destruction at the hands of invading Germans in 1914.

Much of the town's fascinating past is still intact, steeped in an aura of charm and ready to be enjoyed today. You may want to combine this visit with one to nearby Chantilly, quite easily done by getting off to an early start.

GETTING THERE:

Trains depart Nord Station in Paris almost hourly for the 30-minute ride to Chantilly, where you change to a bus for Senlis. These buses, leaving from the north side of the Chantilly station, are operated for the railroad and accept train tickets or passes. The distance is only five miles. Upon arrival at the Senlis bus station, check the posted schedule of return buses to Chantilly, from which trains to Paris operate until early evening.

By car, take the A-1 Autoroute north from Paris to the Senlis exit, a distance of 32 miles.

WHEN TO GO:

Avoid coming on a Tuesday or on a Wednesday morning, when the ancient Royal Palace and the museums are closed.

FOOD AND DRINK:

Senlis has a fair selection of restaurants, including:

> **Le Formanoir** (17 rue du Châtel, 2 blocks from the cathedral) A pleasant restaurant in a 16th-century former convent. X: Sun. $$$

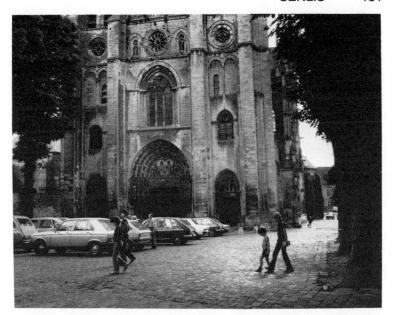

The Cathedral of Notre-Dame

Le Vert Galant (15 Place Henri IV, near the town hall) Good food in a convenient location. X: Sun. eve., Mon. $$

Hostellerie de la Porte Bellon (51 Rue Bellon, near the bus station) A country inn with a charming restaurant. $$

TOURIST INFORMATION:

The local tourist office, phone 44-53-06-40, is located on Place du Parvis-Notre-Dame, in front of the cathedral.

SUGGESTED TOUR:

Leave the **bus station** (1) and follow the map to the **Jardin du Roi** (2), a lovely park built along the remains of the original Gallo-Roman fortifications.

Retrace your steps and turn right on Rue de Villevert to Place du Parvis. This engaging little square facing the cathedral is home to the small but charming **Museum of Fine Arts** *(Musée Vermandois)* (3), which also features an interesting audio-visual presentation. It is open during the same times as the other museums in town. The tourist office, on the west side of the square, can furnish you with information for making a possible side trip to the Gallo-Roman Amphitheater (8).

The 12th-century **Cathedral of Notre-Dame** (4) is one of the earliest Gothic structures in France. Although rather small, it is both handsome and interesting. Examine the carvings over the main portal, which relate to the life of the Virgin, then enter through the splendid south transept, added after a disastrous 16th-century fire. The interior, altered many times throughout the centuries, is noted for its exceptionally beautiful balcony running above the side aisles.

Stroll over to what remains of the **Château Royal** (5), a complex of ancient buildings that were once a principal residence for the early kings of France, particularly during the Merovingian and Carolingian eras. The last king to use the castle was Henri II, while still a 16th-century prince. Following that, the château deteriorated badly and was finally ruined during the Revolution. Enough has survived, however, to be of interest. Against the city wall, on the north side of the grounds, stands the foundations of the original keep.

Also within the castle precincts is the intriguing **Museum of the Hunt** *(Musée de la Vénerie)*, located in the 18th-century Priory of St.-Maurice. Displays of this most royal of sports include costumes, artifacts, paintings and literally thousands of antlers. It may be seen only on guided tours, which begin hourly with an audio-visual show in an adjacent building. Tickets are sold at the entrance to the Château Royal, along with tickets to the grounds alone—take your choice. Both the castle ruins and the museum are open daily except on Tuesdays and on Wednesday mornings; from 10 a.m. to noon and 2–6 p.m., closing an hour earlier during the winter season.

From here, a delightful walk can be made by following the map along colorful old streets and through the ancient **Fausse Porte** (6), a remnant of the original walls. Continue on to the 15th-century **Town Hall** *(Hôtel de Ville)* (7) on Place Henri IV. It is possible to take a side trip to the relics of a **Gallo-Roman Amphitheater** *(Arènes)* (8) unearthed in 1863, but ask about this at the tourist office first.

Return to the cathedral via Due de la Tonnellerie and Rue St.-Frambourg. Along the way you will pass the 12th-century **Church of St.-Frambourg** (9), recently restored by the Hungarian pianist Georges Cziffra as a concert hall.

The former **Bishop's Palace** (10), next to the cathedral, now houses the **Museum of Art and Archaeology**, a fascinating collection of local finds from the Gallo-Roman period onwards, as well as some excellent works of art. Its hours are the same as those of the Museum of the Hunt.

Senlis

200 Yards

Rue du Heaume
Rue Vieille de Paris
TO CHANTILLY
Rue Henri Pi.
R. du Puits-Tiphaine
Walls
Museum
Rue du Chat-Haret
Rue des Cordeliers
Rue St.-Geneviève
Rue de la Tonnellerie
Rue du Châtel
Info.
Rue de Villevert
Pl. du Parvis
Pl. de la Halle
Pl. Notre-Dame
Rue aux Flageards
Rue de la Poterne
Rue de la République
Rue de Meaux
Rue des Bordeaux
Rue Bellon
Rue St.-Pierre
Cours Thore-Montmorency
Rue St.-Yves-à-l'Argent
Ave. Leclerc
Cours Boutteville
Ave. du Maréchal Foch
Ave. Gén. de Gaulle
A-1 TO PARIS
N
Bus Station

Section IV

Daytrips from Paris

Normandy and the North

Normandy, an ancient province lying between the Ile-de-France and the English Channel, is truly a land apart. Molded by its unique history, it offers an amazingly wide variety of sights ranging from some of the prettiest countryside in Europe to dynamic cities, from quaint fishing villages to luxurious seaside resorts. Although the distances are fairly great, an efficient transportation network brings many of its best attractions within comfortable daytrip range of Paris.

Throughout its often turbulent history, Normandy has been a battleground—a place conquered and reconquered by forces outside the mainstream of the French experience. At various times it was held by the Celts, the Romans, the Germanic tribes and, most important of all, the Norsemen—Vikings from Scandinavia—who in the 9th century settled this land for good, thus accounting for the preponderance of tall, blue-eyed Normans today. It was their renowned leader, William the Conqueror, who defeated the English near Hastings in 1066—an event that forever changed the course of European history. As a result, much of our own heritage derives from Norman tradition.

During most of the Middle Ages, Normandy was at best only marginally under the control of French kings. For long periods it was ruled by the English, and its semi-autonomy ended only with the French Revolution. In our own century the Germans again occupied the land, being driven out by the Battle of Normandy in 1944.

The six daytrips in this section can easily be made by trains departing from St.-Lazare Station in Paris. By car, the region is well served via its high-speed lifeline, the A-13 *Autoroute de Normandie*. Those with more time may prefer to stay over and explore its outer fringes, especially the near-magical Mont St.-Michel, a miraculous sight that sadly lies beyond any reasonable daytrip range of Paris.

Outside Normandy itself, this section also includes a daytrip to Amiens, a singularly impressive city in the largely dreary industrial north.

Giverny and Vernon

The Monet Gardens

Born in 1840, the celebrated French painter Claude Monet was one of the founding fathers of Impressionism and a vital force in the modern art movement it led to. After a long period of ridicule and poverty, his talent finally received broad public recognition. Now fairly prosperous, Monet in 1883 created for himself and his family a lovely home surrounded by lush gardens near the Seine, in the tiny hamlet of Giverny. It was in this serene environment that his greatest works were achieved.

Following Monet's death in 1926, the property deteriorated badly until 1966, when it was willed to the *Institut de France* by his son Michel. Generous donations, primarily from the United States, have made possible a stunning restoration of this extraordinary place. Ever since its public opening in 1980 as the Claude Monet Museum, the gardens—along with his remarkably charming house and cavernous studio—have become an extremely popular daytrip destination, indeed a pilgrimage, for art lovers and tourists alike.

Organized bus tours to Giverny are offered by several firms in Paris, which are certainly a convenient way to reach this secluded spot. They have the disadvantage, however, of limiting the amount of time you can spend savoring its enchanting atmosphere. They also overlook nearby Vernon, an ancient town of considerable charm, worthy of a trip in itself. With a little bit of effort it is entirely possible to see both by either train or private car. Giverny, by the way, makes a fine half-day trip, leaving Paris at noon.

GETTING THERE:

Trains depart St.-Lazare Station in Paris several times daily for Vernon, less than an hour away. From here you can take a taxi the three-mile distance to Giverny. It is also possible to walk or rent a bicycle *(Train + Vélo)* at the Vernon station. To make the return easier, there is a public phone at the museum with numbers for the local taxi service posted. Return trains run until early evening.

By car, take the A-13 Autoroute to the Bonnières-Vernon exit, then the N-15 into Vernon, cross the Seine and follow signs to the Monet Museum. It is about 50 miles northwest of Paris.

N

D-313

D-313

Vernonnet

Rue Jules Soret

Rue de Giverny
②
TO MONET MUSEUM

SEINE

Ave. de Rouen

Rue Carnot
Rue Potard

Ave. du Maréchal Leclerc

⑤

Info.

④

Rue St.-Lazare

Ave. Victor Hugo

Rue d'Albufera

Rue Carnot

Rue Steiner

Pl. d'Evreux

Pl. de Gaulle

Ave. Gambetta

Ave. Mendès France

Place de la République

Ave. de Paris
N-15 TO PARIS ➤

Rue du Grévarin

①

Station

TO PARIS ➤

D-181

Ave. Montgomery

Rue de Bizy

Rue du Parc

Ave. de l'Ardèche

⑥
TO BIZY

Rue St.-Louis

Giverny Trip

Vernon

400 Yards

Inside the Water Lily Studio

WHEN TO GO:

The Monet gardens and house are open between April 1st and October 31st, daily except Mondays. Hours for the gardens are from 10 a.m. to 6 p.m., while the house closes between noon and 2 p.m. You will have the place more to yourself in the morning, before the tour buses arrive. Avoid coming on a rainy day.

FOOD AND DRINK:

There are several simple eating places in Giverny—ask at the museum about this. The town of Vernon offers a much wider selection of restaurants, including:

Au Beau Rivage (13 Av. Mar.-Leclerc, near the river) An attractive place for good food. X: Sun. eve., Mon. $$

Les Fleurs (71 Rue Carnot, near the Archives Tower) A local favorite. X: Sun. eve., Mon. $$

Le Strasbourg (6 Place d'Évreux, 2 blocks northeast of the station) Dining in a small hotel. X: Sun. eve., Mon. $

TOURIST INFORMATION:

The tourist office in Vernon is located next to the Church of Notre-Dame, phone 32-51-39-60. You can also call the Monet Museum at 32-51-28-21. They speak English.

SUGGESTED TOUR:

From the **Vernon Train Station** (1) you can take a taxi to the *Musée Monet* in Giverny, a trip of nearly three miles. Walking is also possible

Monet's House at Giverny

by following the map, or you can rent a bicycle at the station. The route is quite level, but may have heavy traffic.

Arriving at the **Claude Monet Museum** (1), you will have a choice of purchasing a ticket for the studio and gardens alone or a combination that includes the house. Buy the latter—it's worth it. Visits begin in the huge **Water Lily Studio**, built in 1916 to accommodate large canvases. The paintings on the wall are, of course, copies; the originals being in leading museums.

Stroll over to the painstakingly restored **house**, surfaced in pink crushed brick with green doors and shutters. Its exquisite interior, looking like the pages from a fashionable architectural magazine, is perhaps a bit too tidy for the home of an artist, but very beautiful nonetheless. It was here that Monet entertained his closest friends, including the French premier Georges Clemenceau and fellow artists Renoir, Degas, Rodin and Cézanne, among others.

The **Clos Normand Garden**, facing the house, is totally French in concept. Monet loved gardens, and as his fortunes improved he employed several gardeners to maintain them. From here, a tunnel leads under the public road to the famous **Water Garden** (3), which he created by diverting a nearby stream. This part of the property exudes a distinctly Oriental aura. Much of it seems familiar, especially the wisteria-entwined **Japanese Bridge**, a subject for many of his best-known paintings, around which clusters of water lilies float on the pond. It was in this miniature universe that Monet, always an innovator, made

The Japanese Bridge in the Water Garden

the stylistic transition beyond Impressionism and came very close to the abstract art of later years.

Returning to **Vernon**, you will have a beautiful view from its bridge of the town, the Seine and the woods beyond. Visit the 12th-century **Church of Notre-Dame** (4), noted for its splendid west-front rose window and lavish interior. In the immediate vicinity stand a number of medieval half-timbered houses, lending atmosphere to this ancient settlement founded by Rollo, the first duke of Normandy, in the 9th century. Stroll along Rue Carnot and Rue Potard. The **Archives Tower** (5) is all that remains of a massive castle built in 1123 by King Henry I of England. Closeby, in another venerable building, is the **Poulain Municipal Museum**, which proudly displays two paintings by Monet along with items of local interest. It is open daily except on Mondays and holidays, from 2–5:30 p.m.

NEARBY SIGHT:

The **Château of Bizy** (6), an 18th-century mansion set in a charming park, may also be visited. Its interior contains many superb pieces in the Empire style along with Napoleonic souvenirs. The château is open from 10 a.m. to noon and 2–6:30 p.m., daily except Fridays, between April 1st and late October. To get there, follow the D-181 for one mile southwest of Vernon.

Rouen

One of the best-preserved medieval cities in all of Europe, Rouen is also a thriving modern commercial center. This unusual combination of past and present results from a deliberate decision on the part of local government to strip away decades of "modernization" in the old part of town and restore its ancient features. At the same time, cars were banned from many of the streets, creating an unusually pleasant—and very beguiling—pedestrian shopping zone. If ever there was a city designed to be explored on foot, Rouen is it.

Over two thousand years ago, Rouen was already in existence as a Celtic encampment on the banks of the Seine. This evolved into a market town known as *Ratuma* to the Gauls and later as *Rotomagus* to the Romans. Its real history, however, begins with an invasion by the Vikings from Scandinavia, who made it the capital of their Norman duchy in 912. The brilliant Norse leader Rollo established an able administration that did much to develop the local economy. His linear descendant, William the Bastard, known to history as the Conqueror, defeated the English near Hastings in 1066 and became king of England, bringing Norman civilization to that island country.

Centuries later it was the English who invaded Normandy. During the Hundred Years War a strange leader arose among the French, Joan of Arc, who persuaded the king to allow her to lead troops in battle. Eventually she was captured by the Burgundians and sold to the English, who brought her to Rouen in 1431 for a mockery of a trial—after which she was burned at the stake in the town's market place.

In the years that followed the re-establishment of French rule, Rouen blossomed into a beautiful and prosperous city with many fine Renaissance buildings. Although it suffered badly during the 16th-century Wars of Religion and again during World War II, it has today regained its place as one of the great cities of France.

There is far more to Rouen than can be comfortably seen in one day. For your own sake, be selective and follow your interests. Time spent leisurely watching the passing parade from a café can be just as rewarding as seeing every last museum.

GETTING THERE:

Trains leave St.-Lazare Station in Paris frequently for Rouen's Rive Droite Station, a trip of about 70 minutes. Return service operates until mid-evening.

By car, Rouen is 86 miles northwest of Paris via the A-13 Autoroute. Don't even *think* of driving in the inner city.

WHEN TO GO:

Rouen may be enjoyed in any season, but avoid coming on a Tuesday or holiday if you plan on visiting any of the major museums.

FOOD AND DRINK:

The city offers an extraordinarily wide range of excellent restaurants, many of which specialize in the rich, highly caloric Norman cuisine. Some good choices are:

Bertrand Warin (9 Rue de la Pie, just west of Place du Vieux-Marché) A highly refined restaurant with inventive cuisine. Reservations needed, call 35-89-26-69. X: Sun. eve., Mon., Aug. $$$

Le Beffroy (15 Rue du Beffroy, 2 blocks east of the Fine Arts Museum) Norman and modern cuisine in a fashionable restaurant. For reservations call 35-71-55-27. X: Sun., Mon. $$$

Gill (60 Rue St. Nicolas, 1 block north of the cathedral) Subtle, contemporary cuisine in a modern setting. X: Sun., Mon. lunch, holidays. $$$

La Couronne (31 Place du Vieux-Marché) Norman specialties, especially duck, in a 14th-century house. X: Sun. eve. $$$

Dufour (67 bis Rue St.-Nicolas, 1 block north of the cathedral) A corner of old Normandy, seafood specialties. X: Sun. eve., Mon., Aug. $$$

La Réverbère (5 Place de la République, 3 blocks southeast of the cathedral) A dependable place favored by local businessmen. X: Sun., late Aug. $$

La Petite Auberge (164 Rue Martainville, 2 blocks east of St.-Maclou) A local favorite for seafood. X: Mon. eve. $$

Les P'tits Parapluies (46 Rue Bourg-l'Abbé, 2 blocks north of St.-Ouen) A stylish restaurant with innovative cooking. X: Sun., Mon. lunch, Aug. $$

La Vieille Auberge (37 Rue St.-Etienne-des-Tonneliers, 3 blocks south of the Great Clock) An exceptional value. X: Mon. $

Pascaline (5 Rue de la Poterne, north of the Palace of Justice) Excellent value in the middle of town. $

Les Flandres (5 Rue des Bons-Enfants, 3 blocks southwest of the Fine Arts Museum) Simple and very popular, with good steaks. X: Sat. eve., Sun., Aug. $

La Tarte Tatin (99 Rue de la Vicomté, 1 block southeast of Place du Vieux-Marché) An outstanding crêperie. X: Sun., Mon. $

TOURIST INFORMATION:

The friendly tourist office, phone 35-71-41-77, is in front of the cathedral.

SUGGESTED TOUR:

Follow the map from Rouen's **Rive Droite Train Station** (1) to Place de la Cathédrale, where the tourist office is housed in an elegant 16th-century Renaissance building. Along the way you will pass many examples of old half-timbered houses that have been put to modern use while still retaining the town's medieval atmosphere.

The **Cathedral of Notre-Dame** (2), one of the finest Gothic structures in existence, is familiar to art lovers as the subject for a series of Impressionist paintings by Monet that captured its spirit under changing atmospheric conditions. Its **west front** displays at a glance the entire history of Gothic cathedral construction. The base of the left tower dates from the early 12th century and, along with two doors, is the only portion of the church that survived the devastating fire of 1200. On the right is the so-called **Butter Tower**, supposedly financed by the sale of indulgences allowing the faithful to eat butter during Lent. This Flamboyant structure was erected in the 15th century. The next hundred years saw the addition of the central portal and the rose window. Construction continued through the 19th century, when the delicate open-ironwork spire, the tallest in France, was completed.

A stroll through the cathedral's majestic interior is impressive. Note in particular the **Booksellers' Staircase** in the north transept and the **tombs** of several historical figures, including those of Rollo, the first duke of Normandy, and Richard the Lionhearted, king of England. Guided tours are conducted through the fascinating 11th-century **crypt** and the ambulatory, several times daily during the summer season, and on weekends and some holidays the rest of the year.

Walk down Rue du Gros-Horloge, a pedestrians-only shopping street of well-preserved houses, many of them half-timbered. The **Great Clock** (*Gros-Horloge*) (3), a famous symbol of Rouen, was relocated here in 1527. Its adjoining 14th-century belfry may be climbed between Palm Sunday and September 30th, from 10 a.m. to noon and 2:30–5:30 p.m., but not on Tuesdays or on Wednesday mornings. The ticket is also valid for the Fine Arts, Wrought Iron, and Ceramics museums. Splendid views of the old city make the climb very worthwhile.

Stroll over to the magnificent **Palace of Justice** (4), one of the great civic structures of Europe. Originally built in the 16th century

Rouen

300 Yards

The Great Clock on Rue du Gros-Horloge

and later modified, its Gothic façade becomes increasingly Flamboyant as it rises above the ground floor. You can visit its Prosecutors' Room, reached via the staircase in the left wing, on weekdays. Recent excavations in the courtyard have unearthed an underground 12th-century synagogue or yeshiva, which can be seen by arrangement with the tourist office.

On May 30th, 1431, Joan of Arc was burned at the stake in Rouen's **Market Place** *(Place du Vieux-Marché)* (5), the next stop on the walking tour. A huge cross now marks the spot where she met her fiery end. The strikingly contemporary **Joan of Arc Church**, adjacent to this, was consecrated in 1979 and contains a large area of marvelous 16th-century stained-glass windows from a previous church on the site. Also in the square is a modern covered marketplace, several inviting outdoor cafés, and the tiny but fascinating **Joan of Arc Museum** (6), a somewhat kitschy waxworks crammed with re-created scenes from the life of the Maid of Orléans. Another nearby sight that might be of interest is the **Pierre Corneille Museum** (7) on the Rue de la Pie, where the famous French playwright was born in 1606 and where he

Inside the Aître St.-Maclou

lived most of his life. It is open daily except on Tuesdays, on Wednesday mornings, and on holidays.

It is only a few steps to the Place de la Pucelle, site of the elegant **Hôtel de Bourgtheroulde** (8). This sumptuous 16th-century mansion, now a bank, combines Gothic with early Renaissance elements. Step into the courtyard to admire the decorations, some of which depict the meeting of François I and England's Henry VIII at the Field of the Cloth of Gold in 1520.

Return to the cathedral via the route shown on the map, which takes you along the right bank of the Seine. Colorful rue St.-Romain, lined with picturesque half-timbered medieval and Renaissance houses, leads past the **Archbishop's Palace**. It was here that Joan of Arc was sentenced to death and, 25 years after the execution, at last found innocent.

The **Church of St.-Maclou** (9) is perhaps the most striking example of Flamboyant Gothic architecture in France. Badly damaged in World War II, it is now completely restored. Don't miss seeing its lovely interior, particularly the remarkable organ loft.

Another absolute "must" sight in Rouen is the **Aître St.-Maclou** (10), a 16th-century cloister that once served as a plague cemetery. Its ossuary galleries, now occupied by an art school, are carved with exceptionally macabre figures of death. Go in for a peek.

Return to the church and follow the gorgeous Rue Damiette to the **Abbey Church of St.-Ouen** (11). This enormous structure, dating mostly from the 14th century, replaces earlier churches on the same site going back as far as the 7th century. Stroll through the gardens behind it and return through the City Hall *(Hôtel de Ville)*.

Now follow the map to the **Le Secq des Tournelles Museum** (12), located in a desanctified former church. Its vast collection of wrought-iron objects dating from the 3rd through the 19th centuries is totally fascinating. The opening times are the same as those of the Fine Arts Museum described below, and the same ticket applies. Continue on to the nearby **Church of St.-Godard** (13), a late-15th-century structure noted for its unusual wooden roof and outstanding stained-glass windows, especially the one depicting the Tree of Jesse at the choir end of the south aisle.

The **Fine Arts Museum** *(Musée des Beaux-Arts)* (14) has one of the best provincial collections in France. There are paintings by Gérard David, Rubens, Ingres, Delacroix, Velázquez, Corot and many others, along with those by native-son Géricault. Impressionism is well represented by Sisley and Monet *(Rouen Cathedral)*. There are also several rooms of contemporary art including one devoted to the local Duchamp family. The museum is open daily except on Tuesdays and holidays; from 10 a.m. to noon and 2–6 p.m., but closed on Wednesday mornings. The same ticket is also valid for the Wrought Iron and Ceramics museums, and for the Clock Tower.

Now amble over to the splendid **Ceramics Museum** (15), located in a former mansion just one block away. The opening times and ticket are the same as for the Fine Arts Museum.

Before leaving Rouen, it would be fitting to visit the **Joan of Arc Tower** (16) near the train station. This former keep is all that remains of a 13th-century castle, and is the place where the Maid of Orléans was confronted with the instruments of torture. You can climb to its top for a nice view. The tower is open daily except on Thursdays, holidays, and all of November; from 10 a.m. to noon and 2–5 p.m.

Rouen offers several other first-rate museums, details of which can be obtained from the tourist office.

Caen

Just enough of old Caen survived the terrible devastation of World War II to make it an attractive daytrip destination. The three monumental structures associated with William the Conqueror remained miraculously intact while the rest of the city has been largely rebuilt in the contemporary mold, with broad boulevards, pedestrian malls and open green spaces.

Caen had virtually no history before Duke William of Normandy, also known as "the Bastard" and "the Conqueror," made it his capital and favorite residence in the 11th century. During the years that followed it developed into both a seaport and a university town, sometimes under English rule. World War II brought ferocious destruction—over three-quarters of the city lay in total ruin after a lengthy battle beginning in June of 1944. Many of its citizens found shelter in the important historical structures, which were spared by the Allies after receiving this information from the Resistance. What has emerged since then is an unusually pleasant, if not very dramatic, city where modern architecture has blended in well with what remains of the past.

GETTING THERE:

Trains depart St.-Lazare Station in Paris almost hourly for the two-hour run to Caen. Many of these are Turbotrains with somewhat limited capacity, so it will pay to claim your seat early or make reservations, especially during peak periods. Return service operates until mid-evening.

By car, it's the A-13 Autoroute all the way. Caen is 150 miles west of Paris.

WHEN TO GO:

Good weather is important for this largely outdoor trip. The two museums are closed on Tuesdays and major holidays.

FOOD AND DRINK:

Some choice restaurants are:

La Bourride (15 Rue Vaugueux, 1 block east of the château entrance) Imaginative variations on classic Norman cuisine. Reservations needed, call 31-93-50-76. X: Sun., Mon. $$$

Relais des Gourmets (15 Rue de Geôle, just west of the château entrance) An elegant place with traditional cuisine. X: Sun. eve. $$$

L'Ecaille (13 Rue de Geôle, just west of the château entrance) Noted for its fine seafood. X: Sat. lunch, Mon. $$

Le Dauphin (29 Rue Gemare, 2 blocks southwest of the château) Classic Norman cuisine with a light touch. X: Sat. $$

Les Quatre Vents (116 Blvd. Mar.-Leclerc, 3 blocks southeast of St.-Sauveur Church) Modern cuisine in a tasteful setting. $$

Relais Normandy (Place de la Gare, by the train station) Long a favorite for good food. $$

Poêle d'Or (7 Rue Laplace, 3 blocks southeast of St.-Jean Church) An exceptional value. X: Sat., Sun. $

Alcide (1 Place Courtonne, at the north end of the Old Port) Good dining at modest prices. X: Sat., July. $

In addition, there are a number of restaurants and cafés of all descriptions in the shopping zone between Place St.-Pierre and Place de la République.

TOURIST INFORMATION:

The local tourist office, phone 31-86-27-65, is located in a lovely Renaissance mansion on Place St.-Pierre, near the castle.

SUGGESTED TOUR:

The **train station** (1) is nearly a mile from Place St.-Pierre, the center of town. You could take a bus or taxi there, although the walk is both level and very pleasant. Along the way you will pass the remarkable **Church of St.-Jean** (2), a 15th-century Flamboyant Gothic structure whose unfinished west tower tilts ever so slightly.

Continue on to Place St.-Pierre. The tourist office occupies a splendid 16th-century mansion, the **Hôtel d'Escoville**, whose richly decorated courtyard should be seen. This feeling of luxury, a reflection of Caen's prosperous past, is mirrored in the **Church of St.-Pierre** (3). Its ornate, almost lush interior is among the most outstanding in Normandy.

The enormous **Castle** (4) begun by William the Conqueror still dominates the city. Stroll up to the massive ramparts, built between the 12th and 15th centuries, cross the moat and climb up on the fortifications for a stunning view of Caen. Little remains of the original

Entrance to the Castle

structures within the walls, most of them having been replaced with later buildings.

The most recent addition to the castle is the **Fine Arts Museum** *(Musée des Beaux-Arts)* (5), whose discreet contemporary architecture harmonizes with its ancient surroundings. A rarity among French provincial museums, its superb collections are exceptionally well lit and displayed. They were begun in the early 19th century when both the Revolution and the Napolenic conquests made large quantities of great art, formerly belonging to the Church and aristocracy as well as to foreign countries, available to public institutions. Artists represented include Van der Weyden, Breughel, Tintoretto, Poussin, Rubens, Van Dyck, Tiepolo and Géricault, among many others. The museum is open daily except on Tuesdays and major holidays, from 10 a.m. to noon and 2–6 p.m., closing at 5 p.m. in winter.

Amble over past the 12th-century **St.-Georges Church** to the **Normandy Museum** (6), also within the castle precincts. Displays here are primarily concerned with local everyday life, particularly during the last century, and with regional arts and crafts along with the archaeological finds. It is open during the same times as the Fine Arts Museum, above.

Wander around to the rear of the castle enclosure for a look at the so-called **Exchequer House**—a rare example of early 12th-century domestic architecture—and at the ruins of an equally old square **keep**, both built by Henry I, king of England and son of the Conqueror.

Caen

300 Yards

N

Now follow the map to the interesting Gothic and Renaissance **Church of St.-Sauveur** (7) and the picturesque Rue Froide. Return on Rue St.-Pierre, passing the **Musée de la Poste** in one of the oldest half-timbered houses left on that street, and turn down Rue Hamon, continuing through a modern pedestrian shopping district with pleasant cafés to Place de la République.

From here the map leads the way through a colorful neighborhood to Caen's premier attraction, the famous **Abbaye aux Hommes**, whose conventual buildings now incorporate the **City Hall** *(Hôtel de Ville)* (8), The esplande in front of this provides a marvelous sight for sore eyes. Interesting guided tours of the old abbey buildings, reconstructed in the 18th century, depart hourly from the City Hall entrance.

Walk around to the rear of the complex and visit the **Church of St.-Étienne** (9), the original church of the abbey. This magnificent structure was founded in the 11th century by William the Conquerer—an illegitimate son of Duke Robert the Devil—as penance for the sin of having married his distant cousin Matilda. Not that the lady was willing—she had in fact made it perfectly clear that she would rather be a nun than marry a bastard. William, feeling his oats, dragged her by the hair and beat her into submission. Both were excommunicated as a result, and later reinstated by the Pope only after promising to build two abbeys and four hospitals. The union actually turned out well, with Matilda becoming queen of England in 1068.

Step inside to visit William's **tomb**, in front of the high altar. His burial was as tempestuous as his life. When he died in 1087 at Rouen, his heirs made a mad scramble for the spoils and neglected his body, which rotted for days before being ignominiously put in the grave after payment of an extortion fee. It did not lie there in peace, either. During the 16th century his bones were scattered by rebellious Protestants, later recovered, and again dispersed during the Revolution. Some parts of it may still be there, but no one is sure. The church offers "computerized audio-visual visits" and is closed between noon and 2 p.m.

Return to the castle area via Rue St.-Mauvieu and Fossés St.-Julien, then follow the map to the **Abbaye aux Dames** (10), the other abbey founded as a result of the illicit marriage. Its **Church of La Trinité** is more richly ornamented than its male counterpart and has an interesting 11th-century **crypt**, which can be reached from the south transept. Matilda was buried here, in the choir, and like that of her husband William, her tomb was desecrated during the Wars of Religion and again in the Revolution. The church is closed between noon and 2 p.m. Its conventual buildings have been recently restored and may be visited at set times.

The Abbaye aux Hommes

The suggested route back to the train station, shown on the map, takes you past the **Old Port** *(Bassin St.-Pierre)*, connected to the sea via the Orne River and a canal. It is now used for pleasure craft, with larger ships docking at the new harbor to the east.

ADDITIONAL SIGHT:

Located in the northwest corner of the city, the new **Memorial of the Battle of Normandy Museum** was opened in 1988. Using the most advanced techniques to document the quest for peace in this century, the museum leads visitors through an historic journey from 1918 to the present, in a variety of languages, with audio-visual shows, weapons displays, and related material. It is open daily except on Tuesdays and certain holidays. Ask at the tourist office for details.

Bayeux

One of the greatest chronicles of the Middle Ages—the famous "Bayeux Tapestry"—is an incredibly lucid history lesson embroidered in cloth. You have surely seen reproductions of it, but to experience the real thing you will have to come to Bayeux, a thoroughly delightful town that is well worth the trip.

Known as the cradle of the Norman dynasty, the town has roots going back much further than the Viking invasions. In Gallo-Roman times it was called *Augustodurum,* and became a bishopric as early as the 4th century. Rollo the Dane, a progenitor of William the Conqueror, married the daughter of the town's ruler early in the 10th century, thus creating the line that gave England some of its most notorious kings. The Norse language continued to be spoken here long after the rest of Normandy adopted French culture, an early sign of Bayeux's stubborn resistance to change. Centuries later, in June of 1944, it was the first town to be liberated by the Allies during the Battle of Normandy, and miraculously suffered no damage.

Bayeux today remains a remarkably well-preserved medieval town whose narrow streets and ancient buildings continue to enchant thousands of visitors. Although well geared to the modern tourist trade, it seems to be amazingly unaffected by it.

GETTING THERE:

Trains *(marked for Cherbourg)* leave St.-Lazare Station in Paris several times in the morning for Bayeux, a run of about $2\frac{1}{2}$ hours. Most of these are Turbotrains with limited seating capacity during peak hours, so either make a reservation, claim your seat early, or ride in the dining car. Return service operates until early evening. Check the schedules carefully.

By car, take the A-13 Autoroute to Caen, the the N-13 into Bayeux, 167 miles west of Paris.

WHEN TO GO:

Bayeux's major attractions are open daily. Good weather will make the trip more enjoyable.

The Covered Fish Market and Old Mill

FOOD AND DRINK:

As an important tourist center, Bayeux has restaurants and cafés in all price ranges. Some of the better choices are:

Lion d'Or (71 Rue St.-Jean, 1 block east of the watermill) A famous old inn serving superb classic Norman dishes since 1770. X: late Dec. to late Jan. $$

Les 4 Saisons (in the Hotel Luxembourg, 25 Rue des Bouchers, 2 blocks northwest of the tourist office) A small hotel with good food. $$

Les Gourmets (Place St.-Patrice, 5 blocks northwest of the tourist office) An excellent value. X: Wed. eve., Thurs. $

La Marmite (in the Hotel Brunville, 9 Rue Genas-Duhomme, 2 blocks northwest of the tourist office) Dining in a small hotel. $

Pizzeria Marsala (17 Rue des Cuisiniers, just south of the tourist office) Italian cuisine. $

TOURIST INFORMATION:

The local tourist office, phone 31-92-16-26, is located in a charming half-timbered medieval house at 1 Rue des Cuisiniers, one block north of the cathedral.

SUGGESTED TOUR:

Leave the **train station** (1) and follow the map to the **William the Conqueror Center** *(Guillaume le Conquérant)* (2), located in a court-yard just off Rue de Nesmond. This is where the world-famous **Bayeux Tapestry**, one of the greatest legacies of the Middle Ages, is displayed. Also known as *La Tapisserie de la Reine Mathilde,* it has long been the subject of two popular misconceptions. First, this is not a tapestry at all, but actually an embroidery on linen. Second, it was almost certainly not made by Queen Matilda herself since the style strongly suggests Saxon craftsmanship, and was probably commissioned by William's half-brother, Bishop Odon of Bayeux, as a decoration for his cathedral. That it survived at all is a miracle. In 1792, when Revolutionary zealots were stripping the churches bare, an observant army officer rescued it from the ignominious fate of being used as a wagon tarpaulin. Seeing its propaganda value, Napoleon had it widely exhibited to drum up support for his planned invasion of England.

The 231-foot-long 11th-century embroidery resembles nothing so much as a gigantic comic strip, and would not look out of place in our Sunday newspapers. Its 58 scenes graphically depict the events leading up to the Norman Conquest of 1066, as well as the Battle of Hastings itself—one of the major turning points in the annals of Western civilization. Of course, the story is seen through Norman eyes; victors do have a way of controlling history.

Be sure to rent one of the earphone devices, which give an engrossing blow-by-blow account in English of the entire complex saga. Without this it is very difficult to understand. You can move along at your own pace, taking plenty of time to absorb it all. The center is open every day, from 9 a.m. to 7 p.m. between May 16th and September 15th; with slightly shorter hours and a 1½-hour lunch break during the rest of the year.

Continue on through the grounds of an ancient hospital and follow the map to the Aure stream. Just across this is the **Lace-Making Center** (3), where yesterday's crafts are still practiced, and where you are welcome to stop in for a look. Walk along the water's edge past a charming **old mill** for a truly gorgeous view with the cathedral's towers rising in the background. The former **Covered Fish Market**, now a cultural center, is at the corner of Rue St.-Jean. Turn right here and follow Rue St.-Martin to the **Tourist Information Office** (4), located in a lovely 14th-century house.

The walking route now takes you through a picturesque neighborhood to the **Baron Gérard Museum** (5), in the former Bishop's Palace, which displays a fascinating collection of local ceramics and lace along with faience from Rouen, furniture and paintings. The latter includes

Museum of the Battle of Normandy

several Italian Primitives, Flemish and French works. Visits may be made daily, from 9 a.m. to 7 p.m. between June and the end of August, with slightly shorter hours and a lunch break during the rest of the year.

Next to this stands the very impressive **Cathedral of Notre-Dame** (6). Parts of it date from the 11th century, when the cathedral was consecrated by Bishop Odon in the presence of the Conqueror. Most of the original church was destroyed in 1105 by William's son, Henry I *(Beauclerc)* of England, and rebuilt in later centuries. The carvings above the west front doors depict the Passion and the Last Judgement, while those in the south transept tell the story of Thomas à Becket's murder in Canterbury Cathedral. Step inside for a look at the magnificent interior and to visit the 11th-century crypt. Just south of the cathedral is the **Diocesan Museum of Religious Art.**

Now follow the route on the map past **Place du Général de Gaulle** (7), a charming square where the famous wartime leader made his first speech on liberated soil in June of 1944.

Continue on to the **Memorial Museum of the Battle of Normandy** (8). This modern structure, surrounded by armor from the participating nations, commemorates the D-Day landings with intriguing displays of the soldiers' lives throughout the conflict. Little touches like cigarette packages and newspaper clippings make the human drama an unforgettable experience. Don't miss seeing this. The museum is open daily from 9 a.m. to 7 p.m. between June and the end of August, with slightly shorter hours and a 1½-hour break for lunch during the rest of the year. The British Military Cemetery is nearby.

Deauville and Trouville

Aristocratic Deauville is Normandy's most elegant seaside resort, while its more down-to-earth neighbor Trouville possesses a charm distinctly its own. A daytrip here in the high season offers a chance to watch the Beautiful People at play. Things quiet down during the rest of the year, but enough activity remains to make the trip interesting.

Trouville is an old resort along the Normandy coast, with a popularity dating from the 1830s, when sea bathing first came into vogue. The court of Napoleon III flocked here, as did a number of famous writers and artists—especially the Impressionists. Its *Belle Époque* atmosphere lingers on amid the unspoiled ambiance of the simple fishing port it once was.

Just across the narrow Touques River, Deauville was developed by speculators in the mid-19th century as an elitist watering place for the smart set, who were presumably tired of plebeian Trouville. Sometimes called the "Twenty-first *arrondissement* of Paris," its aura of chic sophistication has remained pretty much intact to this day.

This trip can easily be combined in the same day with one to the utterly delightful fishing village of Honfleur, described in the next chapter.

GETTING THERE:

Trains for Trouville-Deauville depart St.-Lazare Station in Paris several times in the morning. Check at the information office as a change at Lisieux may be necessary and schedule variations are common. Turbotrains are frequently used, making reservations desirable. Travel time averages about two hours. Return service runs until early evening.

By car, Deauville is 129 miles northwest of Paris via the A-13 Autoroute.

WHEN TO GO:

Deauville's high season lasts from June until September, with less activity during the months before and after this. Crowds are at their maximum on weekends. Trouville can be enjoyed any time during the warm season, provided the weather is good. Its art museum is closed on Tuesdays, on weekdays between Easter and mid-June, and completely between October and March.

FOOD AND DRINK:

Most restaurants in Deauville and Trouville specialize in seafood, and many have outdoor café tables. Some excellent choices are:

Ciro's (Promenade des Planches in Deauville, right on the beach) *The* place to see and be seen. $$$

Le Spinnaker (52 Rue Mirabeau in Deauville, 3 blocks west of the station) Seasonal cuisine with a light touch. $$$

Chez Miocque (81 Rue Eugène-Colas, Deauville, near the tourist office) A very popular and friendly place without pretensions. X: Tues., Jan. $$

Les Vapeurs (160 Blvd. F.-Moureaux, Trouville, by the old port, east of the casino) A favorite old-fashioned brasserie. $$

Le Galatée (on the beach at Trouville, just north of the casino) Friendly and relaxed. X: Thurs. except in July and Aug, entire off-season. $$

La Petite Auberge (7 Rue Carnot, Trouville, 2 blocks northeast of the casino) An excellent value. X; Wed. $

Carmen (24 Rue Carnot, Trouville, 2 blocks northeast of the casino) Dining in a small hotel. X: Mon. eve., Tues. $

TOURIST INFORMATION:

The tourist office in Deauville, phone 31-88-21-43, is located on Place Mairie, two blocks from the Casino d'Été. Its counterpart in Trouville is at 32 Boulevard Fernand-Moureaux, near the bridge. You can phone them at 31-88-36-19.

SUGGESTED TOUR:

Leave the **Trouville-Deauville Train Station** (1), which is shared by both towns, and follow the map past the Floating Basin and the Deauville tourist office to the **Casino d'Été** (2). Open from mid-March through mid-September, this is the "summer" casino—there is a "winter" casino *(d'Hiver)* close by, so you can gamble all year round.

Wander around the opulent shops that fill the neighborhood, then stroll down Rue Gontaut-Biron to the **Promenade des Planches**, a wooden boardwalk where the famous and the infamous come to see and be seen. Follow this to the new marina development of **Port Deauville** (3). A walk out on the breakwater will reward you with some marvelous views.

Return to the Planches and follow the elegant Boulevard Eugène-Cornuché to the yacht basin, where a tiny pedestrian **ferry** *(Bac Pié-*

Port Deauville

tons) (4) crosses the harbor to Trouville. At times of low tide a small footbridge is swung across the river in its place.

Trouville's **Casino** (5), built in 1912 in the grand *Belle Époque* manner, still reflects the days when such notables as Marcel Proust frequented the town—before high society drifted across the river to posher Deauville.

Once again, there is a Promenade des Planches. Stroll along this or on the beach, passing the **Ecological Aquarium**, then follow the map to the **Municipal Museum** (6) in Villa Montebello on Rue Général-Leclerc. Paintings by the early Impressionist Eugène Boudin and others, exhibited here, have captured the spirit of Trouville during its halcyon years. The museum is open from 2:15–6:15 p.m., daily in summer except on Tuesdays, and on weekends only from Easter to mid-June.

Return via rues Pasteur, de la Chapelle and Victor-Hugo to the Old Town. Unlike Deauville, Trouville exists in its own right as a fishing village and remains active all year round. Much of the charming bustle can be enjoyed along its riverside quay, the Boulevard Fernand-Moureaux. From here, the **Pont des Belges** (7) leads across the river to the train station.

Honfleur

If a contest were held to determine the loveliest fishing port in France, Honfleur would certainly be among the top contenders. Its old harbor is so astonishingly picturesque that it defies description. The wonder of it all is that this is not just a tourist attraction but a hard-working port that somehow escaped the march of time. Perhaps this is because Le Havre, just across the bay, has long ago captured the heavy shipping industry, and also simply because Honfleur has no beach to speak of.

Located at the mouth of the Seine estuary, Honfleur was an important port ever since the 14th century, falling into English hands on several occasions. It was from here that Samuel Champlain set sail for the New World in the early 17th century, a voyage that resulted in the founding of Québec as a French colony. Later, during the 19th century, it became popular with artists, particularly with the followers of locally-born Eugène Boudin, including Jongkind and Monet. The attraction still holds, as can be seen by the number of easels lined up along the old port on a nice day.

This trip can be combined in the came day with one to Deauville and Trouville, described in the previous chapter.

GETTING THERE:

Trains depart St.-Lazare Station in Paris several times in the morning for Trouville-Deauville. See page 161 for more information. From there, transfer to a local bus for the nine-mile ride to Honfleur. The bus stop *(Gare Routière)* in Deauville, shown on the map on page 163, is two blocks from the train station. You could also take a taxi. Return trains operate until early evening.

There are also buses to and from Lisieux or Évreux, both of which have train service to Paris. Check the schedules carefully.

By car, take the A-13 Autoroute to the Beuzeville exit, then the D-22 and D-580 into Honfleur—which is 120 miles northwest of Paris.

WHEN TO GO:

Honfleur may be visited at any time in good weather, but note that the art museum is closed on Tuesdays and major holidays, and that some attractions are either closed or have limited hours during the off season.

FOOD AND DRINK:

Many visitors are drawn to Honfleur for its beauty and charm. As a result, the village has quite a few good restaurants and cafés, mostly around the two ports. Some choices are:

> **Le Cheval Blanc** (2 Quai des Passagers, at the north end of the Avant Port) Luxurious surroundings in a 15th-century inn, renowned cuisine. X: Thurs. $$$ and $$
>
> **L'Absinthe** (10 Quai de la Quarantaine, by the Avant Port) Noted for its seafood. X: Mon. eve. and Tues. in the off season. $$
>
> **Le Bistrot du Port** (14 Quai de la Quarantaine, by the Avant Port) Superb seafood in a quaint setting. X: Mon. eve., Tues. $$
>
> **Hostellerie Lechat** (3 Place Ste.-Catherine, near the church) Seafood specialties in a small inn. X: winter. $$
>
> **Au P'tit Mareyeur** (4 Rue Haute, 2 blocks north of Ste.-Catherine Church) A good value. X: Thurs., Fri. lunch. $$

TOURIST INFORMATION:

The local tourist office, phone 31-89-23-30, is at 33 Cours des Fossés, by the bus station.

SUGGESTED TOUR:

The **bus stop** (1) is on Place de la Porte-de-Rouen, close to the tourist office. Stroll over to the exceedingly picturesque **Old Port** (Vieux Bassin) (2), whose quays are lined with quaint houses of wood and slate. The present tidal basin was begun in the 17th century to accommodate the growing maritime development of Honfleur; other harbors being added in the 19th century.

Just a few steps away, the former Church of St.-Étienne, dating from the 14th and 15th centuries, now houses the **Museum of Old Honfleur** (3). Displays here are concerned with the town's illustrious maritime past, going back as far as Gallo-Roman times. Next to this, on Rue de la Prison, the small **Museum of Ethnography and Folk Art** (4) features reproductions of local room interiors. Both museums are open from 10 a.m. to noon and 3–6 p.m.; closed on weekdays out of season.

Continue around the tiny street, little changed since the 16th century. All about you are the ancient slate-roofed houses that recall life

Honfleur

200 Yards

TO DEAUVILLE →

Rue Bucaille

Rue Varin

Rue Haute

Blvd. Charles V

Rue des Capuchins

Rue Albert I

7 Museum

Rue de l'Homme de Bois

Rue Boulanger

Rue Barbel

Rue du Puits

Rue des Lingots

6

Rue Brulée

R. des Logettes

Quai des Passagers

Rue de la Foulerie

Quai St.-Catherine

5

OLD PORT

AVANT PORT

Rue de la République

2

3 Quai St.-Étienne

Museum

Quai de la Quarantaine

4

Rue Cachin

Place Thiers

Rue de la Ville

8

Pl. de la Porte de Rouen

Bus

Info.

1

Quai de la Tour

The Old Port and La Lieutenance

in a small Norman town many centuries ago. Back at the quay, make a right to Place de l'Hôtel-de-Ville, a spot favored by amateur painters trying to recapture scenes made famous by the Impressionists of the 19th century.

Beyond the tidal locks lies **La Lieutenance** (5), a jumble of 16th-century buildings that was once home to the governor of Honfleur. Part of the 13th-century town walls, the Porte de Caen, is incorporated in the side overlooking the square. On your right is the Avant Port, anchorage of the town's fishing fleet.

Follow the map to the **Church of Ste.-Catherine** (6), a very strange sight in this part of Europe. It may well remind you more of Norway than Normandy. Built completely of wood by 15th-century ship-wrights immediately after the Hundred Years War, this double-naved masterpiece has withstood five centuries of continued threat from fire and decay. Its interior is astonishing. Just opposite the church is its detached **Bell Tower**, also built of wood around the same time. A visit inside will only take a few moments and is quite interesting.

Continue on to the **Eugène Boudin Museum** (7). A native of Honfleur, Boudin provided the original inspiration for the Impressionist painters, especially for his friends Jongkind and Monet. Outstanding works by these and other artists, as well as 20th-century painters such as Villon and Dufy, are very well displayed in a contemporary setting.

Place Thiers near the Old Port

The museum is open from 10 a.m. to noon and 2–6 p.m., every day except Tuesdays and major holidays, between mid-March and the end of September. During the rest of the year it is open in the afternoons only, as well as on Saturday and Sunday mornings and afternoons.

Now follow the map to the charming Rue Haute. The house at number 90 was the birthplace in 1866 of the composer Erik Satie. Return to the Old Port and stroll around it to Place Thiers. The **Rue de la Ville** (8) has two interesting 17th-century salt houses. From here it is only a few steps to the bus stop.

Amiens

Relatively few tourists venture into the often-bleak industrial north of France. This region does, however, have some outstanding attractions that make interesting daytrip destinations for experienced travelers in search of the unusual. By far the best of these is Amiens, an ancient riverside city which boasts the largest—and the most perfect—cathedral in all of France. The easy journey there provides an opportunity to experience yet another facet of this complex nation, and to see some sights unique to this town alone.

Throughout much of its long and turbulent history, Amiens was a battlefield lying in the path of invading armies. Once the capital of the Celtic Ambiani tribe, it was subjugated by Julius Caesar in the 1st century B.C. and again by the 9th-century Normans. During the Franco-Prussian War of 1870 Amiens was occupied by German forces, who returned in World War I and left it largely destroyed. The Second World War brought enormous losses as sixty percent of the city was reduced to rubble. Somehow, through all of this, the magnificent cathedral—along with a few other architectural gems—managed to survive unscathed. Postwar reconstruction has added a few interesting, if not exactly beautiful, structures, while current restoration efforts in the medieval quarter by the river are making the town attractive once again.

GETTING THERE:

Trains bound for Amiens leave Nord Station in Paris several times in the morning, the trip taking a little over one hour. Return service operates until mid-evening.

By car, Amiens is 92 miles north of Paris via the A-1 Autoroute and the D-934 and N-29 roads. There is a somewhat shorter route taking the N-1 all the way, but traffic may be heavy.

WHEN TO GO:

Amiens may be visited at any time, noting that the Picardy museum is closed on Mondays.

The Cathedral of Notre-Dame

FOOD AND DRINK:

You can dine very well at moderate prices in Amiens. Some good restaurant choices are:

Le Mermoz (7 Rue Jean-Mermoz, 3 blocks north of the train station) Superb cuisine for the price. X: Sat., Sun., Feb. $$

Les Marissons (68 Rue des Marissons, 3 blocks northeast of the cathedral, across the river) Inventive cuisine in a converted 15th-century workshop. X: Sat. lunch, Sun. eve., Mon. $$

Joséphine (20 Rue Sire-Firmin-Leroux, 2 blocks south of the cathedral) Specializes in seafood. X: Sun. eve., Mon. $$

La Couronne (64 Rue St.-Leu, 1 block north of St.-Leu Church) Straightforward cuisine at good prices. X: Sat., Sun. eve., mid-July to mid-Aug. $$

Le Petit Chef (8 Rue Jean-Catelas, near the Maison de la Culture) Good values with careful choices. X: Tues. eve., Wed., late July. $

La Mangeoire (3 Rue des Sergents, 2 blocks southwest of the cathedral) An atmospheric crêperie. X: Sun., Mon. $

TOURIST INFORMATION:

The local tourist office, phone 22-91-79-28, is located in the Maison de la Culture at the foot of Rue Jean-Catelas, with a summer branch near the front of the cathedral and another in the train station. Ask them about boat trips in the famous *Hortillonnages*.

SUGGESTED TOUR:

Leave the **train station** (1) and amble over to the **Tour Perret** (2), a curious 26-story mini-skyscraper of truly inspired ugliness. At the time of its construction in 1952 it ranked as the tallest office building in Europe. The route now leads through a busy shopping district, passing the beautiful façade of an 18th-century theater. Turn right into the Passage due Logis du Roi, where you will see the 16th-century brick-and-stone Logis du Roi alongside a fine Renaissance façade. Opposite this stands the imposing Palace of Justice.

Continue on to the **Cathedral of Notre-Dame** (3), regarded by many to be the most perfect example of a pure Gothic structure on earth. Its richly carved **west front** merits a long and careful examination, especially the 13th-century statue of Christ and the superb relief of the Last Judgement; both by the central doorway. The two towers flanking the rose window, of unequal height, are later additions. Amiens Cathedral was begun in 1220 and pretty much completed in record time, thus accounting for the truly remarkable architectural unity. A reflection of the town's medieval prosperity, it is the largest cathedral in France.

Step inside to witness its astonishing proportions and noble use of space. Of particular note are the 16th-century **choir stalls**, whose oak carvings depict both religious and secular life, the latter often satirically. Stroll around the ambulatory to admire the marvelous choir screen. The cathedral is closed between noon and 2 p.m.

Walk around to the rear of the cathedral, then visit the **Art and Regional History Museum** (4) in a superb 17th-century mansion, the **Hôtel de Berny**. The furniture and room settings are quite interesting, as are items relating to the author Jules Verne, who lived most of his life in Amiens. The museum is open on Tuesdays through Sundays, from 10 a.m. to noon and 2–6 p.m. From November through April it is open on Wednesdays, Saturdays and Sundays only.

Now follow the map to the **Picardy Museum** (5), which features an excellent collection of art focusing on the 18th-century French style—particularly paintings by Quentin de la Tour and Fragonard. There are also representative works of the Flemish and Dutch schools along with other European masters. The ground floor is devoted to archaeological exhibits. Visits may be made on any day except Mondays, from 10 a.m. to noon and 2–6 p.m.

Amiens

300 Yards

N-1 TO PARIS

R. Mar. de Lattre de Tassigny

R. de Beauvais

6 Info.

R. Jean Catelas

Rue Lavalard

5 Museum

Rue de la République

7

8

R. des Vergeaux

Rue Lamarck

Place Gambetta

R. des Sergents

Rue Flatters

Rue des Jacobins

R. des Trois Cailloux

R. Duseval

Francs Muriers

Rue des

Info.

3

R. St.-Leu

Rue Victor Hugo

R. des Otages

4

Cathedral

Rue du Hocquet

Rue Vanmarcke

9

R. des Archers

R. de l'Amiral Courbet

R. des Augustins

R. Motte

ST.-LEU

R. de Noyon

Rue Lamartine

R. de la Dodane

2

R. des Cannettes

Blvd. du Cange

1

Blvd. d' Alsace-Lorraine

SOMME

Station Info.

N-29 TO PARIS

Rue du Vivier

N

R. Paul Tellier

Rue Serrassaint

Claudius Antoine

Rue de Verdun

Blvd. de Beauville

TO PARIS

Rue Legrand Daussy

10

HORTILLONNAGES

The St.-Leu Quarter

Return to Place Gambetta and turn left to the tourist office in the modern **Maison de la Culture** (6). You may want to ask here about boat trips in the *Hortillonnages* (10), an interesting experience unique to Amiens, which are available at specific times during the summer season.

Retrace your steps as far as the 17th-century **City Hall** *(Hôtel de Ville)* (7). A left here leads past the 16th-century Bailliage (note the dormer windows and Renaissance facade), the equally-old square bell tower, and the **Church of St.-Germain** (8) in the Flamboyant Gothic style.

The medieval **St.-Leu Quarter** (9), cut through with numerous canals, still exudes an aura of the Middle Ages. Much of this area had become quite seedy, but recent efforts at gentrification, including the restoration of many fine old houses, are already yielding results. Stroll through its evocative narrow streets, noting in particular the picturesque 15th-century **Church of St.-Leu**.

From here you can return to the station following the route on the map. Along the way you may want to make a side trip to the extraordinary **Hortillonnages** (10), a curious area of market gardens surrounded by irrigation canals, which have been cultivated since the Middle Ages. To get more than a fleeting glimpse of them requires exploring by boat. Current information about this can be had from the tourist office.

Champagne, Burgundy and Beyond

Wine lovers in particular will savor the five delicious daytrips in this section. Each destination offers a golden opportunity to sample some of France's best vintages right in their own region and return to your Paris base the same evening. But you don't really need a passion for liquid treasures to enjoy the area; even teetotalers will delight in its captivating old towns.

The Champagne district, where all of the world's true champagnes are made, centers on the ancient historical city of Reims. Once you've seen that, you may want to visit other places in the area. Épernay is an especially good choice for its champagne cellars alone, although the town itself is almost without interest.

Throughout most of its long history, Burgundy *(Bourgogne)* has been a land apart; one whose borders remain vague and undefined. Not until the 15th century was it absorbed into France. Much of its colorful past is still highly visible in Auxerre, Dijon and Beaune, the three daytrip destinations chosen to best represent this ancient wine region. Travelers with more time may want to stay over for a few days and explore some of its other attractions, such as Sens, Vézelay, Autun, Nevers or Cluny.

And beyond? That's Lyon—which makes no wine of its own but as the gastronomic capital of France certainly consumes enough; so much so that in fact it is reputed to lie at the junction of not two but three rivers—the Rhône, the Saône, and the Beaujolais.

As an alternative to Paris, Dijon with its excellent rail and highway connections makes a convenient base city for one-day forays throughout Burgundy and to Lyon. Those with cars might also consider staying in Beaune.

Reims

World renowned for its magnificent cathedral, traditionally the coronation site for the kings of France, Reims is also one of the two leading centers of the champagne trade. What better place could there possibly be to sample the bubbly while exploring an intriguing old city?

Reims' grandiose and often turbulent history goes back over two thousand years. Its name derives from a Celtic tribe, the Remi, who lived there long before the Romans changed it to *Curocortorum*. Clovis, king of the Franks, was baptized in a predecessor of its cathedral in A.D. 496, which resulted in the conversion of the Franks to Christianity. Since then, practically every French king received his crown in Reims, the last being Charles X in 1825.

During World War I the city found itself in the middle of a battle zone, being subjected to intense bombardment for four long years. Miraculously, the splendid 13th-century cathedral survived, wounded but still intact, although three-quarters of Reims was reduced to rubble. The Second World War brought great destruction as well, along with another place in history. It was here that the unconditional surrender of the Third Reich was signed in 1945, putting an end to that terrible conflict.

Postwar reconstruction and the restoration of ancient monuments has made Reims once again the fascinating place that it was in the past. Often spelled as "Rheims," the city's name is pronounced as "Rrans," more or less rhyming with *dance*.

It is possible to combine a visit to Reims with one to nearby Épernay, the other major champagne producer, as they are both on the same rail line. The only sights to see there are the champagne *caves*, which are world-famous and absolutely first-rate. Ask the tourist office at 7 Avenue de Champagne in Épernay for details.

GETTING THERE:

Trains depart Gare de l'Est station in Paris several times in the morning for the 90-minute run to Reims. Some require a change at Épernay. Return service operates until mid-evening.

By car, Reims is 88 miles northeast of Paris on the A-4 Autoroute.

WHEN TO GO:

Reims may be enjoyed at any time, but note that the major museums are closed on Tuesdays and holidays. Some of the champagne cellars are closed on weekends and during the winter.

FOOD AND DRINK:

Being a major wine center, Reims offers an extraordinarily high level of cuisine. Some choice restaurants are:

Boyer "Les Crayères" (64 Blvd. Henry Vasnier, 4 blocks east of the St.-Remi Basilica, near the champagne caves) One of the very best restaurants in France, with prices to match. Reservations essential, phone 26-82-80-80. X: Mon., Tues. lunch. $$$+

Le Florence (43 Blvd. Foch, across from the train station) Top quality cuisine in elegant surroundings. X. Sun. eve., mid-July to mid-Aug. $$$

Le Foch (37 Blvd. Foch, across from the train station) Classic cuisine with a modern touch in a nice setting. X: Sun. eve., Mon. $$

Le Vigneron (Place Paul-Jamot, 3 blocks east of the cathedral) Traditional old-fashioned cuisine of the region. X: Sat. lunch, Sun. $$

Le Continental (95 Place Drouet-d'Erlon, across from the train station) Good classic cuisine at fair prices. $$

Le Boulingrin (48 Rue de Mars, just southeast of the Mars Gate) Traditional braserie food. X: Sun., mid-July to mid-Aug. $$

Le Colibri (12 Rue de Chanzy, 2 blocks southwest of the cathedral) Traditional cuisine. $

Flamm' Steak (17 Rue Libergier, 2 blocks southwest of the cathedral) Crêpes, among other items. X: Sun. eve., Sept. $

Le Forum (34 Place du Forum, near the Museum of Old Reims) Offers a low-price *menu* on weekdays. X: Sun. eve., Mon. $

TROUIST INFORMATION:

The local tourist office, phone 26-47-25-69, is located at 2 Rue Guillaume-de-Machault, to the left of the cathedral. Ask them about visits to the champagne cellars.

SUGGESTED TOUR:

Leave the **train station** (1) and follow the map to the **Cathedral** (2). Nearly all of the kings of France were crowned here following a precedent set in 496 by Clovis, king of the Franks. The present cathedral, along with those of Paris, Chartres, and Amiens, is a perfect example of the French Gothic style's golden age. It was begun in 1211 and

Reims

500 Yards

essentially completed within a century, thus accounting for its remarkable stylistic unity.

The richly decorated **west front** with its three deeply recessed doorways recalls the stories of the Bible in carved stone. Its central portal is dedicated to the Virgin, while the right doorway, flanked by the prophets, represents the Last Judgement. Perhaps the most famous symbol of Reims is the enigmatic "smiling angel" in the left doorway, easily worth the small effort of singling out.

Step inside to admire the **stained-glass windows,** some of which are 13th-century originals. Of particular note is the fabulous rose window in the west end. There are also some wonderful modern stainedglass windows by the artist Marc Chagall in the Lady Chapel, installed in 1974. Seventeen marvelous tapestries depicting the life of the Virgin are displayed during the summer months.

Leave the cathedral and stroll around to the rear to witness the almost weightless elegance of its flying buttresses. Next to it is the former **Archbishop's Palace** *(Palais du Tau)* (3), once the residence of the king during coronations and now a museum of the cathedral's treasures. It may be visited on any day, from 10 a.m. to noon and 2–6 p.m., closing an hour earlier in winter.

The **Museum of Fine Arts** *(Musée St.-Denis)* (4) is located in a former abbey just two blocks from the cathedral. Its collections include an outstanding series of 16th-century portrait drawings by both Lucas Cranach the Elder and his son, the Younger. Among the other treasures are two cycles of medieval tapestries and wall hangings, no less than 25 landscapes by Corot, and a marvelous gathering of 19th-and early-20th-century French paintings. The museum is open every day except on Tuesdays and holidays, from 10 a.m. to noon and 2–6 p.m., closing at 5 p.m. in winter.

Now follow the map to the **Basilica of St.-Remi** (5) on Rue Simon. This is the oldest church in Reims, dating from the first half of the 11th century. Much of it is in the Romanesque style, while the huge 12thcentury choir makes a tentative transition into the early Gothic. Behind the altar lies the reconstructed tomb of Saint Remi, a 5th-century archbishop who established the importance of Reims by baptizing Clovis as a Christian and anointing him king of the Franks.

Adjoining the church on the north side is its former abbey, now housing the city's **Archaeological Museum** *(Musée Abbaye St.-Remi)*. Displays here include fascinating artifacts from prehistoric times to the late Middle Ages, along with notable tapestries illustrating the life of Saint Remi. It is open daily except on Tuesdays and holidays, from 10 a.m. to noon and 2–6 p.m.

Now for a real treat—the famous **champagne cellars**, many of which are located in this part of town. The leading ones that offer public

Reims Cathedral

tours without prior arrangement are shown on the map. Those in the immediate vicinity are:

Veuve Clicquot-Ponsardin (6). These *caves* date from Gallo-Roman times.

Pommery (7). An elegant and fascinating tour through ancient pits below the city.

Taittinger (8). A somewhat spooky amble in the crypts of a former abbey, preceded by an excellent audio-visual show.

Piper-Heidsieck (9). Ride a little electric train through the cellars.

All of the tours are free, but do not offer free samples. You may, of course, buy some bottles of the bubbly. Visits are usually conducted in English, French and German. A jacket or sweater is helpful as the *cave* temperatures hover around the 50-degree mark. The cellars are usually open from 9–11 a.m. and 2–5 p.m., but check with the tourist office for current schedules.

Return to the cathedral area via the route on the map. You might want to make a little side trip to the new **French Automobile Museum** *(Centre Historique de l'Automobile Française)* (10) on Avenue Georges-Clemenceau. Some 150 vehicles dating from 1769 up to the present may be seen, daily from 10 a.m. to noon and 2–7 p.m., April through November.

Continuing on beyond the cathedral, you will pass the restored **Place Royale** with its statue of Louis XV. From here it is only a few steps to **Place du Forum**, where parts of the original Roman Forum are visible. The **Museum of Old Reims** *(Musée-Hôtel le Vergeur)* (11), on its north side, displays a splendid collection of antique furniture and art, including a noted set of engravings by Albrecht Dürer of the Apocalypse and Christ's Passion.

The route now leads past several outstanding mansions and the City Hall to the 3rd-century **Mars Gate** *(Porte Mars)* (12), the largest monument left in Reims from the Roman era.

Before returning to the nearby train station you may be interested in a few other sights. The **Salle de Guerre** (13), located in a technical school at 12 Rue Franklin-Roosevelt, is the room in which Germany unconditionally surrendered to the Allies on May 7, 1945. It has been left exactly as it was on that momentous day, when it was a part of General Eisenhower's headquarters. Visits may be made any day except Tuesdays and holidays, from 9 a.m. to noon and 2–6 p.m.; but not between the middle of November and the middle of March.

Another worthwhile sight is the strikingly modern **Foujita Chapel** (14), designed by the Japanese artist Léonard-Tsugouharu Foujita after his conversion to Catholicism in Reims. Just across the street is another champagne house, **Mumm** (15), which also offers a splendid tour of its cellars, this time with free tastings.

Auxerre

You won't find a great many tourists in Auxerre, but that's their loss. This marvelously atmospheric holdover from the Middle Ages is the capital of lower Burgundy and the center of the Chablis wine growing region. The town, as you approach it along the banks of the Yonne River, makes an exceptionally handsome sight with its church spires piercing the skyline above a huddle of ancient houses.

Inhabited since Celtic times, Auxerre was later a Roman fortress called *Autessiodurum,* from which its name derives. The town, converted to Christianity, became the seat of a bishop as early as the 3rd century, and later an important scholastic center. Its medieval heart is today one of the best-preserved in France—an exceptionally attractive place where you can enjoy strolling around the winding, narrow lanes and exploring its picturesque old structures in peace. Auxerre, incidentally, is pronounced *"Ausserre."*

GETTING THERE:

Trains leave Gare de Lyon station in Paris several times in the morning for Auxerre's St.-Gervais Station, less than two hours away. Some of these require a change at Laroche-Migennes. Return service operates until early evening.

By car, take the A-6 Autoroute and enter Auxerre on the N-6 road. The town is 105 miles southeast of Paris.

WHEN TO GO:

A trip to Auxerre can be made at almost any time, but avoid coming on a Tuesday or holiday, when its major attractions are closed.

FOOD AND DRINK:

Some good restaurants are listed below. Naturally, you will probably want to sip *genuine* Chablis, the local wine.

> **Restaurant Maxime** (5 Quai de la Marine, by the river below the cathedral) Excellent food in a nice waterside location. X: Sat. $$$

Le Jardin Gourmand (56 Blvd. Vauban, 3 blocks northwest of the Lapidary Museum) Superb cuisine at a fair price. Highly recommended. $$

Salamandre (84 Rue de Paris, 2 blocks west of the cathedral) Good-value *menus*. X: Sun. eve., Mon. $$

De Seignelay (2 Rue du Pont, near the Church of St.-Pierre) A great value in a small hotel. X: Mon. from Oct. to June. $

TOURIST INFORMATION:

The local tourist office, phone 86-52-06-19, is located along the Quai de la République, by the river, below the cathedral.

SUGGESTED TOUR:

Leave the **train station** (1) and follow the map to the Yonne River, from which you get a splendid view of the old town. A right here leads to a footbridge. Cross this and, passing the tourist office, walk uphill to the **Cathedral of St.-Étienne** (2), a remarkable structure in the Flamboyant Gothic style begun in the 13th century but not completed until the 16th. This was the scene, in 1422, of a fateful meeting in which the English and the Burgundians plotted against the French. In 1429 it was visited by a disguised Joan of Arc on her way to meet the dauphin at Chinon. After defeating the English at Orléans she returned here with Charles VII en route to his coronation at Reims. Another historical event took place in front of the cathedral in 1815 when Napoleon, returning from exile, conspired with Marshal Ney against Louis XVIII, for which Ney was later shot.

The cathedral's interior features some very fine medieval stained-glass windows along with an admirable Gothic choir. Be sure to visit its 11th-century **crypt**, the sole remaining part of an earlier cathedral on the same site. There you will see the famous *Christ on Horseback* fresco, the only one of its kind in the world. Other sights in the church include its treasury of illuminated manuscripts and the **north tower**, which may be climbed for a closeup view of the town.

Now carefully follow the map through a maze of ancient streets to **Place St.-Nicolas** (3), a delightful square in the old marine quarter. Continue on past a handsome 16th-century half-timbered house to the **Abbey of St.-Germain** (4), founded in the 6th century by Queen Clothilde, wife of Clovis, above the tomb of Auxerre's 5th-century bishop and native son, Saint Germain. Rebuilt in later years, the church itself is of minor interest, but the **crypts** are another story. Some of these date from as early as the 5th century. The 9th-century Carolingian chambers contain several fabulous frescoes, among the very earliest yet discovered in France, depicting the martyrdom of Saint Stephen. In the Merovingian part of the crypt there are some oak

Auxerre

300 Yards

Auxerre from the Yonne River

beams that are over 1,100 years old. The crypts may be visited—with a guide—every day except Tuesdays and some holidays, from 9 a.m. to noon and 2–5 p.m. A **Museum of Archaeology and Fine Arts** has recently been added to the abbey complex, making it even more attractive.

Continue on to the **Lapidary Museum** (5) in the former Chapel of the Nuns of the Visitation. Its Gallo-Roman stone sculptures and other archaeological finds may be seen between July 1st and September 15th, daily except on Tuesdays, from 10 a.m. to noon and 2–6 p.m.

Rue de Paris and Rue d'Englény lead to the **Leblanc-Duvernoy Museum** (6), installed in an elegant 18th-century mansion. The magnificent collection of Beauvais tapestries, porcelains, furniture and other items of the 18th-century decorative arts should not be missed. It is open daily from 10:30 a.m. to noon and 2–5:30 p.m., except on Tuesdays and some holidays. Just a few blocks northwest of this and slightly off the map is the new **Paul Bert Natural History Museum**, located at 5 Boulevard Vauban. More interesting, perhaps, for its beautiful setting in a 19th-century mansion surrounded by lovely grounds than for its contents, it is open daily from 9 a.m. to noon and 2–6 p.m., but closed on weekend mornings.

The route goes past the **Church of St.-Eusèbe** (7), noted for its 12th-century Romanesque tower, and winds its way around to Auxerre's famous 15th-century **Clock Tower** *(Tour de l'Horloge)* (8), opposite the Town Hall. This delightfully animated part of town, now

The Clock Tower

pedestrianized, is also its commercial center. All around the tower stand ancient houses, many of them half-timbered, which serve as luxurious shops.

Returning to the station, you will pass the **Church of St.-Pierre** (9) with its highly impressive Renaissance façade. Continue on downhill to the Paul-Bert Bridge for a last look at Auxerre mirrored in the waters of the Yonne before returning to Paris.

Dijon

There is a lot to see in Dijon—if you can just tear yourself away from the pleasures of the table long enough to feast the eyes as well as the palate. Long renowned as the region's gastronomic center, this ancient city is also the traditional capital of Burgundy. Its rulers left behind a rich heritage that today makes it a veritable treasury of the arts. Dijon is an exceedingly likeable place, and an eminently walkable one as well.

Originally a Roman encampment on the military road linking Lyon with Mainz, *Divio*, as Dijon was then known, became the capital of the Burgundian kingdom during the Dark Ages, only to be destroyed by fire in 1137. The late 12th century saw its reconstruction as a fortified city, while the Cathedral of St.-Bénigne was begun a hundred years later.

Philip the Bold, son of King John II of France, inherited Burgundy in 1364, thus starting the powerful line of Valois dukes whose loyalty to the Kingdom of France wavered with each succeeding generation. During this time Burgundy was greatly expanded, making Dijon in effect the capital of much of what is now the Netherlands, Belgium, Alsace and Lorraine as well as the present region of *Bourgogne*. This enormous growth coincided with the beginning of the Renaissance, attracting many leading artists to Dijon, where there was both work and money. The golden days came to an end in 1477 when Duke Charles the Bold was killed fighting Louis XI, thus reunifying Burgundy with France.

GETTING THERE:

Trains for Dijon leave Gare de Lyon station in Paris fairly frequently. The speedy TGVs *(reservations required)* make the run in about 100 minutes; others take about 2½ hours. Return service operates until mid-evening.

By car, Dijon is 195 miles southeast of Paris via the A-6 Autoroute. This may be a bit too far for a daytrip, although Dijon makes an excellent stopover en route between Paris and Provence or the Riviera.

WHEN TO GO:

Dijon may be visited at any time of the year since the walk is short and much of your time will be spent indoors. Most of the major sights are closed on Tuesdays and some holidays.

FOOD AND DRINK:

The overall quality of dining in Dijon is exceptionally high, with such local specialties as *boeuf bourguignon* and *coq au vin* being international favorites. Start you meal with a *kir*, an apéritif made from white wine and blackcurrant liqueur, named after the city's onetime mayor. Burgundy's fabulous Côte d'Or begins just south of Dijon, assuring a plentiful supply of world-class wines at reasonable prices. The city is also very famous for its mustard, a jar of which makes a nice souvenir.

Some outstanding restaurants located on or near the suggested walking route are:

Jean-Pierre Billoux (Hôtel la Cloche, 14 Place Darcy) Regarded as the best restaurant in Dijon, and among the best in France. For reservations call 80-30-11-00. X: Sun. eve., Mon., Feb. $$$+

La Chouette (Breuil) (1 Rue de la Chouette, just north of the Palace of the Dukes) Exquisite dining in an ancient house. X: Mon. eve., Tues. $$$

Le Chapeau Rouge (5 Rue Michelet, 1 block east of the cathedral) Classic dining in a tranquil setting. $$$

Le Toison d'Or (Les Oenophiles) (18 Rue Ste.-Anne, 5 blocks southwest of the Palace of the Dukes) In an old mansion, with ancient wine *caves* and a museum. A unique experience. X: Sun. eve. $$

Le Rallye (39 Rue Chabot-Charny, 2 blocks southeast of the Palace of the Dukes) Fine cooking at a fair price. X: Sun., holidays. $$

La Porte Guillaume (in the Hôtel du Nord on Place Darcy) An old traditional establishment. $$

Le Vinarium (23 Place Bossuet, 2 blocks east of the cathedral) Regional cuisine in a 13th-century crypt. X: Sun., Mon. lunch, Feb. $$

Le Chabrot (36 Rue Monge, 3 blocks southeast of the cathedral) A friendly place with regional specialties. X: Sun., Mon. lunch. $$

Brasserie du Théâtre (Place du Théâtre, 1 block southeast of the Palace of the Dukes) A lively place with outdoor tables in summer. X: Wed. $$

Le Dôme (16 bis Rue Quentin, 2 blocks northwest of Notre-Dame Church) A popular little restaurant facing the Central Market. X: Sun., holidays. $

Au Bec Fin (47 Rue Jeannin, 1 block north of the Church of St.-Michel) An excellent value. X: Sat. lunch, Sun. $

TOURIST INFORMATION:

The local tourist office, phone 80-43-42-12, is located at Place Darcy (2), not far from the train station. There is another office at 34 Rue des Forges, phone 80-30-35-39, near the Church of Notre-Dame.

SUGGESTED TOUR:

Leave the **train station** (1) and follow the map to **Place Darcy** (2), an attractive square with a tourist office, a small park and an 18th-century triumphal arch. Continue on Rue de la Liberté past the venerable Grey Poupon mustard store—which has an exhibit of antique jars on display—to **Place François Rude** (3). In the center of this lively square there is a fountain that once ran with new wine at harvest time, topped by a statue of a naked youth treading the grapes. The Central Market (Les Halles), two blocks north of this, bustles with activity on Tuesday, Friday and Saturday mornings.

Follow the narrow Rue des Forges past several exquisite old houses, the most notable being the 15th-century **Hôtel Morel-Sauvegrain** at number 56; the 13th-century exchange—much restored—at number 40; and the **Maison Milsand** dating from 1561, at number 38. The 15th-century **Hôtel Chambellan** at number 34 houses the main tourist office. A left at place Notre-Dame leads to the **Church of Notre-Dame** (4), a unique jewel of 13th-century Gothic architecture. Its façade is literally covered with hideous gargoyles, while from the roof rises the Jacquemart, a mechanical chiming clock that Philip the Bold brought back as war booty from the Flemish town of Courtrai in 1389. Be sure to visit the remarkably harmonious interior, noted for its ancient stained-glass windows and an 11th-century Black Virgin carved in wood.

Stroll around to the rear of the church on Rue de la Chouetee. At number 8 you will pass the **Hôtel de Vogüé**, a lovely residence in the Renaissance style dating from 1614. Make a left into Rue Verrerie, and the next right on Rue Chaudronnerie, followed by another right on Rue Vannerie—a short walk taking you down three very picturesque streets lined with medieval buildings. At the end you will come to the **Church of St.-Michel** (5), a curious mixture of Gothic and Renaissance styles built during the 15th, 16th and 17th centuries.

The major attraction in Dijon, besides its food and wine, is the **Palace of the Dukes of Burgundy** (6). Begun in the 14th century, it was continually enlarged and modified until the 19th, with much of its classical façade designed by Louis XIV's architect, Jules Hardouin-Mansart of Versailles fame. This enormous complex of structures now houses both the City Hall (Hôtel de Ville), which may be strolled through, and the world-famous **Fine Arts Museum** (Musée des Beaux-Arts), one of the very best of all France.

The entrance to the museum is on Place de la Ste.-Chapelle. Allow

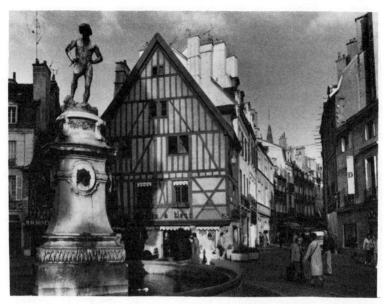

Place François Rude

plenty of time for a visit—an hour at the very least—and carefully study the posted layout maps as it is quite easy to get disoriented and risk missing some of its best treasures. These include the ducal kitchens, the **tombs** of Philip the Bold and John the Fearless; Italian, Swiss, Flemish and German as well as French paintings and sculptures; and, of course, the outstanding galleries of modern and regional art. The museum is open daily except on Tuesdays and major holidays, from 10 a.m. to 6 p.m.

Now stroll into Place des Ducs-de-Bourgogne, a charming square facing the original parts of the palace. A portal at the corner leads back into the palace complex, from which you can climb up the **Tour Philippe-le-Bon** (7) for an excellent view of the city, the mountains beyond and the beginnings of the Burgundy wine district. it is a steep 150 feet to the top of this 15th-century tower, but well worth the effort.

Follow the map through the elegant Place de la Libération to the **Magnin Museum** (8), housed in a fine 17th-century mansion, the Hôtel Lantin on Rue des Bons-Enfants. Step inside to view a sumptuous collection of paintings displayed in the gorgeous environment of original room settings reflecting period bourgeois life. It is open from 9 a.m. to noon and 2–6 p.m., daily except on Tuesdays and major holidays.

Dijon

N

200 Yards

Along Rue de la Liberté

Continue on past the Palace of Justice and turn right on Rue Amiral Roussin. The route now leads through a colorful old part of town to the **Cathedral of St.-Bénigne** (9), a 13th-century example of the Burgundian Gothic style. You can make an interesting visit to its unusual circular crypt, dating from 1002 with some 9th-century segments, which survives from an earlier basilica on the same site.

Next to this is the **Archaeological Museum** (10), housed in the dormitory of a former Benedictine abbey. Displays here include some fascinating Gallo-Roman and medieval artifacts. The museum is open daily except on Tuesdays, from 10 a.m. to 6 p.m. during the summer season and from 9 a.m. to noon and 2–6 p.m. the rest of the year.

On the way back to the train station you may want to stop at the **Jardin de l'Arquebuse** (11), a large and very lovely garden which also houses the **Natural History Museum**. Those with a bit more time can make a short excursion of less than a mile to the famous **Chartreuse de Champmol** (12, off the map). Originally the burial place of the dukes of Burgundy, this 14th-century monastery was destroyed in the Revolution and the site is now occupied by a mental hospital. Some of its fabulous sculptures by the noted medieval master Claus Sluter are still there, and deserve to be seen by anyone interested in the art of the Middle Ages.

Beaune

Beaune is a mecca for wine lovers the world over, and long the center of Burgundy's liquid trade. Its major sight, the 15th-century Hôtel-Dieu, is surely one of the most extraordinary medieval structures in France, or in all of Europe for that matter. Visitors by the thousands are also attracted to its numerous *caves,* where the wines of Burgundy can be sampled in congenial surroundings.

Wine was not always Beaune's sole *raison d'être.* The 14th-century ramparts, still more or less complete, enclose a remarkably well-preserved town that dates from the time of the ancient Gauls. It remained an important political center of the duchy long after the dukes themselves moved to Dijon, with a strategic location between the once-powerful strongholds of warring nobles. All of this changed in the 17th century, when the local citizens finally turned their full attention to wine. That happy development has brought about a prosperity lasting to this day. Beaune (pronounced *Bone*) is indeed a joyful place to visit.

GETTING THERE:

Trains depart Gare de Lyon station in Paris frequently for Dijon, with the TGV types making the run in about 100 minutes. From there take a connecting local to Beaune, a trip of 22 minutes. There is also frequent bus service between the two towns. Some TGV trains run directly from Paris to Beaune, but at rather odd hours. Return service operates until early evening.

By car, Beaune is 196 miles southeast of Paris on the A-6 Autoroute. A daytrip by car is rather impractical, but the town makes an excellent stopover for those driving between Paris and Provence or the Riviera.

WHEN TO GO:

Beaune may be enjoyed at any time. Even if it is raining, the underground *caves* stay dry—at least as far as precipitation is concerned.

FOOD AND DRINK:

As an important tourist attraction, Beaune offers a great many restaurants and cafés in all price ranges. Some particularly good choices are:

Relais de Saulx (6 Rue Louis-Véry, 1 block west of the Hôtel-Dieu) Burgundian cuisine in a lovely rustic setting. Reservations needed, call 80-22-01-35. X: Sun. eve., Mon., holidays. $$$

Jacques Lainé (10 Blvd. Foch, 3 blocks northwest of the Fine Arts Museum) Modernized traditional cuisine in an elegant house. X: Wed. lunch. $$$

Auberge St.-Vincent (Place de la Halle, near the tourist office) Traditional dishes in an ancient house. X: Sun. eve. off season. $$

Les Gourmets (17 Rue Monge, near the tourist office) A busy, popular place. $$

Au P'tit Pressoir (15 Place Fleury, north of the Hôtel-Dieu) Good regional cuisine. X: Tues. eve., Wed. $$

Auberge Bourguignonne (4 Place Madeleine, 4 blocks east of the Hôtel-Dieu, just outside the walls) Traditional cooking in a small inn. X: Mon. $$

Brelinette (6 Rue du Faubourg Madeleine, 4 blocks east of the Hôtel-Dieu, just outside the walls) Local cuisine at low prices. X: Wed. off season. $

Maxime (3 Place Madeleine, 4 blocks east of the Hôtel-Dieu, just outside the walls) A good value. X: Mon., Jan. $

TOURIST INFORMATION:

The local tourist office, phone 80-22-24-51, is next to the Hôtel-Dieu. Be sure to ask them for current information concerning visits to the wine *caves*.

SUGGESTED TOUR:

Leave the **train station** (1) and follow the map through some colorful old streets to the **Tourist Information Office** (2). Here you can get an up-to-date list of the wine *caves* in town that offer tours or tastings (*dégustation*). Many of these are located in ancient cellars dating from as far back as the 13th century and make intriguing places to visit. Some are free while others—often with better vintages—charge a nominal admission. Since the old part of Beaune is quite small you will be able to visit the cellars at your leisure anytime along the walking route. The locations of five of the better-known *caves* are shown on the map as circled numbers. They are:

Marché aux Vins, near the Hôtel-Dieu (8).

Caves des Cordeliers, near the Hôtel-Dieu (9).

Maison Calvet, 6 Blvd. Perpreuil, by the town walls (10).

La Halle aux Vins, facing Square des Lions on Blvd. Foch (11).

Maison Patriarche Père et Fils, on Rue de Collège (12).

N

R. du Fg. Bretonnière

Ave. du Parc

R. Fg. St.-Martin

Blvd. Clemenceau

Walls

R. Maufoux

R. Fraïsse

Ave. République

Blvd. Bretonnière

A-6 TO PARIS

11

Blvd. Mar. Foch

R. Marey

③

Info.

④

⑧ ② ⑤

⑨

R. Monge

⑥

R. du Collège

12

Pl. Carnot

R. Carnot

R. de Lorraine

⑩

R. des Tonneliers

R. Rousseau-Deslandes

① Museum

Walls

Blvd. Perpreuil

R. d'Alsace

R. Thiers

Walls

Walls

Blvd. Mar. Joffre

Rue de Chorey

Blvd. J. Ferry

R. du Fg. Madeleine

R. du Château

Blvd. J. Copeau

St.-Jean

R. A. Colbert

R. Celler

R. du Fg

Ave. du 8 Septembre

① Station

TO DIJON & PARIS

Beaune

300 Yards

The Collegiate Church of Notre-Dame

Now for Beaune's major attractions, the **Hôtel-Dieu** (also known as the *Hospices de Beaune*) (3). This exquisite structure—a major architectural achievement of the 15th century—was founded in 1443 by the chancellor of Burgundy, Nicolas Rolin, as a charity hospital to alleviate the misery of much of the town's population. This was perhaps only too fitting since it was Rolin—acting as tax collector for the dukes—who reduced them to poverty to begin with. Its use as a hospital continued until 1971, with much of it still functioning as an old-age home. Guided tours are conducted through it at very frequent intervals, every day from 9–11:30 a.m. and 2–6 p.m., with slightly shorter hours during the winter season. These end in a small art gallery featuring one of the most fabulous paintings from the Middle Ages, Roger Van der Weyden's great polyptych of the *Last Judgement.*

The Hôtel-Dieu is supported primarily by revenues from the 32 *Côte de Beaune* vineyards it owns, whose wines are sold at its famous auction, held on the third Sunday of each November. These tend to establish the prices for all Burgundy wines of the same vintage. The *Hospices de Beaune* label is highly regarded among lovers of fine wines.

Continue on to the **Collegiate Church of Notre-Dame** (4), begun during the 12th century in the Cluniac tradition. Some of its works of art are truly astonishing—particularly the 15th-century tapestries depicting the life of the Virgin, displayed behind the altar.

The Courtyard of the Hôtel-Dieu

Oenophiles—as well as normal folk—will appreciate the **Burgundy Wine Museum** *(Musée du Vin de Bourgogne)* (5), located in the medieval Mansion of the Dukes of Burgundy. Its many interesting displays cover the history and lore of local wine making from ancient times to the early 20th century. Don't miss the adjacent 14th-century press house *(cuverie)*. The museum is open daily from 9 a.m. to noon and 1:30–7 p.m.; with shorter hours and closed on Tuesdays in winter.

The walk now winds around past the picturesque 15th-century **Belfry** (6) of the former town hall to the **Museum of Fine Arts** *(Musée des Beaux-Arts)* (7). The rather miscellaneous collections, including some Gallo-Roman archaeological finds, are enlivened by a splendid group of paintings by the 19th-century romantic landscapist, Félix Ziem, a native son of Beaune. Another local lad, Étienne-Jules Marey, a 19th-century scientist who pioneered the principles of motion picture photography, has a separate gallery devoted to his work. Visits may be made from 9 a.m. to noon and 2–5:30 p.m. daily, but not on Tuesdays or between November and Easter.

From here you can return to the station by walking along the ancient ramparts or, better still, return to town for another glass of wine.

Lyon

In the past, a daytrip to Lyon would have been nearly unthinkable as the second city of France lies some 288 miles southeast of Paris. All that changed with the introduction of high-speed TGV trains, which cover the distance in an astonishing two hours flat. This is a good excursion for railpass holders—you really get your money's worth—and an excellent reason to purchase one of these bargains (see Section I).

Strangely, Lyon has never been much of a tourist attraction. Visitors yes—about five million a year, nearly all on business—but travelers in search of pleasure have largely avoided it; put off, perhaps, by its image as a large, sprawling industrial center. Lyon deserves better than that. Its older sections are surprisingly beautiful, and endowed with enough first-rate attractions to make just about any other city in France besides Paris pale by comparison.

And then there is the food. Lyon is usually regarded as the gastronomic capital of all France, which in practical terms means that it probably has the best cooking in the world. You could make a trip there just to eat, especially if your object was to indulge in one of the legendary temples of *haute cuisine* the area is famous for.

Over two thousand years old, Lyon was founded in 43 B.C. as the Roman colony of *Lugdunum*. Even before then, the site at the confluence of two rivers had long been occupied by Celts and other people. Under the emperor Augustus it became the capital of Gaul and later, in A.D. 478, the capital of the Burgundians. The city's strategic situation at the crossroads of trade routes favored its development as a mercantile center, a position it still holds. Textile manufacturing took root in the early 16th century, establishing a strong economic base along with banking and printing. Although Lyon—sometimes spelled *Lyons* in English—is now a very modern city with well over a million people in its urban area, the walking tour suggested below is limited to the handsome and very well-preserved older parts of town.

GETTING THERE:

TGV trains *(reservations required)* depart Gare de Lyon station in Paris frequently for the two-hour run (or flight?) to Lyon. Most of these stop at both of Lyon's two main stations, Part-Dieu and Perrache. If your train does this, *do not get off at Part-Dieu but stay on to Perrache.* If your train does not, you will have to get off at Part-Dieu and take another train to Perrache Station, where the walking tour begins. Return service operates until early evening.

By car, the distance from Paris is too great for a daytrip. You may, however, want to make a stopover en route to or from Provence or the Riviera. Lyon is 288 miles southeast of Paris via the A-6 Autoroute.

WHEN TO GO:

Some of the major attractions are closed on Mondays, some on Tuesdays, and other on both days. Good weather will make your trip much more enjoyable.

FOOD AND DRINK:

Lyon abounds in superb restaurants and friendly cafés, with the selections listed below limited to those along or near the suggested walking route. For choices in other parts of town you should consult an up-to-date restaurant guide such as the red-cover *Michelin France.*

Léon de Lyon (1 Rue Pleney, 1 block south of the Fine Arts Museum) Inspired Lyonnais cuisine in the grand tradition. For reservations call 78-28-11-33. X: Sun., Mon. lunch. $$$

Vettard (7 Place Bellecour, on the north side) Highly regarded classical cuisine. X: Sun., Aug. $$$

Bourillot (8 Place des Célestins, 1 block north of Place Bellecour) Excellent classic cuisine at a fair price. X: Sun., holidays, July. $$$

La Tour Rose (16 Rue du Boeuf, in Old Lyon, 3 blocks north of the cathedral) Inventive modern cuisine in a 17th-century house. X: Sun. $$$

La Mère Brazier (12 Rue Royal, in the Traboules district, 7 blocks northeast of the Fine Arts Museum) Traditional old-fashioned cuisine in an unchanged setting. X: Sat. lunch, Sun., Aug. $$$

Les Fantasques (47 Rue de la Bourse, 2 blocks east of the Printing Museum) The best seafood in Lyon. X: Sat., late Aug. $$$

Nandron (26 Quai Jean-Moulin, 3 blocks east of the Printing Museum) Both modern and classic cuisine in a popular restaurant. X: Fri. eve., Sat., Aug. $$$

La Voûte—Chez Lea (11 Place Antonin-Gourju, 1 block northwest of Place Bellecour, near the river) Traditional Lyonnais cooking in an old establishment. X: Sun., July. $$

Boeuf d'Argent (29 Rue du Boeuf in Old Lyon, 2 blocks northwest of the cathedral) Good value *menus.* X: Sat. lunch, Sun., Aug. $$

Daniel et Denise (2 Rue Tupin, 6 blocks south of the Fine Arts Museum) Grand cuisine in the classical style. X: Sun., Mon. lunch, early Aug. $$

Café des Fédérations (8 Rue Major-Martin, 1 block west of the Fine Arts Museum) An old-fashioned place with simple local cuisine. X: Sat., Sun., Aug. $$

Le Bistrot de Lyon (64 Rue Mercière, 5 blocks southwest of the Fine Arts Museum) A real bistro, popular with theater people, local specialties. $$

Garioud (14 Rue du Palais-Grillet, 3 blocks south of the Printing Museum) Fine cuisine at affordable prices. X: Sat. lunch, Sun. $$

La Mère Vittet—Brasserie Lyonnaise (26 Cours de Verdun, between the rail and bus stations at Perrache) Serving good meals 24 hours a day. X: May 1. $$

Le Comptoir du Boeuf (3 Place Neuve-St.-Jean in Old Lyon, 3 blocks north of the cathedral) Great wines by the glass accompany traditional cuisine in this café-restaurant. X: Sun. $$

Chez Sylvain (4 Rue Turpin, 6 blocks south of the Fine Arts Museum) A neighborhood favorite for its local dishes. X: Sun., Mon., Aug. $

La Mère Jean (5 Rue des Marronniers, 1 block east of Place Bellecour) Local home-style cooking at low prices. Always crowded. X: Sat. eve., Sun., Aug. $

Le Blandan (Rue Sergent-Blandan, 4 blocks northwest of the Fine Arts Museum) A good value for quality cuisine. X: Mon., Tues., mid-July to mid-Aug. $

TOURIST INFORMATION:

The main tourist office, phone 78-42-25-75, is located in Place Bellecour (2); with a branch office in the Perrache Train Station and another at the Part-Dieu Station. Ask them about guide maps for the Traboules district.

SUGGESTED TOUR:

Leave the **Perrache Train Station** (1), a huge modern complex that includes a bus terminal, and descend the escalators to Place Carnot. From here the pedestrians-only Rue Victor Hugo leads through a lively shopping district to **Place Bellecour** (2), a vast open space with a flower market, the main tourist office, and an equestrian statue of Louis XIV. Turn left and cross the Pont Bonaparte, a bridge spanning the Saône. Continue straight ahead to the funicular station, buy a ticket from the vending machine, and board the car on the right-hand side marked

The Basilica of Notre-Dame-de-Fourvière

for Fourviére. This will take you to the top of a very steep hill, from which there is a wonderful panoramic view of Lyon.

The monstrous **Basilica of Notre-Dame de Fourvière** (3), at the top of the funicular and overlooking the city, has to be seen to be believed. This marvelously hideous edifice, a curious *mélange* of architectural styles, was begun in 1870 as thanks to the Virgin for saving Lyon from the Germans during the Franco-Prussian War. Step inside for a look at the elaborate stained-glass windows, mosaics, and the crypt. A tower on the left affords an even better view of the city. The basilica is closed between noon and 2 p.m.

The Fourvière hill was the site of the original Roman settlement and is rich in archaeological finds. Follow the map to the **Gallo-Roman Museum** (4), a superb modern structure, mostly underground, which spirals its way down part of the hillside. As you descend its ramps you will pass many fascinating artifacts from Lyon's ancient past. A descriptive booklet in English is available at the entrance. Visits may be made from 9:30 a.m. to noon and 2–6 p.m., daily except on Mondays and Tuesdays.

Remains of a Roman Theater

Leave the museum from its lowest level and stroll over to the two **Roman Theaters** (5), unearthed in the 1930s. The larger of these is the oldest in France and was built by the emperor Augustus in 15 B.C. It is now used for occasional festival performances, but you can usually climb all over it.

Continue down the hill via Montée du Chemin Neuf to the **Cathedral of St.-Jean** (6). Begun in the 12th century, it displays a mixture of styles ranging from Romanesque to Flamboyant Gothic. The interior is noted for its 13th-century stained-glass in the choir, apse and rose windows of the transepts. In the north transept there is an interesting 14th-century **astronomical clock** that puts on a show at noon, 1, 2, and 3 p.m. Don't miss the **Chapel of the Bourbons** on the north side of the nave. The **Treasury**, to the right of the entrance, exhibits rare pieces of religious art. The cathedral is closed between noon and 2 p.m.

Adjacent to the cathedral, on its north side, is an outdoor archaeological garden with excavations of earlier churches. Stroll down Rue St.-Jean and turn left to the **Hôtel de Gadagne** (7), a magnificent 16th-century Renaissance mansion now housing both the **Historical Museum of Lyon** and the intriguing **Marionette Museum**. Puppets have been a tradition of the city since the late 18th century when one Laurent Mourguet, an unemployed silk worker who lost his job after the Revolution made silk undemocratic, created a satirical marionette character named Guignol. The plays, larded with broad humor in the local dialect, are still very popular. Ask at the tourist office for details of performances given in various theaters. Besides the classic Guignol characters, the museum also has puppets from all over the world, notably those from Cambodia. It is open from 10:45 a.m. to 6 p.m., daily except on Tuesdays.

While still in this colorful area, known as Old *(Vieux)* Lyon, you should take the opportunity to explore its numerous tiny streets and alleyways. For many years this was a notorious slum, but recent restoration has made it fashionable once again. Some of its narrowest passages, known as *traboules*, make interior connections between the ancient buildings and adjacent streets, and were used by members of the Resistance during World War II to hide from the Nazis. Maps guiding you through these mazes are available at the tourist office and elsewhere.

Now follow the map across the river to **Place des Terreaux** (8) with its grandoise fountain by the 19th-century sculptor Frédéric Bartholdi, who also created the Statue of Liberty in New York. Those with boundless energy may want to head north up the Croix-Rousse hill and into the evocative quarter of **Les Traboules** (9, off the map), which offers endless possibilities to *trabouler*, as the sport of exploring the tiny passageways is known. As in Old Lyon, these architectural eccentricities are best seen with a specialized and highly detailed map. Don't get lost.

The **Fine Arts Museum** *(Musée des Beaux-Arts)* (10), facing Place des Terreaux, has one of the best collections in France. Originally a Benedictine nunnery, the building is slightly seedy, although not without charm. Its many rooms contain major works covering just about the entire scope of Western art. It is open from 10:30 a.m. to 6 p.m., daily except on Mondays and Tuesdays.

Continue on, following the map down the pedestrianized Rue de la République, to the **Printing and Banking Museum** *(Musée de l'Imprimerie et de la Banque)* (11), installed in a 15th-century mansion on Rue de la Poulaillerie. This is a splendid place to visit if the subject holds any interest to you. It is open daily except on Mondays and Tuesdays.

The walking route now swings over to the banks of the Rhône, then leads past Place Bellecour (2) to two more attractions. The **Decorative Arts Museum** (12) and its next-door neighbor, the **Historical Museum of Textiles** *(Musée Historique des Tissus)*, share the same admission ticket. As its name implies, the Decorative Arts Museum features exquisite room settings, primarily of the 18th century. If you like fabrics you will love the Textile Museum, which has the largest collection in the world. Both are open from 10 a.m. to noon and 2–5:30 p.m., daily except on Mondays and holidays. From here it is only a short walk back to Perrache Station.

Section VI

Daytrips from Paris

The Loire Valley

Few regions of France are as quietly seductive as the Loire Valley. This huge area, whose prime attractions begin about one hundred miles southwest of Paris and extend westward for another hundred, is among the most satisfying of tourist destinations in the country. Drained by a broad, lazy river, the "Garden of France" offers a fine climate, bucolic scenery, unusual wines, a deep sense of history and, best of all, many of the very finest châteaux in the land. Some of these are massive fortifications dating from the Middle Ages, when the Loire Valley was a frequent battleground in the struggles between the French and the English. Others were built in more peaceful times and reflect the unparalleled luxury to which the Renaissance nobility had become accustomed.

Distance and the relative seclusion of many of its attractions do combine to make daytrips from Paris to this enchanting region somewhat of a problem. Fortunately, there are some notable exceptions. Angers, Blois, and Amboise not only sit squarely on major rail lines and highways, but they also rate high among the most fascinating destinations in the area.

Those who would like to explore the valley in greater depth, visiting the fabulous châteaux of Chambord, Chenonceau, Azay-le-Rideau, Loches, Chinon, Saumur and others, should plan on stopping over for a few days. The most convenient base for daytrips in the region is Tours, from which daily bus excursions are offered to the famous sights. You could also rent a car there, which is certainly the ideal way to reach the more remote châteaux.

The Loire Valley is famous, in France at least, for its splendid variety of wines. Not particularly well known in North America, these charming country vintages provide fresh opportunities for new adventures in tasting. Some of the best are Vouvray, Anjou, Chinon, Muscadet and Pouilly-Fumé.

Also included in this section is that quintessential French provincial town, Bourges. Although it lies a bit outside the region itself, it shares many of its characteristics and is served by the same rail line.

Angers

Situated on the Maine River, just north of the Loire, the ancient capital of Anjou attracts visitors with its mighty fortress—one of the most impressive feudal structures in France—and its fine cathedral. Angers is a fairly large and quite animated city that has managed to preserve much of its illustrious past despite heavy wartime damage.

Known to the Romans as *Juliomagus* and later conquered by the Normans, Angers had its true time of glory in the Middle Ages. Between the 10th and 12th centuries its counts had acquired power exceeding that of even the kings of France. One of these Angevin rules, Henri Plantagenet, became Henry II of England in 1154 and fathered both Richard the Lionhearted and bad King John—a story of intrigue that makes for fascinating reading. Henry's wife, Eleanor of Aquitaine, had previously been married to Louis VII of France, thus making her queen of both countries at different times. Another local ruler, born in Angers early in the 15th century, was Good King René, duke of Anjou, count of Provence and king of Sicily. This remarkable man, among the most brilliant thinkers of his age, was largely responsible for the artistic tradition of Angers that continues to this day.

GETTING THERE:

Trains leave Montparnasse Station in Paris several times in the morning for Anger's St.-Laud Station. TGV trains (reservations needed) make the run in 95 minutes, regular trains (possible change at Le Mans) take $2\frac{1}{2}$ hours. Return service runs until mid-evening. This information will change as more of the TGV *Atlantique* network becomes operational.

By car, Angers is 180 miles southwest of Paris. Take the A-10 and A-11 Autoroutes to Le Mans, then the N-23 into Angers.

WHEN TO GO:

The castle is open every day except for a few major holidays, but the museums are closed on Mondays and some holidays.

FOOD AND DRINK:

Angers has an excellent selection of restaurants and cafés. Some good choices along or near the walking route are:

Le Quéré (9 Place du Ralliement, 2 blocks southeast of the Hôtel-Pincé) Considered to be the best restaurant in Angers. X: Tues. eve., Wed., early July. $$$

Le Toussaint (7 Rue Toussaint, near the rear of the cathedral) Local cuisine, especially seafood, in a refined atmosphere. Reservations needed, call 41-87-46-20. X: Sun., Mon., Aug. $$$

Le Logis (17 Rue St.-Laud, 1 block north of the Hôtel-Pincé) Superb seafood. X: Sat. eve., Sun., July. $$

L'Entr'acte (9 Rue Louis-de-Romain,, 2 blocks south of the Hôtel-Pincé) Noted for its seafood. X: Sun., Aug. $$

Plantagenets (in the Hôtel France, 8 Place de la Gare, opposite the train station) Good food in a convenient location. Open daily. $ and $$

Taverne Kanter (in Les Halles food and shopping mall, 2 blocks north of the cathedral) Hearty bistro fare and draft beer. $

TOURIST INFORMATION:

The local tourist office, phone 41-88-69-93, is on Place Kennedy opposite the castle. There is also a branch, phone 41-87-72-50, across from the train station.

SUGGESTED TOUR:

Leave the **Angers St.-Laud Train Station** (1) and head straight for the **Castle** *(Château)* (2), passing both tourist offices along the way. The forbidding bastion facing you was built in the 13th century by Louis IX, known to history as Saint Louis for his famous sense of moral authority. Previous fortresses had existed on the same site since 851; a 12th-century structure having been used by the Plantagenets. The thick curtain wall, over a half-mile in circumference, links 17 massive towers along a deep dry moat in which deer now roam.

With a design based on the crusaders' castles in the Holy Land, this citadel was among the most powerful in the kingdom, and was never successfully taken by assault. It came close to being destroyed in the 16th-century Wars of Religion, however, not by attack but by an order from Henri III to dismantle the fortress before it could fall into enemy hands. Fortunately, the demolition went very slowly and before much damage was done peace had returned and the king was dead.

Angers

300 Yards

Museum

④

R. Lionnaise

R. de la Censerie

Blvd. Arago

Quai Monge

③

MAINE

Quai Gambetta

Rue Thiers

Rue Maillé

Rue Boisnet

Rue

Rue du Mail

R. du Cornet

R. de la Parcheminerie

R. de la Roë

Rue Plantagenet

R. Bodinier

R. St-Laud

Lenepveu

Rue

Quai R. Bazin

Quai des Carmes

R. des Carmes

Blvd. Henri Arnault

Quai Ligny

R. Baudrière

⑥

Pl. du Ralliement

R. d'Alsace

⑤

R. du Vollier

R. St.-Evroult

R. Voltaire

R. St.-Julien

②
Château

R. Toussaint

⑦ Museum

R. -Aubin

Blvd. du Gén. de Gaulle

Info. ⑧

Rue des Lices

Blvd. du Mar. Foch

N

Blvd. du Roi René

R. Hoche

Rue

Delaâge

Ave. de la Blancheraie

Rue Béclard

Rue

Faidherbe

R. M. Richard

R. d'Anjou

Rue Paul Bert

Info. ①

Rue Denis Papin

Station

Rue de Bel-Air

Cross the drawbridge and enter the castle grounds. The most famous sight here, well worth the journey in itself, is the monumental **Apocalypse Tapestry**, housed in a specially built structure. This incomparable 14th-century series of wall hangings present a shattering representation of the text of Saint John in the Book of Revelations. Be sure to allow enough time to carefully study the 70 pieces that survived out of the original 90. An explanation in English will be loaned to you at the door, or you can purchase an illustrated booklet.

More outstanding medieval tapestries are displayed in the **Logis Royal** which, together with the superb **Chapel**, can be seen on guided tours included in the castle admission. The Logis du Gouverneur, beyond the gardens, also exhibits some of this art. A climb to the top of the highest tower, facing the river, reveals a magnificent panorama of the city. From here it is easy to understand why the fortress was so impregnable. A walk around the ramparts and through the gardens will complete your visit. The castle is open every day except for a few major holidays. Its hours are from 9 a.m. to noon and 2–6:30 p.m. in June; from 9 a.m. to 6:30 p.m. from July through September; and from 9:30 a.m. to noon and 2–5:30 p.m. the rest of the year.

Now follow the map across the river and into the colorful old quarter called La Doutre, noted for its ancient half-timbered houses. Turn right at the 12th-century **Church of La Trinité** (3) and continue on to the former **Hospital of St.-Jean** (4). Take a look at the elaborate 12th-century granary, whose cellars have some old wine presses, then enter the ancient hospital. Founded in 1175 by Henry II of England as part of his penance for the murder of Thomas à Becket, it cared for the sick until 1865. The very lovely interior now houses the **Jean Lurçat Museum**, displaying a huge modern 10-piece tapestry completed by Lurçat in 1966. You can also see the old dispensary, a medieval chapel, and the delightful 12th-century cloister.

The route now leads back across the river to the **Cathedral of St.-Maurice** (5). Dating from the 12th and 13th centuries, its unusual design is embellished with a peculiar central tower. Biblical figures decorate the spendid doorway, which opens into a very wide nave illuminated by stained-glass windows from the 12th century to modern times. The treasury, to the left as you enter, has some interesting artifacts including a Roman bathtub used as a baptismal font.

Continue on to the **Hôtel-Pincé** (6), a Renaissance mansion now used as the **Turpin de Crissé Museum**. The collections inside are rather eclectic, but focus mainly on Oriental works, especially Japanese Ukiyo-é. Visits may be made from 10 a.m. to noon and 2–6 p.m., daily except on Mondays and major holidays.

One other major attraction remains before returning to the train station. This is the **Fine Arts Museum** *(Musée des Beaux-Arts)* in the

Within the Castle Grounds

Logis Barrault (7), an impressive 15th-century palace. Medieval and Renaissance items are displayed along with a fine collection of paintings by such artists as Boucher, Tiepolo, Fragonard, David, Géricault, Ingres and Millet. A new annex, just around the corner, houses the outstanding **David d'Angers Gallery** (8) where heroic works by the locally-born 19th-century sculptor are exhibited. Both attractions are open daily except on Mondays and holidays, from 10 a.m. to noon and 2–6 p.m.

Amboise

Rising majestically above the banks of the Loire, the magnificent château of Amboise totally dominates its attractive little town. A castle
has stood on this rocky spur, guarding the strategic bridgehead since
Gallo-Roman times, when it was known as *Ambacia*. The present
structure, however, is a product of the 15th century and incorporates
some of the earliest examples of Renaissance architecture in France.
Charles VIII, who was born and raised at Amboise, had invaded Italy
in 1494. While there, he became captivated by the new Italian style
and brought some of its craftsmen back with him to finish off his favorite château.

The real effect of the Renaissance came with the succession to the
throne of Francois I in 1515. This outstanding king also spent his child-
hood at Amboise and continued residence there during the first years
of his reign. It was he who invited Leonardo da Vinci to France, in-
stalling him in a luxurious home just blocks from the château, where
the great artist and inventor spent the last years of his life.

One of the most notorious carnages in French history occurred at
Amboise in 1560 when Protestant militants plotted to capture the young
king, François II, to demand their religious freedom. The coup was
defeated and all involved were hideously executed, with corpses dec-
orating the château and town for weeks afterward. After that, Amboise was rarely used except as a prison until the 19th century, when
Louis-Philippe, the "Citizen King," lived there on occasion.

Amboise makes a good alternative base for visits to the famous
châteaux of the Loire which lie beyond daytrip range of Paris. Ask at
the tourist office about bus trips to these.

GETTING THERE:

Trains leave Austerlitz Station in Paris in the morning for Amboise,
a trip of under 2½ hours. Be careful to get on the right car as some
trains split en route. Return service operates until early evening. A
change at Orléans or Blois might be necessary.

By car, take the A-10 Autoroute to Blois, then the D-751 or N-152
into Amboise, which is 137 miles southwest of Paris.

The Château and the Loire from the Gardens

WHEN TO GO:

Amboise may be visited at any time. The Clos Lucé is closed in December and January, and the Postal Museum on Mondays and some holidays.

FOOD AND DRINK:

Being a popular tourist center, the town has quite a few restaurants and cafés. Some of the better choices are:

Le Manoir Saint-Thomas (Place Richelieu, 3 blocks south of the château) Superb local specialties in a Renaissance building with a garden. X: Mon. $$$

Au Lion d'Or (17 Quai Charles Guinott, on the river beneath the castle) A quiet inn with a rustic dining room. X: Nov. through mid-Mar. $$

L'Auberge du Mail (32 Quai du Général-de-Gaulle, 4 blocks west of St.-Denis Church) A delightful little country inn. X: Fri. $$

La Brèche (26 Rue Jules Ferry, 2 blocks south of the train station) A small inn with good meals. X: Sun. eve., Mon. in low season, Jan. $

TOURIST INFORMATION:

The local tourist office, phone 47-57-09-28, is located on the Quai du Général-de-Gaulle, near the bridge.

SUGGESTED TOUR:

Leave the **train station** (1) and follow the map across the Loire to the **Château** (2), perched dramatically above the river and town. You may prefer to have lunch before visiting any of the sights as they are closed between noon and 2 p.m. except in July and August. A long ramp leads up to the castle grounds. Climb this and join one of the frequent guided tours, which are given in French with a printed English translation provided. During its time of glory the château was considerably larger than it is today, much of it having been demolished in the early 19th century for lack of maintenance funds. Some of the best parts, however, remained intact and have been beautifully restored to the delight of today's visitors.

The tour begins with the exquisite **Chapel of St.-Hubert**, dedicated to the patron saint of huntsmen. Begun in 1491, shortly before Charles VIII acquired his passion for the Renaissance, it is a triumph of the Flamboyant Gothic style. What are thought to be the bones of Leonardo da Vinci are buried here, under a slab in the north transept.

Following this you will enter the **King's Apartments** (*Logis du Roi*), consisting of two wings, one Gothic and the other Renaissance. These are the only major buildings of any size left at the castle. Their interiors are splendidly decorated in a variety of period styles, ranging from the 15th through the 19th centuries. From the fascinating **Minimes Tower** with its spiral equestrian ramp there is a stunning view up and down the Loire Valley. Don't miss taking a stroll through the **gardens** behind the château after the guided tour has ended. The château is open every day, from 9 a.m. to noon and 2–6 p.m., closing an hour earlier in winter. In July and August it is open daily from 9 a.m. to 6:30 p.m.

A ten-minute walk along Rue Victor Hugo leads to **Clos Lucé** (3). This was the home of Leonardo da Vinci, that visionary genius of the Renaissance, from 1516 until his death three years later. Prior to that it was the residence of Anne of Brittany, the wife of King Charles VIII. The manor house has marvelous period furnishings, worth a visit in themselves, but the main interest lies in the many models of Leonardo's inventions, built by IBM from his original plans. Frequent guided tours, with a printed English translation, are conducted daily between 9 a.m. and noon, and from 2–5 p.m. During the summer the hours are from 9 a.m. to 7 p.m. The house is closed in January.

Return along Rue Victor Hugo and follow the map to the **Postal Museum** (4). Located in an elegant 16th-century mansion, the museum features an intriguing exhibition of the history of transportation from horse-drawn coaches to modern airlines. There are also, of course, many rare stamps to be seen, along with old manuscripts and engravings. The museum is open from 9:30 a.m. to noon and 2–6:30 p.m.,

Some of Leonardo's Inventions at Clos Lucé

closing at 5 p.m. during the winter season. It is closed on Mondays and some holidays.

Continue on to the 15th-century **Clock Tower** *(Beffroi)* (5), a picturesque structure built by Charles VIII on earlier foundations. Now follow the pedestrians-only Rue Nationale to the **Church of St.-Denis** (6). This 12th-century example of the Romanesque style was built on the site of a Roman temple. Step inside for a look at some exceptional works of art including a fine *Pietà* and an astonishingly realistic sculpture of a drowned woman.

Returning via Quai du Général-de-Gaulle you will pass an outstanding modern fountain designed by Max Ernst, the tourist office, the 15th-century Church of St.-Florentin, and the 16th-century Town Hall.

Blois

While certainly not the loveliest château of the Loire, Blois may well prove to be the most interesting. Often called the "Versailles of the Renaissance"—and for a crucial time virtually the capital of France—it exudes a deep sense of history exceeding even that of Angers or Amboise.

Although a castle had stood there since feudal times, it was not until the end of the 15th century that Blois became a royal residence. The first king to move in was Louis XII, in 1498, who promptly added a wing in the Late Gothic style. Another large section, in the new Renaissance style, was built by his successor François I. This flamboyant king later went on to greater architectural triumphs, notably the châteaux of Fontainebleau and Chambord, but he continued to use Blois as a waystop in an endless pursuit of courtly pleasure. Royalty remained in residence there until the Valois line died out in 1589 with the assassination of the miserable Henri III.

After that, the château was used by Louis XIII as a place to get rid of troublesome members of his family. The first to go was his mother, Marie de Medici, who was banished to Blois in 1617 but later managed to escape. He then gave it to his scheming brother, Gaston d'Orléans, to keep him out of political mischief. As did the previous owners, Gaston added a wing, thus completing the château you see today.

The town of Blois has several other nice attractions of its own, including a picturesque old quarter near the river. The name, incidentally, is pronounced "Blwah." It also makes a convenient overnight base for visits to those splendid châteaux which unfortunately lie beyond reasonable daytrip range of Paris, most notably Chambord and Chenonceau. You can ask at the tourist office about bus excursions to these, or rent a car and see them on your own.

GETTING THERE:

Trains for Blois depart Austerlitz Station in Paris several times in the morning. The run takes a bit over two hours, with return service until early evening. Be sure to get on the right car as some trains split en route.

By car, Blois is 112 miles southwest of Paris via the A-10 Autoroute.

WHEN TO GO:

The Château of Blois is open every day, but is less crowded during the week. Good weather will make this trip much more enjoyable.

FOOD AND DRINK:

There are quite a few restaurants and cafés along the walking route, of which some choices are:

Hostellerie de la Loire (8 Rue du Maréchal de Lattre-de-Tassigny, on the river by the bridge) A delightful small inn. X: Sun. in winter. $$

La Bocca d'Or (15 Rue Haute, 2 blocks west of the cathedral) A romantic setting in a 14th-century cellar. X: Sun., Mon. lunch, Feb. $$

La Péniche (Promenade du Mail, along the river northeast of the cathedral) On a moored floating barge, specializes in seafood. $$

Le Monarque (61 Rue Porte-Chartraine, 2 blocks northwest of the top of the Papin steps) A small inn. X: Sun. $

La Tosca (36 Rue de la Foulérie, 3 blocks south of the cathedral) Specializes in hearty alpine dishes. $

TOURIST INFORMATION:

The local tourist office is located at 3 Avenue Jean-Laigret, between the train station and the château. You can call them at 54-74-06-49.

SUGGESTED TOUR:

Leave the **train station** (1) and follow Avenue Jean-Laigret past the tourist office to **Place Victor Hugo** (2). Before climbing the ramp to the château it would be a good idea to check your watch and decide whether you have enough time—well over an hour—to enjoy it properly before lunch, or whether to see some other sights and eat first. The château is open daily from June through September, from 9 a.m. to 6 p.m.; and daily from 9:30 a.m. to noon and 2–6 p.m. the rest of the year. The walking route is quite short so you can always return to the château later.

The **Château of Blois** (3), overlooking the town and the Loire River, is a dramatic study in the evolution of French architecture from the Middle Ages to the Neo-Classical period. After the Valois line of kings died out in the late 16th century it ceased to be a royal residence and was used during Napoleon's time as an army barracks. What you see

The François I Wing of the Château

today is the result of a highly romanticized mid-19th-century restoration, perhaps more theatrical than accurate, but certainly fun to visit.

Pass through the doorway under the equestrian statue of Louis XII and enter the château. You are now in the **Louis XII wing**, built between 1498 and 1503. Purchase your ticket and decide whether to take a guided tour or just wander around on your own, which is entirely practical as there are printed explanations of everything in English.

Stepping into the inner courtyard you will see the famous open staircase of the **François I wing**, dating from 1515–1524. Climb this to the first floor and go in. The route through this wing is well laid out, taking you eventually to the second floor, where a notorious assassination took place in 1588. Henri III, a weak and effeminate king, was able to remain in office only as long as it suited a powerful duke, Henri de Guise, Lieutenant-General of the kingdom and leader of the extremist Catholics. Guise threatened Henri's rule by forcing a meeting of the States-General at the château. While there, the king summoned him to a private meeting, on the way to which he was brutally murdered by 20 of the king's devoted minions. He died at the foot of the royal bed while the cowering Henri looked on through a peephole. The next day the king had the duke's brother, Cardinal de Lorraine, killed as well. But justice was to come. Within days, the king's scheming mother, Catherine de Medici, was dead and Henri III himself fell to an assassin's knife eight months later. He was the last of the Valois line.

The 13th-century **Salle des États**, the oldest surviving part of the château, joins the François I and Louis XII wings together. Take a look inside, then visit the adjacent archaeological museum and the **Fine Arts Museum** in the Louis XII wing.

At the far end of the courtyard stands the 17th-century **Gaston d'Orléans wing**, a Neo-Classical structure designed by François Mansart. Other interesting buildings are the **Charles d'Orléans Gallery** and the **Chapel of St.-Calais**, both dating from the late 15th century. Amble over to the 13th-century **Tour de Foix**, part of the old feudal walls, which offers a splendid panorama of the town.

Leave the château and follow the map down to the lovely **Church of St.-Nicolas** (4), whose interior merits a visit. Built in the 12th century as part of an abbey that was destroyed during the 16th-century Wars of Religion, it is noted for its harmonious blend of Romanesque and Gothic elements.

Continue on to **Place Louis XII** (5), with its Flamboyant Gothic fountain, passing some picturesque old houses on Rue St.-Lubin along the way. Now cut down to the river and stroll out on the elegant 18th-century bridge for a gorgeous view of the town and its château.

Return to the quay and follow the map through a delightful part of old Blois. Rue du Puits-Châtel has two particularly attractive houses at numbers 7 and 5, both dating from the time of Louis XII. When you come to Place Ave-Maria look to your left down Rue Fontaine des Élus, where the noteworthy Hôtel de Jassaud stands at number 5. Now turn hard right and climb Rue des Papegaults. Passing another 16th-century house, the Hôtel de Belot at number 10, this charming street leads to the Petits-Degrés-St.-Louis, which takes you uphill to Place St.-Louis.

The **Cathedral of St.-Louis** (6), facing you, was largely rebuilt in the 17th century. Although the church itself is not particularly outstanding, its 10th-century **Crypt of St.-Solenne** certainly is. Entry to this is from the side of the altar.

Continue around to the rear of the Town Hall, reached via a gate next to the cathedral. The **park** (7) beyond this commands an excellent vantage point for views of the Loire Valley.

Now thread your way through a maze of narrow streets lined with medieval and Renaissance houses, many of which are half-timbered. Follow the map up the Denis Papin stairs to the **Statue of Denis Papin** (8), a local lad of the 17th century who discovered many of the mysteries of steam power. He is shown holding his greatest invention, an

Street Scene near the Cathedral of St.-Louis

early pressure cooker.

Turn left on Rue St.-Honoré past the Hôtel d'Alluye, a splendid Renaissance mansion whose double-galleried courtyard can be seen during office hours. Continue on Rue Porte-Chartraine and return on Rue Chemonton, noting the fine Hôtel de Guise at number 8. This returns you to Place Victor Hugo (2).

If you have a bit more time you may be interested in visiting the 17th-century **Church of St.-Vincent-de-Paul** (9) and, especially, the beautiful **Jardin du Roi** (10), all that remains of the château gardens that once extended all the way to the train station. From here you will get a magnificent close-up view of the château and a last glimpse of Blois before returning to Paris.

Bourges

Located in the very heartland of France, Bourges is an ancient and colorful town whose winding, cobbled streets contain some of the very best medieval architecture anywhere. Although relatively unknown to foreign tourists, it makes an excellent daytrip destination for seasoned travelers looking for a delightful new experience.

Originally populated by Gauls, Bourges fell to Caesar's legions in 52 B.C. and became the Roman town of *Avaricum*. Since A.D. 250 it was ruled by archbishops. Later, as the capital of Aquitaine, it passed into the hands of a succession of counts who in 1101 sold it to King Philip I of France. During the 14th century, Jean, duke of Berry and son of King John the Good, made Bourges the seat of his duchy. For a while the town became a flourishing center of the arts, a role enhanced by the immensely wealthy Jacques Coeur, whose palace there is probably the best example of a medieval town mansion to be found in France.

During the Hundred Years War, Charles VII, cynically referred to by the English as the "King of Bourges," sat in that beleaguered city and slowly gathered the strength, aided by Joan of Arc, which enabled him to drive the English out. His son, Louis XI, born in Bourges, was a brilliant schemer who overcame the feudal system and began development of the modern state. He also founded a university there that became a hotbed of the Reformation, thus plunging Bourges into the Wars of Religion, a catastrophe from which it never recovered.

In the ensuing centuries, Bourges fell into obscurity, far too poor to rebuild its narrow streets and ancient façades. Not until modern times did its economy revive, with industry locating outside the town proper. This newly found prosperity in the setting of a basically unchanged medieval town makes Bourges a fascinating place to visit.

GETTING THERE:

Trains leave Austerlitz Station in Paris several times in the morning for Bourges. Some of these may require a change at Vierzon. Be careful to board the correct car as some trains split en route. The fastest direct run takes a bit under 2½ hours. Return service operates until early evening.

By car, take the A-10 Autoroute to Orléans, then the A-71 to Bourges, which lies 147 miles south of Paris.

WHEN TO GO:
Avoid going to Bourges on a Tuesday or major holiday, when several of its best attractions are closed. One of the sights is closed on Mondays. The trip can be made in any season as the old part of town is quite small and most of your time will be spent indoors.

FOOD AND DRINK:
The cooking in this farmland region tends to be simple and wholesome. Some good restaurant choices are:

Jacques Coeur (3 Place Jacques-Coeur, across from the Jacques Coeur Palace) Traditional classic cuisine. X: Sat., Sun. eve., Aug. $$$

L'Ile d'Or (39 Blvd. de Juranville, 3 blocks southwest of the Maison de la Reine Blanche) Elegant cuisine in a pleasant restaurant. X: Sun., Mon. lunch. $$ and $$$

Au Grand Argentier (9 Rue Parerie, just east of the Church of Notre-Dame) A small hotel with home-style cooking. X: Sun. eve., Mon., also late Dec. through Mar. $$

Au Sénat (8 Rue de la Poissonnerie, just east of Place Gordaine) Regional cuisine in comfortable surroundings. $$

Angleterre (1 Place Quatre Piliers, 1 block south of the Jacques Coeur Palace) A small hotel with good meals. X: Sun., Mon. lunch. $

Le D'Artagnan (19 Place Séraucourt, 4 blocks south of the cathedral) Good-value dining in a hotel $

TOURIST INFORMATION:
The local tourist office, phone 48-24-75-33, is located on Rue Moyenne at the corner of Rue Victor-Hugo, near the cathedral.

SUGGESTED TOUR:
Leave the **train station** (1) and follow the map to the **Church of Notre-Dame** (2), whose brooding atmosphere encompasses a wide variety of styles. Built in the early 15th century, it was badly damaged during the great fire of 1487 that consumed much of Bourges. Reconstruction began in 1520, with considerable latter additions having been made.

Take a look down Rue Pelvoysin, which has some fine old houses, many of them half-timbered. The most noted of these is the **Maison de Pelvoysin** at number 17, built of stone in the 15th century. Con-

A Street Scene near Place Gordaine

tinue on Rue Mirabeau and take the passageway through to Rue Branly, leading to the **Hôtel des Échevins** (3). This 15th-century guildhall features a marvelous octagonal stair tower of unusual design. It now houses the **Musée Estève**, featuring opulent modern works by the noted local 20th-century artist, Maurice Estève. Visits may be made on any day except Tuesdays and major holidays, from 10 a.m. to noon and 2–6 p.m., but not on Sunday mornings.

The **Hôtel Lallemant** (4), just a few steps away on Rue Bourbonnoux, is an outstanding 15th-century mansion built for a wealthy cloth merchant. Heavily altered during the 17th century in the Renaissance style, it is now a museum of decorative art. Step inside to admire the richly decorated rooms, antique furniture and various *objets d'art*. It is open daily except on Mondays and major holidays, from 10–11:15 a.m. and 2–4 or 5 p.m.

Now follow the map past the Grange aux Dimes, a 13th-century tithe barn on Rue Molière, to the **Cathedral of St.-Étienne** (5). The major attraction of Bourges, this is one of the very finest Gothic structures in France. Erected at the same time as the great cathedral at

Chartres, it differs greatly in both layout and concept. Construction began around 1192 as a replacement for a Romanesque basilica that occupied the site. The crypt, which was built first, is like no other. Never intended to house tombs or relics, it is basically a substructure supporting the cathedral over uneven ground. Above this the choir was erected and slowly the new church grew toward the west, surrounding the old building as work progressed. It was consecrated in 1324.

Notice, as you stand in the square facing the cathedral, the five curiously asymmetrical portals that pierce its west front. Take a few moments to examine the magnificent **carvings** depicting the Last Judgment above the central doorway—one of the great masterpieces of Gothic art. To the left, the **north tower** rises to a height of 213 feet, which can be climbed on foot for a splendid view. The south tower, never completed, is supported by a very peculiar buttress.

Inside, the **stained-glass windows**—especially those above the chancel at the east end—are among the best to be found in France and cover a period from the early Gothic to the Renaissance. Be sure to visit the **crypt**, the entrance to which is by the north doorway. Near the reclining figure of Duke Jean of Berry is a stairway leading down to the remains of an earlier 9th-century church. The cathedral closes between noon and 2 p.m.

Stroll over to the 17th-century City Hall *(Hôtel de Ville)*, once the archbishop's palace. The lovely **gardens** *(Jardins de l'Archevêché)* (6) adjacent to this, attributed to Le Nôtre, offer an excellent view of the cathedral's east end as well as being a welcome spot to relax.

Now follow the map past the tourist office to the **Palace of Jacques Coeur** (7), surely one of the most splendid private buildings of the Middle Ages. It was begun in 1443 and completed, at fabulous cost, nearly ten years later for Charles VII's finance minister, a gifted merchant and banker named Jacques Coeur. Alas, poor Jacques never got to enjoy his mansion as he fell from grace in 1451 and was permanently exiled. In 1457 the palace was returned to his heirs and later used by the city as a *Palais de Justice*. Now restored to original condition, its marvelously sumptuous interior may be seen on guided tours. The palace is open from 9–11:15 a.m. and 2–5:15 p.m. between Easter and October, and from 10–11:15 a.m. and 2–4:15 p.m. the rest of the year, every day except major holidays. Don't miss seeing this.

Continue on, descending the steps next to the palace and go into the gardens of Place Berry. From here you can see how the west wall of the mansion was built on top of the original Roman town walls. A short stroll down Rue des Arènes brings you to the **Hôtel Cujas** (8), an elegant mansion built around 1515 for a wealthy merchant and later the residence of Jacques Cujas, a noted jurist. It now houses the

The Palace of Jacques Coeur

Musée du Berry, featuring an archaeological exhibition of artifacts dating from the Roman period back to prehistoric times. Displays of local country life from more recent centuries occupy the first floor, while the rest of the museum is given over to the fine arts. Visits may be made from 10 a.m. to noon and 2–6 p.m., daily except on Tuesdays and major holidays, but not on Sunday mornings.

Cross Place Planchat and turn left onto Rue Gambon. At number 19 stands the ornate **Maison de la Reine Blanche** (9), a 16th-century wooden house decorated with religious motifs. Farther on, at number 32, there is the Hôtel Dieu with its elaborate Renaissance doorway. Return to Place de Mirepied and continue down Avenue Jean-Jaurès past the beautiful **Prés-Fichaux Gardens** (10), where you can spend some delightful moments before returning to the station.

Section VII

Daytrips in
Provence

Going to Provence is like stepping into a different world, one far removed from Paris and the north. This is a Mediterranean region with a distinctly Latin culture reflecting its ancient Roman heritage. It is also a sun-drenched land whose dazzling clarity was made famous by such painters as Van Gogh and Cézanne. Few areas of Europe—or of the world—can begin to match its broad variety of intriguing sights and delicious experiences.

The five destinations in this section are linked by frequent rail service and excellent highways. Any of them could be used as a base for exploring the others without having to change hotels. In terms of convenience, Marseille is the best situated for this purpose since it lies at the hub of major transportation routes. Those who prefer to avoid large cities will find that Arles or Avignon also make excellent bases, with Aix-en-Provence and Nîmes a little less handy, especially for rail travelers.

One-day bus excursions to other attractions in Provence, including the hauntingly beautiful Camargue, mysterious Les Baux, the Roman relics of Orange and the Pont du Gard, or the strange walled town of Aigues-Mortes are available from these base towns. Ask at the local tourist office for current information and schedules. Those with cars can easily visit several of these in one day. Descriptions are not included in this book since these places are a bit difficult to reach by regular public transportation and, being quite small, do not really lend themselves to structured walking tours.

Although it is technically a part of Provence, the Riviera is in a realm of its own, one thoroughly covered in the next section beginning on page 269.

Marseille

No one ever accused Marseille of being charming or quaint, or even lovely, but it certainly is unique—and more than a little intriguing. This brash, noisy, teeming metropolis throbs with such a vitality that to ignore it would be to miss out on a very colorful aspect of Mediterranean life.

Founded around 600 B.C. by Greek colonists from Phocea in Asia Minor, Marseille is the oldest city in France. Depending on how you count heads, it is also the second-largest. Then known as *Massalia*, it developed a network of satellite towns in Nice, Antibes, Arles and other places. Threatened by native tribes, the port later turned to Rome for defense and prospered for centuries afterwards. A major setback came in 49 B.C. when it backed Pompey in his dispute with Julius Caesar. The victorious Caesar got his revenge by shifting trade to Arles, but eventually the 11th-century Crusades brought about an economic resurgence.

Although it became a part of France in 1482, Marseille has always been more a Mediterranean than a French city, caring little for Paris and its kings. It enthusiastically joined the Revolution in 1789, and in 1792 its volunteers sang a new patriotic song with such lusty fervor that the tune became known as *La Marseillaise*, the French national anthem. Commercial development during the 19th century, especially the opening of the Suez Canal in 1869, greatly expanded the city into the metropolis it is today.

With all that history, it is amazing how little of the past remains. The *Marseillais* have never been much interested in antiquity, preferring to focus their energies on trade and the future. For this reason Marseille is more a city to relish for its spicy flavor than for the few bona-fide sights it offers.

Is Marseille really as wicked as its reputation suggests? No, despite the open prostitution that thrives between the Old Port and the Opéra, the drunken sailors and sleazy dives off La Canebière, it is no longer the drug capital of the world—if it ever was. There are, however, a few obvious areas that are best avoided at night.

With its superb transportation facilities and many hotels, Marseille is the most convenient base for daytrips throughout Provence. And it has a few other drawing cards as well, such as the best seafood restaurants in Europe and a truly spectacular setting on steep hills spilling down to the Old Port and the Mediterranean.

GETTING THERE:

Trains connect Marseille's St.-Charles Station with other towns in Provence at fairly frequent intervals. Average running times are: Aix-en-Provence—32 minutes, Arles—45 minutes, Avignon—1 hour *(TGV service also available)*, and Nîmes—75 minutes. For more details consult the chapters for those specific towns. There are also convenient schedules to both the Riviera and Paris, the latter being served by speedy TGVs *(under 5 hours)* as well as conventional trains.

By car, Marseille is 19 miles from Aix-en-Provence, 57 miles from Arles, 62 miles from Avignon and 75 miles from Nîmes. Recommended routes are given in the chapters dealing with those towns.

GETTING AROUND:

You may want to make use of the magnificent **Métro** (subway) or bus service during your exploration of Marseille. Both use the same tickets, sold singly or in a discounted *carnet* package of six. A ticket is valid for one continuous journey, which may combine both the Métro and bus, for a period of 70 minutes after cancellation on first boarding the bus or entering the subway station. The tourist office can supply you with a free map of the system. Rail travelers making Marseille their base will be happy to know that both Métro lines (and several bus routes) stop at St.-Charles Station.

WHEN TO GO:

Marseille may be visited at any time, although good weather will make the suggested tour much more enjoyable. Some of the museums are closed on Tuesdays and on Wednesday mornings.

FOOD AND DRINK:

Bouillabaisse, a fish and seafood stew flavored with saffron, garlic, cayenne and other tasty ingredients, is the classic dish of Marseille—a treat not to be missed by seafood fanciers. As befits one of the world's greatest ports, the city has a wide selection of inexpensive foreign restaurants, particularly North African, Indian, and Vietnamese. Some of the better traditional restaurants are:

> **Michel** (6 Rue des Catalans, near the Jardin du Pharo, facing the sea) Famous for its bouillabaisse and other seafoods. Open daily. $$$

Les Trois Forts (36 Blvd. Charles-Livon, in the Sofitel Vieux-Port Hotel) Inspired contemporary regional cuisine. Open daily. $$$

Chez Brun—Aux Mets de Provence (18 Quai Rive-Neuve, well hidden, near the Old Port) A traditional dining experience sampling seafood. Reservations are essential, phone 91-33-35-38. X: Sun., Mon. $$$

Le Chaudron Provençal (48 Rue Caisserie, 1 block northwest of the Roman Docks Museum) Renowned for its fresh seafood and local wines. X: Sat. lunch, Sun., mid-July to mid-Aug. $$$

Jambon de Parme (67 Rue de la Palud, 2 blocks east of the Cantini Museum) Excellent Italian cuisine in classical surroundings. X: Sun. eve., Mon., mid-July to mid-Aug. $$$

Miramar (12 Quai du Port, at the northeast corner of the Old Port) Inventive seafood cuisine along with other dishes. Inventive seafood cuisine along with other dishes. X: Sun., Aug. $$$

L'Oursinade (in the Hôtel Altéa Bourse, 1 Rue Neuve St.-Martin, overlooking the archaeological gardens) Exceptionally good Provençal cuisine. X: Sun., holidays, Aug. $$$

Chez Caruso (158 Quai du Port, 2 blocks southwest of the Roman Docks Museum) Traditional Italian cuisine of the highest quality. X: Sun. eve., Mon., mid-Oct. to mid-Nov. $$$

Brasserie New-York Vieux Port (7 Quai des Belges, on the Old Port) A local institution since 1932. Everyone comes here. $$ and $$$

La Folie Époque (10 Place Barret, 2 blocks southeast of the Cantini Museum) Home cooking in the style of Lyon. X: Sat. eve., Sun. $$

Piment Rouge (20 Rue Beauvau, 2 blocks south of the tourist office on La Canebière) Cuisine of the Middle East. X: Sun., Aug. $$

Chez Madie (138 Quai du Port, 2 blocks south of the Roman Docks Museum) Regional cuisine, especially seafood, with a view. X: Sun. eve., Mon., Feb. $ and $$

Chez Angèle (50 Rue Caisserie, north of the Roman Docks Museum) Italian and Provençal specialties in a friendly atmosphere. X: Sun. eve., Mon. $ and $$

Chez Antoine (35 Rue Musée, 2 blocks south of La Canebière, near Blvd. Garibaldi) Pizzeria and Italian dishes. X: Tues. $

TOURIST INFORMATION:

The local tourist office, phone 91-54-91-11, is located at the foot of

Selling Fish on the Quai des Belges

La Canebière, near the old Port. They can arrange for hotel reservations and tours, as well as provide you with maps and transit information.

SUGGESTED TOUR:

Rail travelers using another base in Provence will begin their tour at **St.-Charles Station** (1), oddly located at the top of a hill. This marvelous old structure has recently been completely restored, with modern underground levels, while the exterior retains all of its considerable 19th-century charm. Walk outside for a panoramic view across the harbor, then descend the steps to Boulevard d'Athènes and walk downhill to **La Canebière**. Long known to foreign sailors as "The Can o' Beer," this once-glamorous main street of Marseille has faded somewhat in recent years, but its vitality remains as alive as ever.

Turn right and continue downhill past the tourist office to the Quai des Belges and the **Old Port** *(Vieux Port)* (2), the real start of this tour. Those in a hurry could also get here from the train station by Métro, although doing so misses a lot of the city's character. Until 1844 this was the only harbor at Marseille, but large ships now dock beyond the breakwater and the Old Port is used for fishing and pleasure vessels. If you arrive fairly early in the morning you will be treated to the sight of fishermen hawking their fresh catch right off the boats. Excursions by boat through the harbors or to the outlying islands are avail-

able here, but it is perhaps better to wait until you return to this spot for that exciting experience.

Follow the map along the Quai du Port past the elegant 17th-century **Town Hall** *(Hôtel de Ville)*, easily singled out among the hideous modern apartment blocks lining that side of the port. This was once a fascinating warren of narrow alleyways and fetid slums, but all that ended in 1943 when the occupying Germans blew the area up in an attempt to deny the Resistance a base of operations. They only got two blocks inland, however, and the rest of the colorful old quarter still survives intact.

Continue on to the 17th-century bastion of **Fort St.-Jean** (3), which guards the narrow entrance to the harbor, and take the pedestrian promenade around it. In a few blocks you will come to a huge, remarkably ostentatious neo-Byzantine church, the **Cathédrale de la Major** (4). Built in the late 19th century, it replaces the much smaller **Old Major Cathedral**, which fortunately still stands directly to its side. This 12th-century Romanesque structure, erected on the site of a Roman stadium and no longer used as a church, is in rather poor condition but contains some outstanding works of religious art. It may be visited any day except Tuesdays, from 9 a.m. to noon and 2–6:30 p.m.

The walk now enters the old Panier quarter and follows an uphill route to the **Old Charity Hospice** *(La Vieille Charité)* (5), a magnificent 17th-century almshouse that has been beautifully restored and is now used for temporary art exhibitions. You can stop in for a look on any day, between between 10 a.m. and 5 p.m.

This is the very heart of Old Marseille, a colorful but somewhat seedy area of tiny alleyways that is slowly yielding to gentrification. Follow the map through Place des Moulins and downhill past the belfry of the 12th-century Notre-Dame des Accoules Church. In a few more steps you will come to the **Museum of Old Marseille** *(Musée du Vieux Marseille)* (6) on Rue de la Prison. Housed in a 16th-century mansion with an unusual stone façade, the fascinating displays here are devoted to local life in former times and include a model of the highly intriguing Transporter Bridge, which until World War II carried traffic across the harbor entrance in a most unorthodox manner. The museum is open on Thursdays through Mondays, from 10 a.m. to noon and 2–6:30 p.m.; and on Wednesdays from 2–6:30 p.m.

The **Roman Docks Museum** (7), nearby, features the *in situ* remains of Roman port installations discovered when the neighborhood was rebuilt in 1947. There are also interesting displays of ancient maritime artifacts. Visits may be made on any day, from 10 a.m. to 5 p.m.

Now return to the Old Port and follow the map to an enormous modern indoor shopping mall, the Centre Bourse. Just in front of this is a lovely **archaeological garden** where remains of the Greek port

The Archaeological Garden by the Centre Bourse

from the 3rd century B.C. may be explored. These were discovered only recently, and digs are still going on. Adjoining this, on the lower level of the shopping mall, is the **Museum of the History of Marseille** (8). The very well-displayed artifacts include a 2nd-century Roman merchant ship unearthed on the spot in 1974. The museum is open from 10 a.m. until 7 p.m., daily except on Sundays and Mondays.

Continue past the former stock exchange *(Bourse)*, which now houses an interesting **Marine Museum** (9) devoted to the city's long tradition of maritime trade, from the Greek era to the present. The ship models alone are worth the visit. You can see this between 10 a.m. and noon and 2–6 p.m., any day except Tuesdays.

Turn the corner onto La Canebière and return to the Quai des Belges (2). Several establishments along the quay offer very enjoyable boat excursions to the **Château d'If** (10, off the map), a 16th-century military fortress on a small island well beyond the breakwater. Long used as a prison, it was made famous by its description in *The Count of Monte Cristo* by Alexandre Dumas. Many of these boats also call at the nearby **Frioul Islands**, where a pleasant resort village offers numerous outdoor cafés. Allow at least 90 minutes for the round trip and be prepared for a rough ride. Anyone foolish enough to sit on the outdoor deck will probably get wet.

Back at the Quai des Belges you will find a wide selection of restaurants and cafés in all price ranges. Stroll over to the adjacent Cours

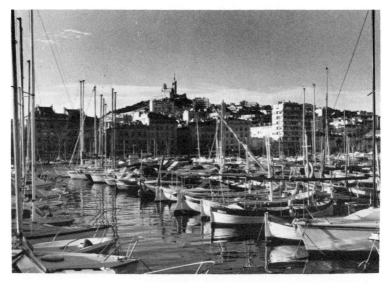

The Old Port and the Basilica of Notre-Dame

d'Estienne-d'Orves and board bus number 60—running every 30 minutes—for the very steep climb to Marseille's most spectacular landmark. The **Basilica of Notre-Dame de la Garde** (11), crowned with a huge golden statue of the Virgin, is yet another 19th-century neo-Byzantine monument. It is visible from virtually everywhere in the city, even at night, and after a while you may actually get to like it. Step inside to see the literally thousands of interesting sailors' ex-votos. The real reason to come up here, however, is for the fabulous panorama it offers of the port, city, islands and seacoast.

Marseille does have at least one genuinely superb ancient church. Follow the map down a stepped path and along city streets to the **Abbey of St.-Victor** (12). The above-ground portion of this dates from the 11th to the 14th centuries and looks like a fortress, but the main interest lies in its spooky 5th-century crypt, which may be visited from 10–11:30 a.m. and 3–6 p.m. It is closed on Sunday mornings. Filled with a mysterious early-Christian atmosphere, the catacombs contain the relics of two 3rd-century martyrs. Don't miss exploring this strange, dark and wonderful place.

Continue on, following the map. When you come to a short tunnel be sure to use the sidewalk to the left; otherwise you will be caught in horrendous traffic. Just beyond this there is a Foreign Legion post, whose sidewalk recruiting office is open day and night—in case you feel so inclined. Those who would rather rest in a beautiful park with an unusually good view of the harbor will enjoy a visit to the nearby **Jardin du Pharo** (13). Luckily, it has an outdoor café overlooking the yacht basin, a perfect spot to unwind before walking or taking a bus back to the Quai des Belges. If you are heading for St.-Charles Station, you can take the Métro from there and avoid a long uphill climb.

ADDITIONAL SIGHTS:

Travelers staying in Marseille may want to see some of these attractions on another day:

The **Fine Arts Museum** *(Musée des Beaux Arts)* (14) has an extensive collection of works by major artists, especially those of native son Honoré Daumier. Located in the splendid 19th-century Longchamp Palace, it is a fairly long walk from the top of La Canebière, or can be reached by taking Métro line 1 to Cinq-Avenues Longchamp. The museum is open from 10 a.m. to noon and 2–6:30 p.m.; but closed on Tuesdays, some holidays, and Wednesday mornings. The same building also houses the Natural History Museum.

The **Grobet-Labadié Museum** (15) displays the private collections and furniture of a wealthy musician in his own 19th-century mansion. It is very close to the front of the Longchamp Palace, above, and his similar hours.

The **Cantini Museum** (16), close to downtown and just off Rue Paradis, features contemporary art along with traditional objects. It is open daily from noon to 7 p.m. The closest Métro stop is Estrangin Préfecture on line 1.

Unité d'Habitation (17). The famous architect Le Corbusier built this noted—and controversial—complex in 1952 as part of a larger project, the *Cité Radieuse,* which was never completed. Architectural mavens will find it fascinating, although its social goals failed to materialize. To get there, take bus 21 or 22 from the La Canebière area to the Le Corbusier stop.

Visits to the modern commercial **harbor installations** (18) beyond the Cathédrale de la Major may be made on Sundays and holidays only. You may want to ask at the tourist office about this first.

Aix-en-Provence

Only nineteen miles from Marseille, Aix-en-Provence is light years removed in character. Elegant, refined, gracious, dignified, sophisticated—all of these adjectives and more can be honestly used to describe the former capital of Provence, which many consider to be nothing less than the loveliest town in France. Whether you feel the same depends, of course, on your interests, but a few hours spent sitting at an outdoor café on the Cours Mirabeau does leave most visitors with a contended perspective on life.

First settled by the Romans in 122 B.C. after their victory over a local tribe, *Aquae Sextiae,* as it was then called, was already famous as a warm spring spa. By the 6th century A.D., however, it was nearly abandoned, the ancient buildings being used as a convenient stone quarry. Good King René, that marvelous figure who keeps popping up in French history, made it his capital in the 15th century. René was the count of Provence, the duke of Anjou, and more or less the king of Sicily, albeit in exile. He was also a true Renaissance man—one of the most civilized, diversely educated and decent men of his age.

Though united to France in 1482, Provence retained much of its independence and maintained a parliament at Aix until the Revolution. After that the town declined in importance until the recent post-war era, which has seen a nearly explosive growth in population. Much of this is due to the development of modern light industries in the outlying areas, but some of the credit goes to both its university and to its world-famous summer music festival held annually during July and August.

Those with cars will find Aix to be a good base for exploring the rest of Provence, although it is somewhat inconvenient for rail travelers.

GETTING THERE:

Trains depart St.-Charles Station in Marseille nearly hourly for the 30-minute run to Aix-en-Provence, with returns until mid-evening. To get anywhere else in Provence or the Riviera by rail requires a change at Marseille. There is also fairly frequent bus service to other areas of Provence, leaving from near the tourist office.

By car, Aix is 19 miles north of Marseille via the A-7 and A-51 Autoroutes. Other distances are: Arles—47 miles, Avignon—50 miles, Nîmes—66 miles; all via the A-8 and A-7 Autoroutes followed by local roads.

WHEN TO GO:

Good weather will make a stroll around Aix much more pleasant. Some of the major sights are closed on Tuesdays and holidays. Hotel rooms are scarce during July and August.

FOOD AND DRINK:

The many restaurants of Aix reflect a broad range of cuisines and prices. Some of the better choices are:

Clos de la Violette (10 Ave. Violette, 4 blocks north of the cathedral) Superb and imaginative regional cuisine in a garden setting. Reservations needed, phone 42-23-30-71. X: Sun., Mon. lunch. $$$

Vendôme (in the Casino on Place du Général-de-Gaulle) Contemporary cuisine with impeccable service. X: Tues. eve., Wed, except in July and Aug. $$$

Poivre et Sel (9 Rue Constantin, 3 blocks northeast of the Town Hall) Original variations on Provençal cuisine. X: Tues. except in July and Aug. $$ and $$$.

L'Abbaye des Cordeliers (21 Rue Lieutaud, 2 blocks west of the Town Hall) Traditional cuisine in a former abbey, with outdoor tables available. Reservations needed, phone 42-27-29-47. X: Sun. eve., Mon. $$

La Brocherie (5 Rue Fernand-Dol, 2 blocks east of the Paul Arbaud Museum) Seasonal specialties and grilled meats in a rustic atmosphere. X: Sun., Mon. $$

Chez Joe—Le Bar des Augustins (59 Rue Espariat, 1 block north of the lower end of the Cours Mirabeau) Italian and Provençal cuisine, excellent pizza. Very popular, always crowded. X: Sun., Aug. $$

Le Vieux Tonneau (6 Rue des Bernardines, 2 blocks north of Place du Général-de-Gaulle) Good value in a friendly atmosphere. X: Sun. lunch. $ and $$

L'Hacienda (7 Rue Mérindol, 3 blocks west of the Town Hall) Home cooking in a family-style restaurant. X: Sun., Aug. $

TOURIST INFORMATION:

The local tourist office, phone 42-26-02-93, is conveniently located on Place du Général-de-Gaulle, near the foot of the Cours Mirabeau. Ask them about local bus service to Cézanne's studio, the Vasarely

Foundation, and about short regional tours. They can also find you a hotel room.

SUGGESTED TOUR:

Leave the **train station** (1) and follow the map to Place du Général-de-Gaulle, also called La Rotonde, where the tourist office and gambling casino are located. In a few more steps you will be on the **Cours Mirabeau** (2), one of the most utterly delightful avenues on earth. It was named for the unscrupulous Count Mirabeau, a popular 18th-century demagogue who represented the common people of Aix in the States-General of 1789 that led to the French Revolution. Although only a quarter of a mile in length, it is very wide and completely shaded by four rows of ancient plane trees forming a cool green canopy. There are several fountains along its length, the most intriguing being the curious moss-covered Fontaine Chaude at the intersection of Rue Clemenceau, which runs with the warm thermal waters that made Aix famous. The south side is lined with strikingly elegant mansions while the north is the preserve of trendy shops and a great many outdoor cafés. One of the great pleasures of a trip to France is to sit at one of these and just watch the world go by.

Stroll north on Rue Clemenceau and follow the map through a colorful old district of narrow streets to the **Town Hall** *(Hôtel de Ville)* (3), a 17th-century classical building with a lovely courtyard. Step into this, then climb the inside staircase to the first floor where there are some interesting displays in the Bibliothèque Méjanes. The handsome 16th-century **clock tower** in the adjacent square is topped with one of those ornate wrought-iron bell cages so typical to Provence. In a niche below this is a mechanical "calendar" that rotates wooden figures representing the seasons four times a year. A fountain graces the square, where an outdoor **flower market** is held on Tuesday, Thursday and Saturday mornings.

The **Museum of Old Aix** *(Musée du Vieil Aix)* (4), reached in a few minutes, has one of the best folklore collections in the south of France. Particularly noteworthy are the traditional *santons*—colored clay figures used in home Christmas displays—and larger puppets made to be drawn through the streets in the now-discontinued Corpus Christi processions. The museum is open from 10 a.m. to noon and 2:30–6 p.m. (5 p.m. in winter), but is closed on Mondays and during the entire month of February.

Continue on to the **Tapestry Museum** (5) in the former archbishop's palace. The inner courtyard of this building is the center of the annual music festival held in July and August. You may be interested in the outstanding collection of 17th- and 18th-century Beauvais tapestries, some of which depict the life of Don Quixote. Visits may be

Aix-en-Provence

300 Yards

made from 10 a.m. to noon and 2–5 p.m., daily except on Tuesdays, some holidays, and the month of January.

Next to this stands the **Cathedral of St.-Sauveur** (6), a curious architectural *mélange* incorporating elements from the 5th century onwards. Enter through an enchanting 12th-century Romanesque cloister, then step inside to enjoy the richly varied interior. The main attraction here is the famous *Triptych of the Burning Bush,* painted about 1476 by Nicolas Froment for King René, who appears on the left panel, with his wife on the right panel. These are usually closed, but will be opened for you by the caretaker on request. Outside again, take a look at the west front. All of the sculptures except one are replacements, the originals having been destroyed in the Revolution. The sole survivor is that of the Virgin on the central pillar of the main portal, which escaped harm when some quick-witted person crowned her with a red cap of Liberty.

Art lovers might want to make a side trip at this point to the **Atelier Paul Cézanne** (7, off the map), the small studio where the renowned painter worked until his death in 1906. Although everything here is pretty much as he left it, the effect is curiously unmoving. Still, if you are an admirer of Cézanne—a native of Aix—this is a worthwhile stop, which can be made from 10 a.m. to noon and 2:30–6 p.m. (2–5 p.m. off season), except on Tuesdays and holidays. To get there on foot continue straight ahead and follow Avenue Pasteur a short distance, then make a right uphill on Avenue Paul Cézanne to the studio on the left. The distance is about three-quarters of a mile. It is also possible to take bus number 1 from the front of the tourist office to the Cézanne stop, which follows an entirely different route.

Return to the cathedral and follow the map through a highly picturesque old part of town to the eastern end of the Cours Mirabeau. Continue on Rue d'Italie and turn right at the 13th-century **Church of St.-Jean-de-Malte**, the first Gothic structure in Provence—worth a visit for its stained-glass windows. Adjacent to this stands the **Granet Museum** (8), whose collections of fine art and pre-Roman archaeological artifacts are among the best in Provence. Some of the more outstanding paintings on display include a magnificent self-portrait by Rembrandt, several works by the locally-born early-19th-century artist François Granet, a portrait of Granet by Ingres, and a few works by Cézanne. The museum is open from 10 a.m. to noon and 2–6 p.m. (5 p.m. in winter), daily except on Tuesdays and major holidays.

You are now in the Mazarin Quarter, laid out in the 17th century by the archbishop of Aix, a brother of the great statesman. Stroll past the charming Fountain of the Four Dolphins, which has been merrily splashing away since 1667.

A right turn leads to the **Paul Arbaud Museum** (9), featuring inter-

Along the Cours Mirabeau

esting displays of local Provençal ceramics, art and culture. Visits may be made from 2–5 p.m., any day except Sundays and certain holidays. From here it is only a few steps back to the Cours Mirabeau.

ADDITIONAL SIGHTS:

The **Vasarely Foundation** (10, off the map), in the suburbs of Aix, is devoted to the work of the contemporary Hungarian Op-artist Victor Vasarely. Housed in a stunningly modern building of hexagonal shapes, the vibrant displays appeal to some, while others find them literally painful to the eye. The foundation is open from 9:30 a.m. to 12:30 p.m. and 2–5:30 p.m., every day except Tuesdays and certain holidays. You can get there via local bus from near the front of the tourist office. Ask them about current route information. You might also inquire about their bus excursions along the "Route Cézanne," seeing places made famous by the painter.

Arles

Few towns in France are as rich in ancient monuments as Arles, yet it remains a delightfully unpretentious country place, captivating in its honest simplicity. Virtually everyone who goes there enjoys the experience.

Founded by Greeks from Marseille in the 6th century B.C., Arles became an important Roman colony in 49 B.C. after it sided with Julius Caesar in his victorious struggle against the rival general, Pompey. Having backed the wrong man, Marseille was humbled and its wealth transferred to Arles.

At that time the town was already a major port, linked to the Mediterranean by canal and set astride the main highway between Italy and Spain. The prosperity that followed brought about the construction of major public projects, several of which still stand today. Christianity came to Arles at an early date, along with political importance as the capital of Gaul. With the fall of the empire, however, the city fell to the barbarians from the north and was invaded by the Arab Saracens. Although later a kingdom in its own right, it never really recovered and soon drifted into the dreamy backwater that it is today.

Arles is probably best known for its association with the artist Vincent van Gogh, who created some 200 of his greatest works while living there in 1888 and 1889, just prior to his insanity and suicide.

As an alternative to Marseille, Arles is an excellent base for daytrips throughout Provence, particularly for those with cars. Ask at the tourist office for information about bus excursions to the Camargue region, Les Baux, Aigues-Mortes and other nearby attractions. They can also make hotel reservations for you.

GETTING THERE:

Trains depart St.-Charles Station in Marseille several times in the morning for the 45-minute run to Arles, with returns until late evening. There is also convenient service to and from Avignon and, less frequently, with Nîmes. Aix-en-Provence is reached via Marseille.

By car, Arles is connected via the N-113 road and the A-7 Autoroute to Marseille, 57 miles to the southeast. Other distances are: Aix-en-Provence—47 miles, Avignon—23 miles, and Nîmes—19 miles.

WHEN TO GO:

Good weather, which fortunately is common in Provence, will make this trip much more enjoyable. All of the major sights, except the Museon Arlaten, are open every day except January 1st, May Day and Christmas. An economical all-inclusive "global" ticket is available. With a few minor variations, each attraction is open from 8:30 a.m. to 7:00 p.m. during the summer, with shorter hours and a lunch break the rest of the year.

FOOD AND DRINK:

Arles has a wide variety of restaurants and cafés, particularly near the Arena, on the Boulevard des Lices, and at Place du Forum. Some outstanding choices are:

> **Lou Marquès** (in the Jules César Hôtel on Blvd. des Lices, by the tourist office) Excellent classical and Provençal specialties as well as seafood. X: Dec. $$$

> **Le Vaccarès** (9 Rue Favorin, by Place du Forum) Traditional Provençal cuisine in a romantic setting. X: Sun. eve. and Mon. from Oct. to June. $$$

> **La Paillote** (28 Rue Dr.-Fanton, 1 block north of Place du Forum) Good value in an old part of town, specializes in seafood. X: Wed., Thurs. lunch (low season), mid-Jan. to mid-Mar. $$

> **Le Tambourin** (65 Rue Amédée-Pichot, 2 blocks north of the Arena, just off Place Voltaire) Home-style Provençal cooking. X: Thurs. $$

> **Hostellerie des Arènes** (62 Rue du Refuge, northeast side of the arena) Very popular for its Provençal cuisine at modest prices. X: Tues. eve. in low season, Wed., Jan., late June.$

TOURIST INFORMATION:

The local tourist office, phone 90-96-29-35, is along the Boulevard des Lices, near the center of town.

SUGGESTED TOUR:

Leave the **train station** (1) and stroll down to Place Lamartine, a good place to park if you came by car. Vincent van Gogh lived in a bistro here, sharing his place with the painter Gauguin for a while, and it was here that he cut off his ear. The house, alas, was destroyed by a bomb in 1944.

Continue on through the town gates and follow the map to the **Arena** *(Les Arènes)* (2), one of the largest, oldest and best-preserved Roman amphitheaters in existence. Probably built around A.D. 80 to seat some 25,000 spectators, it is now used for bullfights. During the Middle Ages the amphitheater was converted into a fortress, with the

TO MARSEILLE

TO MARSEILLE

Avenue Victor Hugo

Allée des Tombeaux

⑦

Blvd. Emile Combes

③

R. de la Madeleine

Ave. des Alyscamps

R. Vauban

Montée Vauban

Boulevard des Lices

Arena

④

Theatre

R. de la Calade

R. du Cloître

Blvd. G. Bizet

⑤

Info.

Blvd. Emile Zola

R. des Arènes

a Hôtel de Ville

Pl. de la
République

Forum

⑥

⑩

Rue Balze

⑨

République

R. de la

⑧

R. du Prés. Wilson

Blvd. G. Clemenceau

R. Gambetta

Arles

300 Yards

top rows of arches being demolished to furnish stones for the defensive towers. An entire town with a church and some 200 houses was built within it, and this provided some measure of safety from the marauding bands and incessant wars of those troubled times. The arena was restored to its present condition only during the 19th century. Step inside and make a circular tour through the various passageways, exploring the inner chambers, then climb to the top of the medieval tower for a splendid view.

Walk up the stepped Rue Renan to the Romanesque **Notre-Dame-de-la-Major Church** (3), now closed. Directly aside of this there is a good lookout spot above the ancient ramparts that offers a spectacular panorama of the region.

Return via the arena and amble over to the nearby **Roman Theater** (*Théâtre Antique*) (4). It was built during the reign of the emperor Augustus, toward the end of the 1st century B.C., and was used for elaborate theatrical productions, which often tended to be obscene. The Christians put an end to all that and tore the place down, using most of the stones to build churches and convents. Miraculously, two Corinthian columns survived *in situ* and are still there. Excavations in the 18th century revealed the long-forgotten structure that, only partially restored, is now used for festival productions. You can wander inside for a close look at the stage and seating arrangements.

Continue on to Place de la République and the Romanesque former **Cathedral of St.-Trophîme** (5), now used as a parish church. Although parts of it may date from the Carolingian era, it is basically an 11th-century structure, much altered in later years. The marvelous west front is richly carved with a *Last Judgement* above the portal, a procession of the redeemed on the left frieze and, on the right, figures of the damned being marched naked into hell.

Next door to the cathedral is the entrance to the incomparable **St.-Trophîme Cloister** (*Cloître*), considered to be the best in Provence. Be sure to go upstairs to see the many small exhibits, and to carefully examine the marvelously sculpted details of Biblical stories and local legends on the pillars.

Just across the square, next to the Town Hall, is the **Museum of Pagan Art** (*Musée Lapidaire Païen*) (6), which features Greek and Roman statues and mosaics dug up nearby. The head of *Venus of Arles*, found in the Roman Theater, is a cast—the original is in the Louvre in Paris.

Follow the map past the tourist office to **Les Alyscamps** (7), the strangely evocative remnant of what was once a great necropolis. Begun in pagan times and later taken over by Christians, it formerly covered an immense area nearly a mile in length, with many thousands of tombs. Desecrated during the 16th century, it fell to ruin, and what

Inside the Roman Arena

few sarcophagi survived were lined up along the sole remaining alley. Dante described the place in his *Divine Comedy*, while both Van Gogh and Gauguin painted its melancholy beauty. At the end of the lane stands the fittingly ruined remains of an ancient church.

Return to the animated Boulevard des Lices and take Rue du Président-Wilson to the extraordinarily fascinating **Museon Arlaten** (8), whose name is appropriately in the Provençal language. Allow yourself at least an hour to get lost in this vast storage attic of a museum, filled to the brim with just about everything imaginable that might relate to Provençal folklore. It was founded by the noted writer Frédéric Mistral using funds he received for winning the Nobel Prize in 1904, and many of the faded display cards are still in his hand. The total disregard for conventional museum values is what makes this place so intriguing, like a perverse visit to a huge junkshop. It is open from June through September, daily from 8:30 a.m. to 7 p.m.; and on Tuesdays through Sundays from 9 a.m. to noon and 2–4:30 or 6:30 p.m. the rest of the year. Don't miss seeing this.

Turn the corner to the **Museum of Christian Art** (*Musée Lapidaire Chrétien*) (9). By this time you may be weary of old sarcophagi, but don't let that discourage you from entering. In the midst of all those burial pieces is a staircase leading down to the **subterranean galleries** (*Cryptoportiques*), a very spooky place built by the Romans in the 1st Century B.C. as a storage center for grain. The passageways were probably the substructure of the original Roman forum, near today's Place du Forum. If it is closed just ask the caretaker to turn on the lights.

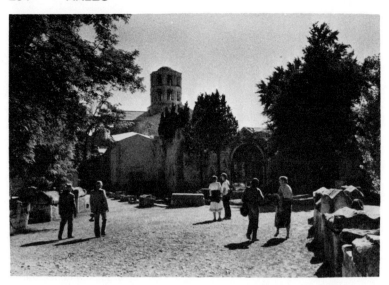

Les Alyscamps

Continue on through the **Place du Forum** (10), a charming square with several inviting outdoor cafés, a statue of Frédéric Mistral, and a few relics of the Roman forum. The **Baths of Constantine** *(Palais des Thermes)* (11), nearby, are all that remain of a great 4th-century bathing establishment built by the emperor Constantine. The water came via an aqueduct some 40 miles long that crossed the wide Rhône River.

The last important sight to visit in Arles is right next door, the **Museum of Fine Arts** *(Musée Réattu)* (12). Located in the 15th-century former priory of the Knights of Malta, it is best known for its collection of late Picasso drawings, donated by the artist just prior to his death in 1973. There is also a fine collection of other modern works by French artists as well as local art, 17th-century tapestries, and a famous section devoted to photography. From here you can walk along the banks of the Rhône to the town gates, or return through the town.

Avignon

Lively, cosmopolitan Avignon is far more sophisticated than its size would suggest. Ever since the 14th century, when it was the capital of Christendom, it has retained a worldly atmosphere that today makes it a popular tourist and convention center as well as the setting for one of Europe's major theatrical festivals.

Although the town has existed since Gallo-Roman times, and its famous bridge has stood since the 12th century, Avignon did not really gain significance until 1309. Pope Clement V, a Frenchman, was driven from Rome by the endless wars between the Guelfs and the Ghibellines. Desiring to be closer to the French king, he moved the Papacy to a territory it owned on the banks of the Rhône, on the edge of France. Avignon, although a part of Provence, bordered on this, and was the town best suited as their new capital. The "Second Babylonian Captivity" had begun, lasting through seven French Popes, until Gregory XI moved back to Rome in 1377. This did not sit well with a faction of Cardinals who preferred to remain in Avignon. They resisted by electing their own Pope, thus creating the "Great Schism" in which the Pope in Rome and the Antipope in Avignon hurled anathemas at one another until 1403.

After that, Avignon became a peaceful but still worldly place. Having been purchased from Provence in 1348, it remained the property of the Papacy right up until the French Revolution, when it was annexed to France.

With its superb tourist facilities, Avignon makes a fine base for daytrips throughout Provence. Those staying there may want to explore the city in greater depth, or make short excursions to nearby Villeneuve-lés-Avignon, Orange, Pont du Gard, Tarascon or Les Baux. Avignon plays host to its famous drama festival from early July until early August.

GETTING THERE:

Trains, including speedy TGVs, connect St.-Charles Station in Marseille with Avignon at fairly frequent intervals, with return service until late evening. Regular trains take about one hour, TGVs at bit less. There is also direct service to and from Arles (under 20 minutes) and with Nîmes (about 30 minutes, with faster TGV service available). To get to Aix-en-Provence requires a change at Marseille.

Avignon is connected with Paris by direct TGV service, taking a bit under four hours.

By car, Avignon is 62 miles northwest of Marseille via the A-7 Autoroute and the N-7 road. Other distances are: Aix-en-Provence—50 miles, Arles—23 miles, and Nîmes—27 miles.

WHEN TO GO:

The Palace of the Popes is open daily except for a few major holidays. Most of the museums close on Tuesdays and holidays. Good weather will make this trip more rewarding. The town is crowded during the international drama festival held from early July until early August.

FOOD AND DRINK:

Sophisticated Avignon is endowed with an exceptional range of restaurants and cafés in all price ranges. Some excellent choices are:

Hiély-Lucullus (5 Rue de la République, at the Place de l'Horloge) Traditional gastronomy in an upstairs dining room. For reservations phone 90-86-17-07. X: Mon. except July, Tues., late June, early Jan. $$$

Brunel (46 Rue de la Balance, 1 block northwest of the Palace of the Popes) Refined regional cuisine in a pleasant atmosphere. X: Sun., Mon. off season, early Aug. $$$

Auberge de France (28 Place de l'Horloge) Excellent Provençal cuisine in a modern setting. X: Wed. eve., Thurs., late June, Jan. $$$

Le Vernet (58 Rue Joseph-Vernet, opposite the Calvet Museum) Modern cuisine in a luxurious old house or garden. X: Sun. except for summer, Jan., Feb. $$$

Le Saint-Didier (41 Rue Saraillerie, behind the Church of St.-Didier) Superb cuisine at affordable prices, especially fish. X: Mon., Tues., May. $$$

Les Trois Clefs (26 Rue des Trois Faucons, 2 blocks northeast of the tourist office) A lovely little restaurant with imaginative cuisine. X: Sun. except July, Nov. $$ and $$$

Le Salon de la Fourchette (7 Rue Racine, 1 block west of Place de l'Horloge) Superb cuisine at moderate prices. Reservations needed, phone 90-82-56-01. X: Sun., Mon. $$

La Fourchette II (17 Rue Racine, 1 block west of Place de l'Horloge) An annex of *Le Salon,* above. Good food at moderate prices brings in crowds. For reservations phone 90-85-20-93. X: Sat., Sun., late June. $$

The Palace of the Popes

La Férigoulo (30 Rue Joseph-Vernet, 1 block west of St.-Agricol Church) A traditional restaurant with inventive cuisine. X: Sun. eve. & Mon. off season. $$

Le Patio (2 Rue Petite-Calade, 2 blocks north of the Calvet Museum) A very popular garden restaurant with Provençal specialties. X: Sat. $

Le Pain Bis (6 Rue Armand de Pontmartin, 3 blocks east of Place de l'Horloge) A pleasant vegetarian restaurant with organic dishes. X: Sat., Sun. $

Crêperie du Cloître (9 Place du Cloître St.-Pierre, 3 blocks east of Place de l'Horloge) Crêpes, salads and the like. X: Sun. $

The local wines are those from the Côtes du Rhône, especially Châteauneuf-du-Pape.

TOURIST INFORMATION:

The helpful tourist office, phone 90-82-65-11, is located at 41 Cours Jean-Jaurès, not far from the train station. They can make hotel reservations for you.

SUGGESTED TOUR:

Leave the **train station** (1) and follow the map through the 14th-century ramparts, which completely encircle the old part of town. They were restored in the 19th century by Viollet-le-Duc, the architect who did so much to preserve medieval France. Continue past the tourist office to **Place de l'Horloge** (2), a delightfully animated spot on the site of the ancient Roman forum, with many outdoor cafés, a 14th-century clock tower and the Town Hall.

Just beyond this is Avignon's stellar attraction, the **Palace of the Popes** (Palais des Papes) (3). Looking more like a mighty fortress than the residence of a religious leader, it is really two very different structures joined together. The austere **Old Palace**, to the left, was built by Benedict XII between 1335 and 1342. His successor, Clement VI, was a more flamboyant Pope, as the **New Palace** (1342—1352) on the right suggests. Both buildings were badly damaged and looted during the Revolution, then used as a prison and, later, as an army barracks until 1906. An enormous amount of restoration has been done since then, but most of the rooms are still pretty much devoid of furnishings. Still, they are extremely interesting and well worth the visit. One-hour guided tours are offered in French, English, or German; but you can just walk through on your own if you wish. A descriptive brochure in English with detailed floor plans will be given to you at the entrance. The palace is open daily from 9 a.m. to 6 p.m. between July 1st and September 30th; from 9–11 a.m. and 2–4 p.m. from October 1st until the Easter holidays; and from 9–11 a.m. and 2–5 p.m. between then and June 30th. It is closed on New Year's Day, May Day and Christmas.

The **Cathedral of Notre-Dame-des-Doms** (4) stands next to the palace. Dating from the 12th century, it was greatly altered in later years. The gilded statue of the Virgin atop the steeple, added in 1859, is visible from all over town. Step inside to see the 12th-century white marble archbishop's throne and the fine canopied tomb of Pope John XXII.

Stroll down to the nearby **Petit Palais** (5), built in 1317 as a palace for the Archbishop of Avignon and greatly altered in later centuries. It now houses the splendid **Museum of Medieval Painting and Sculpture** (Musée du Petit Palais). Aside from the quality of the art, which is quite high, this is a beautiful example of museum organization at its very best—a situation all too rare in provincial France. Don't miss ambling through the lovely rooms. Visits may be made from 9:30–11:50 a.m. and 2–6:15 p.m., daily except on Tuesdays and holidays.

Climb up to the **Rocher des Doms** (6), a beautiful park on the site of Avignon's prehistoric origins. The highest point in town, it overlooks a bend in the river and the famous **Pont St.-Bénézet** (7), a 12th-

Avignon

300 Yards

The Pont St.-Bénézet

century bridge known to generations of French children as the *Pont d'Avignon* of the familiar nursery rhyme. Storms and floods over the centuries have reduced the original 22 arches that were once the only stone span across the Rhône south of Lyon to a mere four, but these certainly make a spectacular sight. According to legend, the bridge was begun after a young shepherd lad named Bénézet experienced a Divine vision, then by performing a miracle convinced the authorities to construct the span. It turned out to be a good investment, bringing prosperity to Avignon for centuries to come. If you wish to walk out on it you can follow the map—steeply downhill—to its foot, where the entrance is hidden in a souvenir shop. It is usually open daily except for a one-hour lunch break.

Return to Place de l'Horloge (2), using the route on the map if you went down to the bridge. A right on Rue St.-Agricol leads to the interesting **Church of St.-Agricol** (8), up a flight of stairs, rebuilt in the 14th century and much altered since. It contains several excellent works of art including a superb altarpiece.

Continue on Rue Joseph-Vernet to the **Calvet Museum** (9), housed in a magnificent 18th-century mansion. The collections of art, displayed in an old-fashioned manner, are certainly an eclectic lot, with several great masterpieces by such talents as Breughel, David, Géricault, Manet, Corot, Toulouse-Lautrec, Dufy and Utrillo scattered among a mass of decidedly lesser works, some of which are just awful.

In the Palace of the Popes

There is also a fascinating collection of medieval wrought-iron objects. The museum has a certain charm about it that is difficult to describe but worth experiencing. Visits may be made from 10 a.m. to noon and 2–6 p.m., daily except Tuesdays and holidays.

Follow the map to the 14th-century **Church of St.-Didier** (10). In the first chapel on the right you will see a noted altarpiece of 1478, called *"Our Lady of the Spasm"* for its realistic depiction of the Virgin in anguish. There are also some outstanding 14th-century frescoes in the first chapel on the left.

The route now wanders through a picturesque old part of town to the **Rue des Teinturiers**, an ancient cobbled street running along a stream lined with old water wheels once used in the production of dyed fabrics. Stop in at the **Chapel of the Grey Penitents** *(Pénitents Gris)* (11) to admire its splendid 17th-century golden glory. Continue on to the ramparts, then return to the tourist office, following the map. You may be interested in visiting the nearby **Lapidary Museum** (12) on Rue de la République, which features Gallo-Roman and prehistoric archaeological finds from the region. Housed in a former Jesuit chapel of the 17th century, it is open during the same times as the Calvet Museum. From here it is only a short stroll back to the station.

Nîmes

Some of the most remarkable Roman structures outside Italy are to be found in Nîmes, a handsome city on the fringe of Provence that bills itself as *"La Rome Française."* A visit here will be made even more enjoyable by the magnificent gardens, the fine museums, and by a stroll through the colorful medieval quarter.

Centered around a sacred spring, Nîmes was already a large tribal settlement with the Romans came in 121 B.C. Then known as *Nemausus,* it flourished as a colony of veterans set at the junction of several trade routes. During this time it became a showplace of the Roman Empire, with many fine buildings, some of which are still in excellent condition.

Occupation by the Visigoths in the 5th century A.D. prevented the spread of Christianity, which did not arrive until the 8th century. After that the town was annexed to the Counts of Toulouse. During the 16th century Nîmes became a Protestant stronghold, with religious strife continuing until the Revolution. Since then it has prospered with the development of various light industries.

The city is noted for the manufacture of textiles, particularly of a rough twill fabric long marketed abroad as being *"de Nîmes,"* from which we get the word denim.

Nîmes can be used as a base for daytrips in Provence, although it is not as convenient for this purpose as Marseille, Arles or Avignon. Other short excursion possibilities are to the ancient walled town of Aigues-Mortes or the famous Roman aqueduct at Pont du Gard, both served by regional buses. Ask at the tourist office for current schedules.

GETTING THERE:

Trains depart St.-Charles Station in Marseille in the morning for Nîmes, a trip of about 75 minutes. Return service operates until early evening. Most of these also stop at Arles en route. There are direct trains between Nîmes and Avignon, including TGVs, taking about 30 minutes. To get to Aix-en-Provence requires a change at Marseille.

Nîmes is connected to Paris with direct TGV service, the run taking about 4½ hours.

By car, Nîmes is easy to reach following local maps. Distances are: 75 miles northwest of Marseille, from Aix-en-Provence—66 miles, Arles—19 miles, and Avignon—27 miles.

WHEN TO GO:
The attractions in Nîmes are open every day except for a few major holidays. The Roman Arena cannot be visited on bullfight days. Good weather will make this trip much more enjoyable.

FOOD AND DRINK:
Nîmes offers a fairly good selection of restaurants, several of which are in hotels. Among the best choices are:

Le Magister (5 Rue Nationale, 2 blocks west of the Augustus Gate) Considered to be the best restaurant in town. X: Sun., early Aug. $$$

L'Enclos de la Fontaine (in the Hôtel Impérator on Place Aristide Briand, 1 block southeast of the Fountain Gardens) Imaginative cuisine in lovely surroundings. X: Sat. lunch. $$$

Le Carrousel (in the Hôtel Cheval Blanc, 1 Place des Arènes, facing the south side of the Arena) Traditional food, with an outdoor dining terrace available. X: Wed. $$

Le Louvre (2 Square de la Couronne, 2 blocks southeast of the Archaeology Museum) Elegant dining at moderate prices in a small hotel. $$

Le Lisita (2 Blvd. des Arènes, just north of the Arena) A popular favorite. X: Sat., Aug. $$

Carrière (6 Rue Grizot, 1 block east of the Archaeology Museum) Good-value dining in a small hotel. $

There are quite a few inviting sidewalk cafés behind the arena and along Boulevard Victor-Hugo.

TOURIST INFORMATION:
The local tourist office, phone 66-67-29-11, is located at 6 Rue Auguste, close to the Maison Carrée. They can find hotel rooms for you and provide bus schedules for nearby excursions. There is also a regional office in front of the arena.

SUGGESTED TOUR:
Leave the **train station** (1) and follow the map to the **Roman Arena** *(Arènes)* (2). Built around A.D. 50, it is a bit smaller than the similar amphitheater in Arles, but is actually in better condition. Following

Nîmes

300 Yards

The Roman Arena

the fall of the empire it became a fortress, and during the Middle Ages a slum with some 150 houses erected within its walls. As a result of a complete renovation carried out in the 19th century, the amphitheater is now used for bullfights, concerts and other events. You may explore the interior—when it is not in use—from mid-June to mid-September, daily from 8 a.m. to 8 p.m.; and the rest of the year daily from 9 a.m. to noon and 2–6 p.m., closing at 5 p.m. in winter. An economical all-inclusive "global" ticket for the Roman monuments is available. If you happen to come on a bullfight day, don't despair—the running of the bulls down Boulevard Victor-Hugo is an exciting event in itself.

Continue along Boulevard Victor-Hugo to the **Maison Carrée** (3) which, despite its name, is rectangular in shape. This splendid Greek-style temple was built around 20 B.C. and is probably the best-preserved Roman temple anywhere. Unlike most structures from antiquity, it has been in continuous use for a variety of functions for over two thousand years, which no doubt accounts for the fine shape it is in today. In the late 18th century it even provided inspiration for Thomas Jefferson in his design of the Virginia State Capitol. The Maison Carrée now serves as a museum of local Roman artifacts and may be visited during the same hours that the Arena is open, with a few minor variations.

Now follow the map past the tourist office to the very impressive

The Maison Carrée

Fountain Gardens *(Jardins de la Fontaine)* (4), laid out in the 18th century around the sacred spring of Nemausus. Stroll over to the exquisite **Temple of Diana** (5), a highly romantic 2nd-century ruin that may have been part of a long-vanished Roman bath.

The route now climbs through a park to the **Tour Magne** (6), a massive Roman defensive tower that was once part of the town walls. At the time of its construction, about 16 B.C., it was some 30 feet taller than it is today, but it is still a fairly stiff climb to the top. The magnificent panoramic view from up there, extending as far as the Pyrenees on a clear day, makes it all worth the effort. The ascent may be made during the same hours that the Arena is open, with slight variations.

Return to the Fountain Gardens (4) and follow Quai de la Fontaine to Boulevard Gambetta. Those interested in early Roman plumbing may want to make a short side trip up Rue du Fort and Rue de la Lampèze to the **Castellum** (7), an ancient distribution center for water flowing in via the Pont du Gard aqueduct.

Continue along to the **Augustus Gate** (or *Porte d'Arles*) (8), a well-preserved part of the Roman ramparts from the 1st century B.C. A few blocks beyond this lies a 17th-century Jesuit monastery that now houses the intriguing **Museum of Archaeology** (9), displaying many artifacts from prehistoric as well as Roman times. The Natural History Museum, in the same building, is also worth a visit. Both are open from

9 a.m. to noon and 1:30–6 p.m. daily, but closed on certain holidays and on Sunday mornings.

You are now on the edge of **Old Nîmes** *(Vieux Nîmes)*, the medieval core from which the modern city emerged. Follow the map to the **Cathedral of St.-Castor** (10), a small and much-altered structure with its roots in the 11th century. The partly Romanesque frieze on its west front depicts scenes from the Old Testament.

Step over to the former Bishop's Palace, a 17th-century mansion that now houses the **Museum of Old Nîmes** (11). Open daily from 10 a.m. to 6 p.m., its collections include some truly magnificent furniture in beautiful surroundings. In addition, there are interesting displays devoted to textiles and bullfighting.

The route now leads through some highly picturesque streets lined with nicely restored houses of mixed ages, several of which are medieval. Take a look into the courtyard at number 14 Rue de l'Aspic, noted for its magnificent double staircase. There are many other pleasant surprises in this charming neighborhood, best seen by just wandering around and poking your head into doorways.

Return to the station via the Arena. You may be interested in making a slight detour to the **Fine Arts Museum** *(Musée des Beaux-Arts)* (12), open daily from 9 a.m. to noon and 1:30–6 p.m. The most remarkable item there is a major Roman mosaic on the ground floor. There are also a number of paintings representing various European schools from the 16th through the 19th centuries.

Section VIII

Daytrips on

The Riviera

There is something for everyone on the French Riviera. Whether your tastes run to hedonistic resorts, half-hidden hill towns, vibrant art colonies, medieval strongholds, golden beaches, mountains and forests, sophisticated urban centers or gambling casinos, you're sure to find some little corner of this enchanted, sun-drenched land that will call you back again and again. And that, precisely, is the reason why daytrips throughout the region are such a good idea. They allow you to sample many different facets of the Riviera in a relatively short time and at reasonable cost, so when you return—and you probably will return—you'll know just where to head.

There is no exact definition of what constitutes the Riviera or, as it is often called, the Côte d'Azur. For the purposes of the book, however, it includes the Mediterranean seacoast from St. Tropez to the Italian border, and extends north to the beginnings of the Alps.

For lovers of modern art, a trip to the Riviera is virtually a pilgrimage. This is where Picasso painted, as did Renoir, Chagall, Matisse and many others. Museums abound along with the homes of the artists themselves.

Although almost any of the coastal towns can be used as a base for your daytrips, there is no denying that Nice is the most convenient for those traveling by rail or bus since it is the transportation hub of the entire region, with frequent services to the other attractions. A large and very attractive city with a Mediterranean flair all its own, Nice has a broad range of hotels and restaurants in every conceivable price bracket, as well as a major airport with connections to all of Europe and beyond. Other towns that make particularly good bases are Cannes, Antibes, Monaco and Menton.

Old Nice

Nice is, well, nice. That is probably the best possible word to describe this appealing city—the fifth-largest in France—beautifully situated on the edge of the Mediterranean and practically in the shadow of the Alps. Not extravagantly spectacular in any one aspect, its harmonious blend of qualities makes it quite endearing to the many visitors who return year after year. A great commercial center in its own right, Nice does not have to depend on tourists for a living and is all the more attractive for that.

Since there is an excellent chance that Nice will be the base for your Riviera daytrips, two walking tours are included that cover the most interesting parts of town. Either of these can be done in just a few hours, leaving the rest of the day free for a possible half-day excursion to a nearby uncomplicated destination such as Cagnes-sur-Mer or Menton. Or for taking the other tour, or for just relaxing.

The first walking tour explores the picturesque narrow alleyways, outdoor markets, hilltop fortress and bustling port of Old Nice, a delightful district that retains much of its ancient charm. The second tour—described in the next chapter—turns inland to the relics of Roman Nice on the Cimiez hill.

Founded as a trading post by the Phocean Greeks of Marseille around 350 B.C., the settlement was first called *Nikêa* in honor of Nike, the goddess of victory, following a defeat of the local Ligurian tribes. Two centuries later, the Romans established a town—*Cemenelum*—on the Cimiez hill, but this was later destroyed by the Barbarians and the Saracens. In the 10th century A.D. Nice came to life again and prospered, first as a part of Provence and later under the Italian House of Savoy. Although it changed hands several times, the city remained essentially a Savoyan one until 1860, when it was ceded to France after a popular plebiscite. Much of its ancient heritage still lingers in the twisting lanes of Old Nice, and especially on the menus of many of its best restaurants.

GETTING THERE:

Trains connect Nice with virtually all coastal towns along the Riviera, from St. Raphaël to the Italian border, at frequent intervals, with service operating until late evening. Expresses stop at major towns including St. Raphaël, Cannes, Antibes, Monaco and Menton; while locals (*omnibus*) make halts virtually everywhere. Typical running times to Nice are: from Cannes—under 30 minutes; from Antibes—15 minutes; from Monaco—20 minutes; and from Menton—under 30 minutes.

There is direct train service to and from Paris, with the TGV types making the run in 7 hours.

The main station in Nice (*Gare Nice-Ville*) is about a 10-to 15-minute stroll from the starting point of this walking tour, Place Masséna. There is also frequent bus service, as well as taxis. You can get a free city map at the tourist office adjacent to the train station.

By car, Nice is 11 miles from Monaco, 17 miles from Menton, 8 miles from Cagnes-sur-Mer, 15 miles from Antibes and 21 miles from Cannes. Recommended routes are given in the chapters dealing with those and other towns.

By air, the Nice-Côte d'Azur Airport is only four miles southwest of the city center and has frequent flights to Paris on both Air France and Air Inter. There are also flights to all over Europe, North Africa, the Middle East, and North America.

WHEN TO GO:

Old Nice may be explored at any time, but note the schedules of the museums if these are of interest to you.

FOOD AND DRINK:

Nice is blessed with an exceptionally wide range of restaurants at every possible price level. Many of these feature seafood, Niçoise or Italian cuisine. The choices listed below are located in or near the old part of town covered by this walking tour. For restaurants in other parts of Nice you should consult a reliable guide such as the red-cover *Michelin France*.

Ane Rouge (7 Quai des Deux-Emmanuel, 1 block beyond the east side of Port Lympia) Exquisite seafood. X: Sat., Sun., holidays, late July, Aug. $$$

Chez Les Pêcheurs (18 Quai des Docks, on the east side of Port Lympia) Famous for its seafood. X: Wed., lunch in summer, Nov. $$$

Don Camillo (5 Rue des Ponchettes, near the base of the elevator to Le Château) Italian specialties in a relaxed setting. X: Sun., Mon. $$$

Chez Rolando (3 Rue Desboutins, 2 blocks southwest of Place Masséna) Italian cuisine. X: Sun., holidays, July, lunch in Aug. $$$

Les Dents de la Mer (2 Rue St.-François-de-Paule, just east of the Opéra) Contemporary classical seafood dishes in a very nautical environment. $$$

Au Chapon Fin (1 Rue du Moulin, 2 blocks west of the cathedral) Niçoise specialties in pleasant surroundings. X: Sun., holidays, Jan. $$

La Coquille (36 Cours Saleya, by the Flower Market) A simple and popular seafood restaurant. X: Mon. $$

La Merenda (4 Rue de la Terrace, 2 blocks northwest of the Flower Market) A tiny and very popular restaurant with authentic Niçoise cuisine. X: Sat. eve., Sun., Mon., holidays, Aug., Feb. $$

Le Lympia (4 Place Guynemer, near the southwest end of Port Lympia) Well known for its grilled fish in a maritime setting. X: Sun. $$

La Nissarda (17 Rue Gubernatis, 6 blocks north of the Opéra) Niçoise, French and Italian dishes in a traditional neighborhood restaurant. X: Wed., early July. $

Taverne du Château (42 Rue Droite, near the Lascaris Palace) Home-style Niçoise cooking. $

TOURIST INFORMATION:

Nice has several tourist offices. One of these is located next to the main train station and can be phoned at 93-87-07-07. Another convenient branch, phone 93-87-60-60, is at 5 Avenue Gustave V, at the west end of the Jardin Albert I near the Old Town and Place Masséna. There is also an office on the road leading in from the airport.

Be sure to ask for a city map—essential for finding your way around the parts of town not covered by these walking tours—and for their helpful brochure *Museums of Nice*.

SUGGESTED TOUR:

Begin your walk at the very heart of Nice, the elegant **Place Masséna** (1), located near the beach and many of the city's best hotels and shopping areas. It can be easily reached from other parts of town by bus or on foot. For those lucky enough to be in Nice during the annual Carnival, held during the last two weeks of February, this is the best possible place for viewing the festivities.

Continue around the **Jardin Albert I**, a lovely garden filled with exotic plants and palm trees. The Quai des États-Unis is an extension of the world-renowned **Promenade des Anglais**, a seaside avenue laid out by the resident English colony in the early 1800s and soon taken over by the town. The beach along here is certainly pretty to look at but not very comfortable for sunbathing since it is all pebbles.

Le Château from the Quai des États-Unis

A left turn at the handsome, late-19th-century **Opéra** leads to the Cours Saleya and the outdoor **Flower Market** (2), a colorful spot that comes to life with the vending of flowers and produce from early morning until mid-afternoon, every day except Mondays and Sunday afternoons.

Follow the map to the base of a steep, rocky plateau overlooking the city, port and seacoast. An **elevator** (*ascenseur*) (3), reached through a short tunnel, will quickly lift you some 300 feet for a marvelous view from the top. It is also possible to walk up. Still known as **Le Château** (4), its summit is crowned with the ruins of a 16th-century fortress, destroyed in 1706 on orders from Louis XIV. Close by are the foundations of an 11th-century cathedral and some early Greek structures. A stroll through the lush gardens leads to a viewing platform, several outdoor cafés, and an utterly delightful artificial waterfall (*cascade*).

On the way back be sure to stop at the **Bellanda Tower**, a 16th-century circular bastion near the elevator, now housing the **Naval Museum**. Step inside to admire the splendid ship models and nautical artifacts, which may be seen from 10 a.m. to noon and 2–5 p.m. (7 p.m. in summer), every day except Tuesdays, some holidays, and the period between mid-November and the end of December. Interestingly, the tower was once occupied by Hector Berlioz, who composed the music to *King Lear* in these rooms. From here you can easily walk down or rejoin the elevator—it makes a special stop at the museum, part way down the hill.

Continue around the base of the hill to **Port Lympia** (5), the lively old harbor of Nice. Begun in 1750, it provides a safe haven for boats which, prior to that, just docked along the foot of the castle hill. Regular cruises are offered to other points along the Riviera, as well as to Corsica. The north end of the harbor, known as Place de l'Ile-de-Beauté, is very reminiscent of Italy, and it was in fact near the Customs House that Giuseppe Garibaldi, the hero of the Italian Revolution, was born in 1807.

Now follow the map to the **Church of St.-Martin and St.-Augustin** (6), a richly-decorated 17th-century baroque structure that contains a wonderful *Pietà* by Louis Bréa. It was here that Garibaldi was baptized.

Continue down the narrow alleyways to **Place Garibaldi** (7), a magnificent arcaded square in the 18th-century Savoyan style with a statue of Garibaldi.

Rue Pairolière leads to **Place St.-François** (8), where an animated outdoor fish market is held in the mornings. Nearby, on Boulevard Jean Jaurès, is the modern bus terminal *(Gare Routière)*, which you might be using for some of the other daytrips.

A stop at the **Lascaris Palace** (9) on Rue Droite is a "must" for visitors to Old Nice. This 17th-century mansion in the Genoese style has been well restored and furnished with period pieces along with fascinating displays of folk traditions. The palace is open from 9:30 a.m. to noon and 2:30–6 p.m., daily except Mondays and some holidays. It is closed in November.

Wander around to the **Cathedral of Ste.-Réparate** (10), a mid-17th-century classical building with a fine dome of glazed tiles and an 18th-century tower. Step inside to view the marvelous baroque carvings, then continue on to the **Church of St.-Jacques** (11), also known as the Gesù Church. Again, there is a truly magnificent baroque interior well worth inspecting. One other church you may be interested in is the Chapel of St.-Giaume (12), another splendid example of baroque decoration. From here follow the map back to Place Masséna.

Nice-Cimiez

When the Romans came to Nice around 150 B.C., they immediately moved inland to the heights of Cimiez, commanding a view of the surrounding countryside. Previously, this had been the site of a Ligurian fort. Known as *Cemenelum*, the Roman town rapidly grew to an estimated population of 20,000, and soon acquired the usual features including an arena, baths and so on. This gradually fell to ruin during the Barbarian invasions and was abandoned by the 6th century A.D.

Cimiez is now an attractive residential area with many splendid homes. During the 19th century it was especially favored by the British. Queen Victoria was a frequent winter guest, staying at the old Hôtel Régina at the top of the main boulevard, from which her statue still surveys the scene.

Scattered among the elegant homes and gardens on the Cimiez hill are two outstanding art museums, some fascinating Roman ruins, and an interesting monastery. This trip can easily be done in half a day, leaving the remaining hours to explore Old Nice.

GETTING THERE:

City buses *(Route #15)* leave from Place Masséna in downtown Nice (see map on page 273) very frequently for the starting point of this tour, the Marc Chagall Museum (1). Get off at the "Chagall" stop. The same bus continues on to the Roman Arena (2), whose stop is marked "Arènes."

Those starting at the **main train station** in Nice can easily walk to the Chagall Museum, using the city map offered by the tourist office as a guide. This should take about ten minutes but does involve a short, steep climb. Taxis are also available.

By car, start at the wide promenade between Place Garibaldi and the Palais des Congrès, then follow Boulevard Carabacel and Boulevard de Cimiez to the Chagall Museum. Ample parking is available everywhere.

In the Marc Chagall Museum

WHEN TO GO:

The Chagall Museum is closed on Tuesdays, while the Matisse and Archaeological museums close on Mondays, some holidays, Sunday mornings, and the month of November. The Franciscan Museum is closed on Sundays and holidays. Good weather will make this trip much more enjoyable.

FOOD AND DRINK:

There are virtually no restaurants in the Cimiez area, so plan on eating in Nice proper (see page 271). Snacks and drinks are available outdoors at or near each of the attractions.

TOURIST INFORMATION:

See page 272 for the location of tourist offices in Nice.

SUGGESTED TOUR:

The **Marc Chagall Museum** (1) was opened in 1973 as the only national museum dedicated to a then-living artist. It is devoted primarily to a series of large canvases created during the 1960s in which Chagall depicted his own unique version of stories from the Bible. These were donated to the State on the condition that the government would erect a suitable museum. Chagall's strange and colorful fantasies are enormously popular, attracting a great many visitors to this rather out-of-the-way spot. The museum itself is a delightful place—modern, well lit and beautifully arranged. In addition to the Biblical series, don't miss the sculptures, tapestries, stained-glass windows, graphic works and, especially, the outdoor mosaic of the prophet Elijah rising to Heaven. Chagall, who died nearby in 1985 at the age of 97, was himself a sometime visitor to the museum. It is open every day except Tuesdays, from 10 a.m. to 7 p.m. between July 1st and September 30th; and from 10 a.m. to 12:30 p.m. and 2–5:30 p.m. between October 1st through June 30th.

From here it is a pleasant but slightly uphill walk of a bit less than a mile to the **Roman Arena** (2), located in a public park. You can also get there by taking bus number 15 from the stop on the far side of Boulevard de Cimiez. One of the smallest amphitheaters in the Roman world, it probably dates from the 1st century A.D. and could seat some 5,000 spectators after its enlargement in the 3rd century. Although in poor condition, the arena is still used for occasional performances.

Stroll over to the charming 17th-century **Villa des Arènes** (3), the home of the **Matisse Museum**, whose collections span the entire career of the famous artist Henri Matisse. Born in 1869, Matisse spent much of his life around Nice and died in Cimiez in 1954. It is absolutely fascinating to see such a broad scope of artistic talent, covering such a long period of time, displayed in just a few rooms. Don't miss his sketches and models for the Chapel of the Rosary in Vence (see page 322). Close to this is the **Archaeological Museum** with its exhibits of local artifacts from the 7th century B.C. through the Roman era. Both museums are open from 10 a.m. to noon and 2:30–6:30 p.m. between May 2nd and September 30th; and from 10 a.m. to noon and 2–5 p.m. between October 1st and April 30th. They are closed on Mondays, some holidays, Sunday mornings, and November.

Step outside and visit the adjacent **Archaeological Site** (4), where you can wander around a large area of Roman ruins. The 3rd-century A.D. baths, one of which is incorrectly called the "Temple of Apollo," are possibly the best to be found in Gaul. Just south of the villa are the remains of a 5th-century Palaeo-Christian bascilica. A guide booklet in English is available at the museum entrance to help you understand the ongoing digs.

A short stroll through the park leads to the **Cimiez Monastery** (5), heavily rebuilt in the 19th century. This originally dates from the 16th century, when it replaced a 9th-century Benedictine monastery erected on the site of a temple of Diana. The church interior contains some remarkable works of art including both a 15th-century *Pietà* and a *Crucifixion* by Louis Bréa. Guided tours of the complex are conducted at 10 and 11 a.m. and 3, 4 and 5 p.m. daily, except Saturday afternoons, Sundays, and holidays.

Nice-Cimiez

500 Yards

The "Temple of Apollo"

The **Franciscan Museum** (6), next to this, tells the story of the order's life and works in several intriguing displays, with a re-created 17th-century monk's cell and an 18th-century chapel as highlights. A descriptive brochure in English is available. The museum is open from 10 a.m. to noon and 3–6 p.m., daily except on Sundays and holidays.

Be sure to stroll out into the magnificent terraced **gardens** that overlook the city and the Mediterrean. The view from here is just fabulous. Before leaving, you may want to stop at the little **cemetery** just north of the church. Both Matisse and his fellow artist Raoul Dufy are buried here. Return to the arena to take bus number 15 back to Nice proper. You can also take bus number 17 from the opposite corner, whichever comes first.

Monaco

Somewhat less than a square mile in size, the Principality of Monaco is an independent country that thrives on tourism. Its casino is world famous, and the palace adds a touch of theatricality that only a ministate could muster. The panoramic view from its heights is simply stupendous. Not surprisingly, the two towns of Monaco-Ville and Monte-Carlo, separated by a small harbor, offer more than their share of attractions.

The Grimaldi family has more or less ruled Monaco since 1308, when they bought it from the Genoese. They also once controlled other choice pieces of real estate along the coast, including Antibes and Cagnes. The last of their holdings, Menton, was sold to France in 1860 at the same time that Nice was ceded and the French-Italian border moved eastward. The family did, however, manage to hang on to Monaco, which was then practically bankrupt. Financial salvation came with the opening of the Principality's first successful casino in 1865 and the arrival of the railroad in 1868. Growth since then has been spectacular, with much of the land now covered by concrete highrises. Gambling is no longer the major industry, having been replaced by tourism, conventions, and more traditional businesses.

Although it is not a part of France, French money is used in Monaco along with its own coinage. There are no customs to go through between the two countries; in fact the border is practically invisible. As you probably know, the lucky *Monégasques* pay no taxes.

GETTING THERE:

Trains connect Monaco/Monte-Carlo with virtually all coastal towns along the Riviera at frequent intervals. Service operates until late evening. From Nice the ride takes about 20 minutes.

By car, Monaco is best reached via the N-7 road, the famous *Moyenne Corniche*. It is 11 miles northeast of Nice. There are many underground parking lots—just follow the "P" signs.

GETTING AROUND:

Two-dimensional maps make Monaco seem like a walker's paradise. It isn't. Most of the Principality is extremely hilly, so much so that public elevators have been installed between some streets. You will probably wind up using buses for part of the walking tour. These run quite frequently, with route maps at the bus stops. Fares may be paid directly to the driver.

WHEN TO GO:

Monaco is always open for business, but some of the sights may be closed in winter or on major holidays. Visits to the Prince's Palace can be made from June through September.

FOOD AND DRINK:

Sumptuous dining in Monaco can be a very expensive proposition. Those with thinner wallets will find adequate meals in the many bistro-type places near the station, by the harbor, and in the alleyways behind the Prince's Palace. Some outstanding choices are:

In the Old Town:

Castelroc (in front of the Prince's Palace) Monégasque specialties, with outdoor tables overlooking the palace. Open for lunch only. X: Sat., Dec., Jan. $$

L'Aurore (8 Rue Princesse Marie-de-Lorraine, 2 blocks north of the Oceanographic Museum) Italian specialties including pizza. X: Dec., Jan. $ and $$

L'Estragon (6 Rue Emile de Loth, behind the cathedral) Pleasant budget dining with outdoor seating. X: Fri., Dec., Jan. $

Saint-Nicolas (6 Rue de l'Eglise, on the west side of the cathedral) Traditional Monégasque and French cooking at modest prices. X: Thurs., Feb. $

In Monte-Carlo:

Le Louis XV (in the Hôtel de Paris, across from the casino) The finest and most luxurious dining imaginable. For reservations phone 93-50-80-80. X: Tues., Wed. $$$+

Le Grill (in the Hôtel de Paris, across from the casino) On the rooftop of a sumptuous hotel, an experience to remember. For reservations call 93-50-80-80. X: Late May to mid-June. $$$+

Le Saint-Benoît (10 ter, Av. de la Costa, 5 blocks southwest of the tourist office) Noted for its seafood and grilled meats. X: Mon., Dec. $$$

Toula (20 Blvd. de Suisse, 4 blocks southwest of the tourist office) Superb Italian cuisine. X: Sun., Jan. $$

The Prince's Palace

Rampoldi (3 Ave. des Spélugues, 1 block north of the casino) A chic place for fine Italian and French cuisine. X: Nov. $$$

Polpetta (2 Rue Paradis, 5 blocks southwest of the tourist office) Fine Italian cuisine in a romantic atmosphere. X: Tues., late Oct., mid-Feb. to mid-Mar. $$

TOURIST INFORMATION:

The Monaco tourist office, phone 93-30-87-01, is at 2 Boulevard des Moulins in Monte-Carlo, near the casino. They can make hotel reservations for you.

SUGGESTED TOUR:

Leave the **train station** (1) and walk straight ahead to Place d'Armes. From here you can climb up the Rampe Major to the **Old Town** *(Monaco-Ville)*, perched high above the port on a promonotory rock *(Le Rocher)*. Alternatively, you can take a bus that drops you off a few level blocks from the first attraction. However you get there, you will have the first of many spectacular views.

The **Prince's Palace** (2), surveying the entire domain, is open to tourists from June through September, when the reigning prince is not in residence. Guided tours are then conducted daily between 9:30 a.m. and 6:30 p.m. Even if you miss this, however, you can still enjoy the slightly ludicrous operetta-like changing-of-the-guard ceremony

The View from the Old Town

held daily at 11:55 a.m. in front of the palace. Several outdoor cafés are grouped around here so you can watch in comfort. The palace itself was begun in 1215 and greatly altered during the ensuing centuries. Besides being home to Prince Rainier III, whose wife, Grace Kelly, was tragically killed in a car accident in 1982, it also houses the small but interesting **Napoleonic Museum**. Step inside to see the many personal effects of the great French leader along with items relating to the history of Monaco. It is open daily from 9:30 a.m. to 6:30 p.m., with somewhat shorter hours in the off season, but closed on Mondays and during November.

Several of the narrow lanes in Monaco-Ville are now reserved for pedestrians. Stroll down Rue Basse to the **Historial des Princes de Monaco** (3), a beautifully arranged wax museum that depicts the history of the Grimaldi family in 24 life-size scenes. The costumes are authentic and were donated by the family. Visits may be made from 9:30 a.m. to 6:30 or 7:30 p.m., with shorter hours off season, every day except in December and January.

Continuing down the street, you will pass the **Misericord Chapel** (4), a 17th-century structure whose interior features a fine high altar in polychrome marble and a splendid statue of Christ, which is carried through the Old Town on Good Fridays.

The **Cathedral of Monaco** (5), built at the end of the 19th century in a somewhat ostentatious Neo-Romanesque style, reflects the sudden prosperity brought about by the opening of the casino. It inherited several excellent works of art from the 13th-century church that stood on the same site, including a superb 16th-century altarpiece by Louis Bréa in the right transept. The tomb of Princess Grace is among those of the princes of Monaco.

A stroll through the lovely St.-Martin Gardens leads to the renowned **Oceanographic Museum** (6), considered to be the best of its kind in the world. Now directed by the noted underwater explorer Jacques Cousteau, it was founded in 1910 by Prince Albert I, who had a passion for the sea. The large aquarium in its basement is a fascinating treat for all visitors, while the upper floors are devoted to the many aspects of oceanography. The museum is open daily from 9 or 9:30 a.m. to 7 p.m., and until 9 p.m. during July and August.

Now follow the map back to Place d'Armes and continue on past the bustling harbor. This is a good place to stop for a rest as there are many outdoor cafés along the waterfront. From here the route leads uphill along Avenue d'Ostende to the town of **Monte Carlo**. You may prefer to take a bus and avoid the rather steep climb.

The **Casino of Monte-Carlo** (7) is undoubtedly the most famous gambling establishment in the world. The older section of this highly elaborate structure was designed in 1878 by Charles Garnier, the architect of the Paris Opéra—which it somewhat resembles. To your left as you enter are the gambling rooms, whose extravagant décor is worth seeing even if you're not a gambler. Admission to the first section requires only a passport to prove that you are over 21 and not a local citizen. An entrance fee is charged for the more exclusive—and much more intriguing—*salons* beyond that. Don't miss the bar with its fantastic ceiling depicting naked ladies puffing on cigars. The casino also contains a magnificent opera house, which can only be seen by attending a performance.

A short walk through the gardens brings you to the tourist office on Boulevard des Moulins. From here you may want to make a little side trip to the **National Museum** (8), housed in a charming mansion also designed by Charles Garnier. Appropriately enough for a toy nation, the enchanting displays here feature hundreds of dolls and mechanical toys *(automata)* in exquisite settings. To reach the museum just follow the map and take the elevator down the hill. It is open from 10 a.m. to 12:15 p.m. and 2:30–6:30 p.m., daily except on some holidays.

From the corner near the tourist office you can take a bus to the next attraction, the **Exotic Gardens** *(Jardin Exotique)* (9). It is also possible to get there on foot, but the walk is long and boring. Clinging to the side of a cliff overlooking the entire Principality, the gardens contain literally thousands of varieties of weird and wonderful plants, es-

In the Exotic Gardens

pecially a broad range of cacti from Africa and Latin America. Near the bottom of this are the **Observatory Caves** *(Grottes de l'Observatoire)*, where prehistoric man once lived. Guided tours are conducted through this magic world of stalactites and stalagmites at frequent intervals, a great treat for the energetic who don't mind all the hoofing involved.

Back at the entrance to the gardens is the **Museum of Prehistoric Anthropology** (11) with its collections of ancient relics. One combined ticket covers the gardens, caves and museum. They are open from 9 a.m. to 7 p.m. in season, closing at sunset out of season. The museum closes at 5:30 p.m. in the off season. The entire trio is open every day except May 1st and November 19th.

The easiest way to get back to the station is by taking a bus to Place d'Armes. You could also walk part of the way, then take the escalator and elevator down to the port.

Menton

The last town before the Italian border, Menton is a pleasantly picturesque resort blessed with the mildest climate on the Riviera. Long favored by British vacationers, it has become somewhat of a cultural center in recent years. The old quarter, remarkably well preserved, exudes a quiet charm. Menton is famous for its citrus fruits, particularly lemons. It makes a good half-day trip since all of the sights can be seen in a few hours; unless you would rather linger and enjoy yourself—not a bad idea.

GETTING THERE:

Trains link Menton with other coastal towns on the Riviera at frequent intervals, with returns until mid-evening. From Nice, the trip takes about 30 minutes.

By car, Menton is on the N-7 road, 17 miles northeast of Nice.

WHEN TO GO:

Sunny Menton may be savored at any time, but note that the museums are closed on Mondays, Tuesdays and holidays.

FOOD AND DRINK:

This old resort offers a good selection of restaurants and cafés, especially along the Promenade du Soleil and near the port. Some choices are:

Chez Francine (1 Quai Bonaparte, just north of the port) Noted for its excellent seafood. X: Tues. in winter. $$$

La Calanque (13 Square Victoria, just north of the port) Traditional local cuisine in a lovely setting. X: Tues. eve., Wed., early Nov., Jan. $$

Roc Amadour (1 Square Victoria, just north of the port) Traditional cuisine, with a nice terrace. X: Mon. $$

L'Artisan Gourmand (32 Rue St.-Michel, 3 blocks west of the Jean Cocteau Museum) Specializing in vegetable dishes, but not exclusively. X: Sun. $$

Les Arches, Chez Diana (31 Quai Bonaparte, just north of the port) A popular and very lively bistro, with French and Italian dishes. X: Wed. $

Au Pistou (2 Rue Fossan, 2 blocks east of the Town Hall) An excellent value. X: Mon., Nov. $

TOURIST INFORMATION:

The local tourist office, phone 93-57-57-00, is at 8 Avenue Boyer, near the casino.

SUGGESTED TOUR:

Leave the **train station** (1) and follow the map through the lovely Biovès Garden along Avenue Boyer. Turn around for a splendid view of the nearby mountains framed by exotic trees. Along the way you will pass the impressive **Palais d'Europe** (2), a cultural center in the *Belle Époque* style that houses the tourist office.

Continue on past the casino to the **Promenade du Soleil**, an elegant avenue running alongside the beach. Follow this to the **Municipal Market** brimming with morning activity in an old Victorian structure. The **Jean Cocteau Museum** (3) lies just beyond this, housed in a small fortification erected during the 17th century by the rulers of Monaco, which once owned Menton. Cocteau, who died in 1963, was primarily known as a talented poet, writer, film maker and general leader in French avant-garde circles. His reputation as a graphic artist is less secure, but the works displayed here are nonetheless fascinating. There is also an outstanding drawing of him by Picasso. The museum is open on Wednesdays through Sundays, from 10 a.m. to noon and 2–6 p.m., with slightly shorter hours from November through March.

Stroll out on the **Quai Napoléon III Jetty** (4), climbing the steps next to the museum for a marvelous view of the Old Town. When you get to the lighthouse at the end, descend to the lower level and return.

Continue along the port and climb the steps to Quai Bonaparte, a broad street supported by arches. From here you can make a short side trip to the **Tropical Garden** *(Jardin Botanique)* (5, off the map) in the suburb of Garavan. Turn left on Chemin St.-Jacques to enter the magnificent gardens, located one-half mile from the Italian border. They are open from February through September, daily from 9 a.m. to noon and 3–8 p.m., closing at sunset when earlier.

Back at the port, climb the massive staircase to the **Church of St.-Michel** (6) in the Old Town. Facing a charming little Italianate square where outdoor concerts are given in August, the 17th-century baroque church has a richly decorated interior that should be seen. At

View of the Old Town from the Jetty

the end of the square stands another interesting church, the Chapel of the Pénitents-Blancs.

Now follow Rue du Vieux Château to the **Old Cemetery** (7), built on the site of a former castle, which offers splendid views from its grounds. Return via Montée du Souvenir and descend the steps as far as Rue Longue. A right leads through a picturesque neighborhood to the new town.

Stroll down Rue St.-Michel and turn right to the **Municipal Museum** (8). The displays here are concerned with local history, folk art and archaeology; and may be seen from 10 a.m. to noon and 3–6 p.m., daily except on Mondays, Tuesdays and holidays. The hours are shorter in winter.

Continue on to the **Town Hall** *(Hôtel de Ville)* (9), which features a fantastic Marriage Room wildly decorated by Jean Cocteau in 1957. Step inside and ask to see it. The doors are open from 9 a.m. to noon and 3–6 p.m. (2–6 p.m. in winter), daily except Saturdays, Sundays and holidays.

While in Menton you may be interested in visiting the **Palais Carnolès Museum** (10, off the map), a walk of nearly a mile from the casino. There is also bus service to it. Devoted to the fine arts, and located in a gorgeous old mansion once used by the princes of Monaco, it is noted for its exceptionally lovely **gardens**. Visits may be made on Wednesdays through Sundays, from 10 a.m. to noon and 2–6 p.m., but not on holidays.

Cagnes-sur-Mer

Primarily a modern seaside resort, Cagnes-sur-Mer offers two magnificent attractions that make a daytrip there highly worthwhile. First, there is Haut-de-Cagnes, an ancient walled village perched high atop a hill overlooking the Riviera. The other lure is Les Collettes, the enchanting country villa of the famous Impressionist painter Pierre-Auguste Renoir. Both can be seen in a few hours, making this an ideal half-day trip. You may, however, want to linger there and have dinner at one of the attractive restaurants in the upper town. This trip could be combined with one to Antibes or Cannes.

GETTING THERE:

Trains connect Cagnes-sur-Mer with other coastal Riviera towns at frequent intervals, with returns until late evening. Not all expresses stop at Cagnes.

By car, take the coastal road or the A-8. Cagnes is 8 miles west of Nice.

WHEN TO GO:

Cagnes may be visited at most any time, but note the opening times of the castle and the Renoir villa. Avoid coming between mid-October and mid-November.

FOOD AND DRINK:

The walled hilltop village of Haut-de-Cagnes offers a number of charming restaurants and outdoor cafés. Among the better choices are:

> **Le Cagnard** (Rue du Pontis-Long, 2 blocks southwest of the castle) A famous old inn with classic cuisine. X: Thurs. lunch, Nov. $$$

> **Josy-Jo** (2 Rue Planastel, near the Chapel of Notre-Dame) Excellent uncomplicated cuisine in pleasing surroundings. X: Aug. $$$

Les Peintres (71 Montée de la Bourgade, 3 blocks southeast of the castle) This rustic and highly romantic restaurant doubles as an art gallery. Inventive variations on classic cuisine. X: Wed. $$

Le Jimmy's (Place du Château, just north of the castle) Charming outdoor tables, a good place for snacks or drinks. $

TOURIST INFORMATION:

The local tourist office, phone 93-20-61-64, is at 6 Boulevard Maréchal Juin in the lower town.

SUGGESTED TOUR:

Stepping out of the **train station** (1) may leave you with that awful "what-ever-brought-me-*here*" feeling. Don't despair. A few minute's walk past the highway intersection and tacky modern developments will bring you to the foot of one of the nicest hilltowns on the Riviera. You could also take a taxi, which would eliminate the interesting but somewhat strenuous climb.

Follow the map up the steep Montée de la Bourgade to **Haut-de-Cagnes**, the well-preserved medieval village whose history as a fortress dates from pre-Roman times. Overlooking the mouth of the Var River, which until 1860 was the Italian border, this has long been a strategically important stronghold.

The present **Castle** *(Château)* (2), around which the village developed, was originally begun in 1302 by Rainier I Grimaldi, ruler of Monaco and other Riviera towns. Transformed into an elegant residence in 1620, it remained in the Grimaldi family until 1789. The château now contains two museums, one of which is devoted to everything you could possibly want to know about olive cultivation. Stroll through the delightful inner courtyard and visit the 17th-century banqueting hall on the main floor, noted for its *trompe l'oeil* fresco of the *Fall of Phaeton*, a triumph of contrived perspective.

The rest of the castle in an **art museum**, focusing on modern works of Mediterranean inspiration. One room contains an unusual display of 40 portraits of Susy Solidor, a popular French singer, each by a different well-known 20th-century painter. Be sure to climb to the top of the tower for a spectacular view. An exhibition of contemporary art from all over the world is held in the château during the summer months. The castle is open daily from Easter through mid-October, from 10 a.m. to noon and 2:30–7 p.m.; and during the rest of the year daily except Tuesdays, from 10 a.m. to noon and 2–5 p.m. It is closed on some holidays and from mid-October to mid-November.

An amble up and down the stepped passageways within the walls—too small to be shown on the map—leads to serendipitous discover-

Chemin des Collettes

6 ▪
Museum

Ave. Marcel Pagnol

Ave. des Tuilières

Route de la Gaude

Pas. A. Renoir

Chemin des Salles

Ave. Auguste Renoir

Ave. Cyrille Besset

4

3   2

Rue Jean Feraud

Ave. A. France

Ave. de l'Église

Montée de la Bourgade

5

HAUT-DE-CAGNES

Rue des Combes

R. Gén. Bérenger

Ave.

Ave. de Verdun

Blvd du Mar. Juin

info.

TO NICE ►

N

Ave. de la Gare

Cagnes-sur-Mer

Route de la Pénétrante

Autoroute (Elevated)

A-8

Station

1

Ave. de la Gare

400 Yards

Renoir's Studio at Les Collettes

ies. Find your way to **Place du Château** (3), a delightful spot with outdoor cafés. Nearby is the **Chapel of Notre-Dame-de-Protection** (4), a 14th-century structure whose charming setting inspired Renoir. Step inside to see the primitive 16th-century frescoes.

Return to the château and visit the **Church of St.-Pierre** (5), whose double-nave interior contains some interesting works of art.

Follow the map downhill to the lower town. From here it is a relatively short walk to Renoir's country villa, **Les Collettes** (6), where the great painter spent the last 12 years of his life. Now housing the **Renoir Souvenir Museum**, it has been faithfully restored to the condition it was in when he died there in 1919. Although Renoir was very ill during his last years, he continued to paint from a wheelchair with brushes tied to his fingers. This touching scene is lovingly evoked in the studio, and throughout the property. The few works on display are, of course, minor pieces, but that in no way distracts from the wonderful experience of a visit here. The museum is open from April through October, daily from 2:30–6:30 p.m.; and from November through March on Wednesdays through Mondays, from 2–5 p.m. Don't miss seeing this.

Antibes

Dating from the 4th century B.C., the ancient Greek trading post of *Antipolis* grew up to become the delightfully unpretentious Antibes of today. The narrow streets of its picturesque Old Town are an open invitation for pleasant wanderings, particularly to the seaside promenade and its castle, which today houses the fabulous Picasso Museum. Ambitious walkers, or those with cars, can also explore the lovely Cap d'Antibes, a place of great natural beauty.

A trip to Antibes can easily be combined in the same day with one to Cannes or Cagnes-sur-Mer.

GETTING THERE:

Trains link Antibes with other Riviera coastal towns quite frequently, with returns until late evening. The ride from Nice takes about 15 minutes.

By car, use the N-7 or N-98 road. Antibes is 15 miles southwest of Nice.

WHEN TO GO:

The Picasso Museum, which should not be missed, is closed on Tuesdays, some major holidays, and during November. Good weather is essential for a pleasant side trip to Cap d'Antibes.

FOOD AND DRINK:

Antibes has a broad range of restaurants in all price brackets. Some excellent choices are:

Bacon (Blvd. de Bacon, near Pointe Bacon) Renowned for its fresh seafood. X: Sun. eve., Mon., mid-Nov. through Jan. $$$

La Marguerite (11 Rue Sadi Carnot, 2 blocks southeast of the train station) Inventive contemporary cuisine in elegant surroundings. X: Mon., Tues. lunch from mid-June to mid-Sept., Sun. eve. off season, early May. $$$

L'Auberge Provençale (61 Place Nationale, 3 blocks west of the Picasso Museum) A charming country inn with modern variations on traditional cuisine. X: Mon. $$

Restaurant du Bastion (1 Ave. du Général Maizière, next to the Archaeological Museum) Regional specialties in a picturesque garden restaurant. X: Mon., Sun. eve. off season. $$

L'Oursin (16 Rue de la République, 6 blocks west of the Picasso Museum) A very popular place for seafood. X: Sun. eve., Mon., Aug. $$

Le Dauphin d'Or (16 Blvd. d'Aguillon, 5 blocks northwest of the Picasso Museum) A bright, unpretentious place with excellent seafood and other dishes. X: Sun. eve., Wed., late Jan. $$

Le Caméo (Place Nationale, 3 blocks west of the Picasso Museum) A friendly inn with good seafood. X: Sun. eve., Tues. $$

Josse (8 Blvd. James Wyllie, on the way to Pointe Bacon) Good-value dining in a small hotel. X: Wed. except July & Aug., mid-Oct. to mid-Mar. $

TOURIST INFORMATION:

The local tourist office, phone 93-33-95-64, is at 11 Place du Général de Gaulle.

SUGGESTED TOUR:

Leave the **train station** (1) and follow the town map, passing the tourist office on Place du Général de Gaulle. Rue de la République leads to Place Nationale. You are now entering the **Old Town** with its picturesque maze of narrow streets.

Thread your way through past the colorful market place on Cours Masséna to the **Grimaldi Castle** (2), home of the marvelous **Picasso Museum**. Built between the 13th and 16th centuries, this medieval stronghold overlooking the sea was for centuries home to a branch of the ruling Grimaldi family of Monaco. After seeing service as a governor's residence and later as an army barracks, the castle was bought by the town after World War I for use as a museum.

In 1946, Pablo Picasso was invited to use part of it as a studio. During the months that followed he produced some of his greatest works, many of which the artist later donated to the museum in memory of the happy times he had there. Although primarily devoted to Picasso, the museum also displays works by other contemporary artists along with some archaeological pieces. To wander through its well-arranged rooms and passageways is a sheer joy. Don't miss the sculpture-filled terrace overlooking the sea. The museum is open daily from 10 a.m. to noon and 2–6 p.m., but closed on Tuesdays, some holidays, and during November.

PORT

TO NICE

Station

Ave. de la Libération

Ave. du 11 Novembre

Soleau

Pasteur

Ave. Thiers

Ave.

Mistral

Rue F.

Ave. de Verdun

Blvd. de l'Aiguillon

Rue Robert

Ave.

Rue Vauban

Pl. des Martyrs

Rue Thuret

Info.

Pl. du Gén. De Gaulle

Rue de la République

Pl. Nationale

Rue Sade

Masséna

③

②

Rue James Close

Rue Fersen

Cours

Prom. Amiral de Grasse

N

Blvd. Albert

Blvd. du Mar. Foch

④

MEDITERRANEAN

Antibes
Town

⌐————— 200 Yards —————⌐

SEE NEXT MAP FOR
CONTINUATION

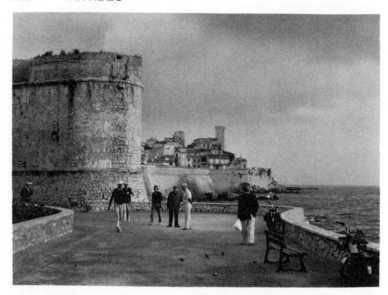

A Game of Boules *at the Bastion St.-André*

The **Church of the Immaculate Conception** (3), next door, is still referred to as a cathedral although it lost that status as far back as 1244. Much of the present structure is from the 17th century, but the 12th-century belfry is original. Step inside to see the noted altarpiece in the south transept, attributed to Louis Bréa.

Now meander through the oldest parts of Antibes and follow the 16th-century ramparts to the **Archaeological Museum** (4) in the 17th-century Bastion of St.-André. The collections here, covering some 4,000 years of local history, include jewelry, coins and pottery; among other finds. They may be seen from 10 a.m. to noon and 2–6 p.m. (7 p.m. in summer), daily except on Tuesdays, some holidays, and during November.

Ambitious walkers have a real treat ahead of them. Turn to the area map and follow the coastal road past the public beach to **Pointe Bacon** on Cap d'Antibes (5), a distance of slightly over one mile. The views from here are marvelous, encompassing the Bay of Angels as far as Nice. Those with cars can, of course, drive there and continue completely around the wooded peninsula, long a haunt of the very rich.

Retrace your steps and turn into a stepped path called Chemin du Calvaire. This leads uphill past some Stations of the Cross to the **La Garoupe Plateau**, which offers a sweeping panorama of the seacoast, extending from Cannes to Nice, with part of the Alps in the back-

Antibes
Area

500 Yards

TO NICE Station

Ave. R. Soleau

ANTIBES TOWN

Info.

Rue de la République

TO CANNES

Blvd. du Prés. Wilson

Blvd. Mar. Foch

Blvd. Albert I

SEE OTHER MAP
FOR DETAIL

N

Blvd. Mar. Leclerc

MEDITERRANEAN

Ave. des Sables

Blvd. du Cap

Blvd. James Wyllie

Chemin du Calvaire

Ave. H. Duvernois

Pointe
Bacon

Blvd. de Bacon

The Chapel of Notre-Dame-de-la-Garoupe

ground. The delightful **Chapel of Notre-Dame-de-la-Garoupe** (6), dating in part from the Middle Ages, has a strange and wonderful interior. Its walls are covered with touchingly naïve ex-votos offered by sailors and others in thanks for deliverance from some awful fate. You could literally spend hours examining the tales they so graphically depict. The chapel is open from 10:30 a.m. to 12:30 p.m. and 2–5 p.m., with shorter hours in the winter. Nearby is a **lighthouse** *(phare)* (7), which may also be visited. The plateau can also be reached by car.

The route shown on the map takes you past the interesting **Thuret Gardens** (8), a research center for exotic trees and plants. These may be seen from 8 a.m. to 12:30 p.m. and 2–5:30 p.m., daily except on Saturdays, Sundays, and some holidays.

Return to Antibes via Boulevard du Cap. The route indicated on the town map follows the seacoast all the way to the train station, although it is shorter to go by way of Boulevard Albert I.

Cannes

Cannes was just a sleepy fishing village until that fateful day in 1834 when Lord Brougham, an English ex-chancellor en route to Italy, was turned back at the then-nearby border on account of an outbreak of cholera. Determined to have his vacation in the sun anyway, he built a villa near Cannes and spent the next 34 winters there, encouraging other aristocrats to follow suit. By the time the railway arrived in 1863, the town's destiny was sealed and the rush to build hotels began.

What was once upper class has now become commercial chic, existing for sensual pleasure. Cannes' main thoroughfare—La Croisette—is lined with luxury hotels, its harbor a flotilla of sumptuous yachts. This is truly the playground of the rich and famous. Fortunately, there are other diversions as well—the nearby Lérins Islands, the Old Port and the tiny medieval quarter each offer their own special charms.

A daytrip to Cannes could be combined with one to Antibes or Cagnes-sur-Mer; or by really rushing, with one to Grasse.

GETTING THERE:

Trains connect Cannes with other Riviera coastal towns, with frequent service operating until late evening. The ride from Nice takes about 30 minutes. Cannes also has direct TGV service with Paris, a ride of $6\frac{1}{2}$ hours.

By car, Cannes is best reached via the A-8 Autoroute or the N-7 road. It is 21 miles southwest of Nice.

WHEN TO GO:

You can enjoy yourself in Cannes at any time. It may be crowded during festivals, but that's part of the fun. Boat service to the Lérins Islands is excellent from June through September, but reduced the rest of the year.

FOOD AND DRINK:

Cannes has an enormous selection of restaurants and cafés, not all of which are expensive. Some of the better choices are:

Royal Gray (in the Hôtel Gray d'Albion, 38 Rue des Serbes, 3 blocks northeast of the Convention Center) Luxurious dining in an elegant modern décor. For reservations phone 93-68-54-54. X: Sun., Mon. except in July and Aug., Feb. $$$+

La Palme d'Or (in the Hôtel Martinez at 73 La Croisette, 10 blocks southeast of the Convention Center) Innovative modern cuisine in a 1930s setting. For reservations phone 93-98-30-18. X: Mon., Tues. lunch, Feb. $$$+

La Rescator (7 Rue du Maréchal-Joffre, 3 blocks north of the Boat Terminal) Reliable contemporary cuisine in elegant surroundings. X: Sun. $$$

La Poêle d'Or (23 Rue des États-Unis, 4 blocks east of the Convention Center) A good value in the luxury category. X: Mon., Tues. lunch. $$$

Le Croquant (18 Blvd. Jean-Hibert, 3 blocks south of the La Castre Museum) Excellent regional cuisine from the Périgord. X: Mon. $$

Au Mal Assis (15 Quai St.-Pierre, 3 blocks east of the La Castre Museum) A colorful large bistro with superb seafood. $$

Caveau 30 (45 Rue Félix-Faure, 3 blocks northwest of the Boat Terminal) An old-fashioned bistro with sidewalk tables and good food. $$

L'Olivier (9 Rue Rouguière, 3 blocks north of the Boat Terminal) A good value for classic Provençal cuisine. X: Mon. $$

La Coquille (65 Rue Félix-Faure, 3 blocks northwest of the Boat Terminal) An old bistro noted for its fine seafood. $$

Le Monaco (15 Rue du 24-Août, 2 blocks southwest of the train station) A popular neighborhood restaurant with good food at modest prices. X: Sun. $

Au Bec Fin (12 Rue du 24-Août, 2 blocks southwest of the train station) An unpretentious place for good home cooking. X: Sat. eve., Sun. $

La Pizza (3 Quai St.-Pierre, 3 blocks east of the La Castre Museum) A large and lively pizzeria. $

TOURIST INFORMATION:

The local tourist office, phone 93-99-19-77, is in the train station. There is another office, phone 93-39-24-53, in the Convention Center by the port.

SUGGESTED TOUR:

The **train station** (1) has a tourist office upstairs, reached by an outdoor staircase. Stop there for a map that lists the schedule of boats to the Lérins Islands along with other useful information. Now follow

View of Le Suquet from the Harbor

Rue des Serbes to **La Croisette**, an elegant seaside promenade of world renown.

From here you may want to take a delightful walk along the bay to the **Palm Beach Casino** (2, off the map), a distance of less than a mile and a half. Along the way you will pass beaches, gardens, and several opulent marinas.

Returning along the sandy beach will bring you to the modern **Convention Center** *(Palais des Festivals)* (3), home to the famous International Film Festival held each year in May, as well as many other events. Stroll through the lovely gardens behind it and over to the **Boat Terminal** *(Gare Maritime)* (4), where you can take an enjoyable cruise to the nearby **Lérins Islands** (5). For many, this is the highlight of a visit to Cannes.

There are two islands in the group, and it is quite possible to visit both. Most tourists, however, are content to explore just the first, **Sainte-Marguerite**, reached in 15 minutes. About two miles long by a half-mile in width, it is mostly covered with a dense forest cut through with charming pathways. A massive 17th-century **fortress** lies near the dock. Within its forbidding walls you can visit the prison cell of the enigmatic "Man in the Iron Mask," confined there for 16 years by Louis XIV, along with those of several Protestants locked up after the revocation of the Edict of Nantes. There is also a small **museum of marine archaeology**. Returning to the docks, you can either take a boat back to Cannes or continue on for another 15-minute cruise to

Disembarking at Ste.-Marguerite

the second island, **Saint-Honorat**. Considerably smaller but more enchanting, it contains an ancient 11th-century fortified monastery that
may be explored. The newer Abbaye de Lérins, still in use, opens its
church and museum to visitors. Boat service to both islands operates
quite frequently from June through September, with reduced schedules the rest of the year.

Back in Cannes, step over to the **Allées de la Liberté** (6), alive with
a flower market in the mornings and games of *boules* in the afternoons. From here it is a short climb up to the old part of town known
as **Le Suquet**. Follow the map to the **La Castre Museum** (7), a former
citadel containing an interesting—and highly eclectic—assemblage of
art, antiquities, and items of ethnographic interest from around the
world. It is open daily except on Tuesdays, from 10 a.m. to noon and
2–5 p.m. (3–7 p.m. in summer). The medieval tower next to it may be
climbed by asking at the museum entrance.

Continue around to the 16th- and 17th-century **Church of Notre-
Dame-de-l'Espérance** (8), a late-Gothic structure featuring some fine
polychrome statues. The route now leads downhill through the old
town to the port. Quai St.-Pierre is a particularly colorful spot with its
popular restaurants and outdoor cafés. Wander around the lively old
market area and follow Rue Meynadier—the former Main Street when
Cannes was still a village—back in the direction of the train station.

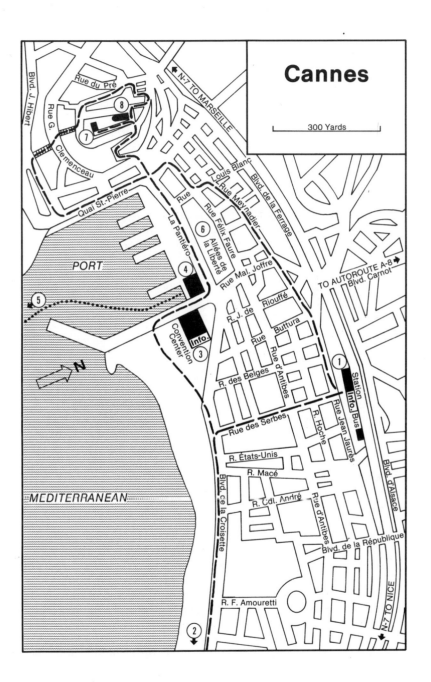

Cannes

300 Yards

Blvd. J. Hibert

Rue du Pré

Rue G.

Clemenceau

⑧

⑦

Quai St.-Pierre

N-7 TO MARSEILLE

Louis Blanc

Blvd. de la Ferrage

Rue Meynadier

Rue

La Panthéro

Rue Félix Faure

Allées de la Liberté

⑥

PORT

④

⑤

Convention Center

Info. ③

Rue Mal. Joffre

R. J. de Riouffé

Rue Buttura

Rue d'Antibes

TO AUTOROUTE A-8

Blvd. Carnot

N

R. des Belges

① Station

Info./Bus

Rue des Serbes

R. Hoche

Rue Jean Jaurès

Blvd. d'Alsace

R. États-Unis

R. Macé

R. Cdl. André

Rue d'Antibes

MEDITERRANEAN

Blvd. de la Croisette

Blvd. de la République

N-7 TO NICE

R. F. Amouretti

②

Grasse

The medieval hill town of Grasse is widely known as the undisputed world center of perfume essences. A visit to one of its scent factories is a must, of course, but don't miss out on exploring the enchanting town itself. A veritable maze of ancient alleyways and half-hidden passages wind their way along the hillside, opening here and there for magnificent views. With its interesting cathedral and three small but highly intriguing museums, Grasse offers enough attractions to entertain you for an entire day, although it is possible to combine this daytrip with one to Cannes.

GETTING THERE:

Buses to Grasse depart fairly frequently from the east side of the train station in Cannes, easily reached from other Riviera towns (see page 303). The bus ride takes about 45 minutes, with return service running until early evening. There is also direct bus service with Nice.

By car, take the N-85 north from Cannes, a distance of 10 miles. Grasse is 26 miles from Nice. Park by the bus station.

WHEN TO GO:

At least one museum is closed on Sundays, another on Tuesdays, and some in November.

FOOD AND DRINK:

Grasse has an adequate number of rather modest restaurants, some good choices being:

> **Amphitryon** (16 Blvd. Victor-Hugo, 2 blocks west of the Fragonard Villa Museum) Light classical cuisine from the Southwest of France in a small traditional restaurant. X: Sun., holidays, Aug. $$

> **Maître Boscq** (13 Rue de Fontette, 2 blocks east of Place aux Aires) A tiny and very romantic restaurant with traditional local cooking. X: Sun., Mon. off season, Nov. $

Place aux Aires

La Voute (Rue du Thouron, 2 blocks west of Place aux Aires) Provençal cuisine. $
Crêperie Bretonne (3 Rue des Fabreries, just southeast of Place aux Aires) Delicious crêpes in a colorful setting. $

TOURIST INFORMATION:

The local tourist office, phone, 93-36-03-56, is on Place de la Foux, near the bus station.

SUGGESTED TOUR:

Leave the **bus station** *(Gare Routère)* (1) and follow the map past the tourist office to **Place aux Aires** (2). This thoroughly delightful open area has some fine arcaded 18th-century houses and several sidewalk cafés arranged around a bubbling fountain. A lively outdoor market is held there in the mornings.

Follow the map down Rue des 4 Coins and descend the steep Rue de Fontette to Place Jean-Jaurès. Continue on, trying not to get lost in the tiny alleyways, to the 12th-century **Cathedral of Notre-Dame-du-Puy** (3), heavily restored in the 17th century. Step inside to view the two paintings by Rubens in the south aisle, an altarpiece attributed to Louis Bréa and, above the sacristy door, one of Fragonard's rare religious works, the *Washing of the Feet*.

The square in front of the cathedral has an impressive square tower from the 12th century. Stroll around to **Place du 24 Août** (4), which offers a sweeping panorama of the countryside.

A series of steps leads to Rue Mirabeau and the **Museum of Provençal Art and History** (5). Housed in an 18th-century mansion, its splendid collections are mostly concerned with the folk arts and traditions of the region, although there are also some fine paintings and archaeological displays. These may be seen on Mondays through Saturdays, from 10 a.m. to noon and 2–6 p.m., closing earlier in winter. A bargain joint ticket is available.

Grasse produces most of the world's supply of the essences used in perfume manufacturing. This industry had its origin in the 16th-century fashion for scented gloves, which were made locally. It grew with the nearby cultivation of roses, jasmin and other plants; with more exotic ingredients now being imported from all over the world. Several of the larger factories offer free guided tours explaining their operations. One of the most interesting of these is the **Parfumerie Fragonard** (6), conveniently located a few steps away, whose tours in English are given daily at frequent intervals.

Now wander past a lovely park to the **Fragonard Villa Museum** (7). If that name seems common around here, it is because the famous painter Jean-Honoré Fragonard was born in Grasse in 1732. Although he lived most of his life in Paris, he returned to his hometown during the Revolution and spent a year in this villa. Most of the paintings on display are copies, albeit very good ones; the originals being in the Frick Museum in New York. Still, a visit to this charming small museum is very worthwhile and can be made on weekdays from 10 a.m. to noon and 2–5 p.m., and also on the first and last Sunday of each month.

The new **International Perfume Museum** (8) at 8 Place du Cours is now open, with displays on the history of perfume making and marketing. It is open on Wednesdays through Mondays, from 10 a.m. to 6 p.m.

American tourists will be particularly interested in the **Maritime Museum** (9), devoted primarily to the life of Amiral de Grasse. Born in nearby Bar-sur-Loup, this 18th-century French Naval hero is remembered for his role in the American War of Independence, when he blockaded the British at Yorktown, Virginia. Souvenirs of the battle are on display along with ship models and related items. The museum is open on Mondays through Fridays, from 10 a.m. to noon and 2–5:30 p.m. It is closed in November. From here follow the map back to Place aux Aires and the bus station.

Bus Station

Rue P. Goby

Info.

Pl. de la Foux

R. des
4 Coins

Ave. Mar. Juin

Ave. Yves Baudoin

Blvd. Gambetta

R. de Fontette

Droite

Place aux Aires

R. de
l'Oratoire

Rue

Pl. J.
Jaurès

R. de la
Poissonnerie

Blvd. du Jeu de Ballon

Rue Amiral de Grasse

R. M. Journet

R. Sans Peur

Rue J. Ossola

R. Tracastel

Rue Mirabeau

Blvd. Fragonard

Blvd. Carnot

Blvd. Crouët

N

Grasse

100 Yards

St. Tropez

Fame and notoriety have not managed to spoil St. Tropez, which preserves all of its considerable charm. Isolated by geography from the main stream of the Riviera and far off the highways and rail line, this deliciously hedonistic place is well worth the effort of reaching.

There are many faces to St. Tropez. It is at one and the same time an art colony, a haunt of the intelligentsia, a bohemian resort, a center of fashion, and—yes—even a sleepy old fishing port. These and other facets of its paradoxical existence may or may not appeal to you, but the easiest way to at least sample its heady lifestyle is to go there for a day and try the place on for size. Who knows? You may decide to return for a real vacation. If you do, you'll be happy to know that there are sandy beaches for every taste, all within a short distance of the town.

GETTING THERE:

Trains in the morning connect coastal towns along the Riviera with St. Raphaël, a one-hour ride from Nice. From the St. Raphaël station you can get a **bus** for the 80-minute ride to St. Tropez. Return service operates until early evening. During the summer there are also **boats** from the St. Raphaël port (not far from the station) to St. Tropez, a cruise of about 50 minutes and not much costlier than the bus.

By car, take the A-8 Autoroute to the Fréjus exit, then the N-98 to St. Tropez. It is 68 miles southwest of Nice.

WHEN TO GO:

Good weather is essential for a visit to St. Tropez. The art museum is closed on Tuesdays, major holidays, and in November; while the Maritime Museum closes on Thursdays, major holidays, and from November 15th through December 15th. Unlike the rest of the Riviera, St. Tropez faces north and experiences cold winters.

FOOD AND DRINK:

As you might expect, St. Tropez abounds in restaurants and outdoor cafés. Some choices are:

Along the Breakwater

Le Chabichou (Ave. Foch, one block east of Place des Lices / Place Carnot) Fabulous contemporary cuisine in cheerful surroundings. For reservations phone 94-54-80-00. X: mid-Oct. through April. $$$+

L'Échalote (35 Rue Allard, 2 blocks south of the art museum) An elegant modern garden restaurant. For reservations phone 94-54-83-26. $$$

Bistrot des Lices (3 Place des Lices / Place Carnot) A trendy bistro with classical and modern dishes, live music. $$$

Le Girelier (Quai Jean-Jaurès, near the tourist office) Seafood specialties in the Provençal style, also meat dishes. X: mid-Jan. to early Mar. $$$

La Marjolaine (Rue François-Sibilli, 2 blocks southeast of the tourist office) A very popular trattoria and pizzeria. X: Mon, except in July & Aug. $$

Café des Arts (Place des Lices / Place Carnot) A long-time favorite for simple bistro food. X: Oct. through March. $$

TOURIST INFORMATION:

The local tourist office, phone 94-97-45-21, is on the quay by the port, with a branch on the road into town, phone 94-97-41-21.

SUGGESTED TOUR:

Leave the **bus station** (1) and follow the map to the port. Filled with all kinds of boats, from humble fishing vessels to luxury yachts, this is the very heart of St. Tropez. Don't be surprised to see ocean-going sailboats with American registrations docked here. The quays are often the scene of uninhibited exhibitionism or joyous revelry, which can be best savored by sitting down at one of the seemingly endless sidewalk cafés, especially **Le Gorille** or **Sénéquier's**.

Be sure to stroll out to the end of the **Môle Jean Réveille** (2), a massive breakwater that encloses the harbor. The panoramic vistas from its upper level are fantastic.

Return to the quay and turn left on Rue de la Mairie, passing the Suffren Castle and the **Town Hall** (3). You are now in the picturesque Old Town, where several narrow passageways lead to lovely views. Continue on Rue de la Ponche to its end, poke around the alleyways there, then follow the map uphill to a path that goes to the nearby Graniers beach. Stroll a short way down this to a **point** (4) where you will be treated to a magnificent perspective of the town and the sea.

Walk uphill to the **Citadel** (5), a 16th-century fortress that now houses the fascinating **Maritime Museum**. Step inside to see the marvelous reconstruction of a Greek galley, displays on the manufacture of torpedoes (a local industry), and a section devoted to the Allied landing of 1944—when this bastion was the last stronghold of German resistance. A climb to the roof reveals yet another fabulous panorama. The museum is open from 10 a.m. to 6 p.m. (5 p.m. in winter), daily except on Thursdays and some holidays.

Returning to town, you may want to make a little side trip to witness a more traditional aspect of life in St. Tropez. Known to residents as **Place des Lices** (6) but called Place Carnot on maps, the town's main square is a delightfully shady spot where men play *boules* all day and a market is held on Tuesday and Saturday mornings. Stop in for a drink at the Café des Arts, then stroll over to the 18th-century **Parish Church** (7) to see its remarkable bust of Saint Tropez himself.

No visit to St. Tropez is complete without a stop at the **Annonciade Museum** (8), housed in a 16th-century chapel right by the port. Surprisingly, this is one of the best small museums of modern art in all France. Most of the artists represented in its permanent collection have had some connection with the town, and include Signac, Matisse, Van Dongen, Derain, Bonnard, Dufy, Vuillard, Roussel and others. It is open from 10 a.m. to noon and 3–7 p.m. (2–6 p.m. in winter), daily except on Tuesdays, some holidays, and all of November.

TO ST.-RAPHAËL

Ave. Mar. Leclerc

① Bus Station

Ave. du 11 Novembre

Rue du Gén. Allard

Blanc

Blvd. Louis

Rue J. Quaranta

Blvd. Vasserot

Rue G. Clemenceau

Ave. Grangeon

Place Carnot

Quai de l'Epi

② Môle Jean Réveille

PORT

⑧

Quai G. Péri

Quai Suffren

Quai J. Jaurès

Info.

Quai F. Mistral

R. de la Marie

③

⑦ Neuf

R. de la Ponche

Rue Sibilli

Rue Gambetta

R. du Portail-Neuf

Rue de la Citadelle

R. des Remparts

Blvd. d'Aumale

⑥

→ N

Ave. P. Signac

④

⑤ Citadel

St. Tropez

200 Yards

St. Paul

Totally enclosed by its ancient ramparts, the tiny fortified hill town of St. Paul is today both an art colony and a magnet for discerning tourists. Often referred to as St.-Paul-de-Vence after its larger neighbor, this charming village is home to one of the world's greatest museums of contemporary art.

Once occupied by Ligurians, and then Romans, St. Paul was converted into a military stronghold in the 16th century by François I, who needed to defend his frontier against the dukes of Savoy. Its importance declined after the Revolution, only to be rediscovered by artists in the 1920s.

This classic daytrip is customarily combined with one to nearby Vence, described in the next chapter.

GETTING THERE:

Buses depart the bus station *(Gare Routière)* on Boulevard Jean Jaurès in Nice about every hour for the 45-minute ride to St. Paul. They then continue on to Vence. Return buses run until early evening. A special round-trip ticket allowing stops at both towns is available.

By car, take the A-8 Autoroute or other coastal roads to Cagnes-sur-Mer, then the D-6 and D-107 north to St. Paul. From there the D-102 continues on to Vence, three miles to the north. St. Paul is 12 miles northwest of Nice.

WHEN TO GO:

This trip can be made at any time. Good weather will make it much more enjoyable.

FOOD AND DRINK:

The village of St. Paul has several restaurants, most of which are quite simple. A few of the better choices are:

> **La Colombe d'Or** (at the entrance to the town) World-famous for its magnificent collection of modern art, given to the owner by the painters in payment for meals. The terrace restaurant of this inn is enchanting. For reservations phone 93-32-80-02. X: mid-Nov. through Dec. $$$

> **Le Bougainvillier** (7 Rempart Ouest, on the western ramparts) A charming restaurant with exceptionally good contemporary cuisine. X: Nov. $$$

Rue Grande near the North Gate

La Marmite (Rue Grande) Local cuisine in nice surroundings.
   $$
Le Tilleul Menthe (Place du Tilleul, by the north gate) A simple
   café with outdoor tables. Sandwiches and the like. $
Snacks and drinks are also available at the Maeght Foundation.

TOURIST INFORMATION:

The local tourist office, phone 93-32-86-95, is at 2 Rue Grande, just
inside the town gate.

SUGGESTED TOUR:

Leave the **bus stop** (1) and stroll past the famous Colombe d'Or
inn to the North Gate of the village. Just inside this is the **tourist office**
(2) and a small art museum.

The narrow pedestrians-only Rue Grande, lined with antiques shops,
art galleries, boutiques and restaurants, is the main street of the vil-
lage. Follow it to the utterly delightful urn-shaped **fountain** (3) that
splashes away merrily in a tiny square.

Turn left and climb the steps to the 13th-century **Church** (4), heavily
rebuilt during the 17th century. Its attractive interior contains some
remarkable works of art, including a painting of St. Catherine at-
tributed to Tintoretto at the far end of the north aisle. Step into the

In the Maeght Foundation

Treasury for a look at a few unusually fine items dating from the 12th to the 15th centuries.

Amble over to the east ramparts. It is possible, if you're feeling sure-footed, to walk along the top of these for some good views. Continue on to the **South Gate Bastion** (5), from which you may—in clear weather—have a sweeping panorama from the Alps to the Mediterranean.

Now meander back to the North Gate, exploring the hidden stepped alleys along the way. Return to the bus stop and follow the secondary road to the left. This leads, in half a mile (800 meters), to St. Paul's major attraction. Those with cars should follow the road signs instead.

A visit to the **Maeght Foundation** (6, off the map) is an experience no lover of modern art should miss. Established in 1964 by a Paris gallery owner and publisher to promote an understanding of contemporary art, it is housed in a stunning cluster of buildings set atop a hill surrounded by pine forests. More than just a museum, the foundation embraces a wide range of artistic endeavors, with theaters, libraries, studios and other facilities on the premises. Its permanent collections cover works by many of the leading artists of this century. More important than this, however, are the renowned temporary exhibitions, usually devoted to the work of one particular artist. The Maeght Foundation is open daily, from 10 a.m. to 7 p.m. between July 1st and September 30th; and from 10 a.m. to 12:30 p.m. and 2:30–6 p.m. between October 1st and June 30th. You can phone them at 93-32-81-63 for information about current shows.

Return to the bus stop. from which you can continue on to Vence or head back to Nice.

To Vence →

← To Nice

Maeght Foundation ½ Mile

La Colombe d'Or

Bus Stop

Info.

Rue Grande

Remparts Ouest

Walls

Rue Grande

Remparts Est

Walls

Walls

Bastion

N

St. Paul

NOT TO SCALE

Vence

Once a Ligurian tribal capital of some importance, Vence, then known by its Roman name of *Vintium,* became the seat of a bishop as early as A.D. 374—a distinction it retained until 1790. Its ancient town walls and medieval quarter are still virtually intact, complete with a maze of quaint little passageways and picturesque squares.

Sheltered from the north winds by a mountain range, Vence is noted for its mild climate and luminous air. This, together with its charming Old Town, has long attracted artists and writers as well as numerous tourists. A daytrip here can easily be combined with one to St. Paul, described in the previous chapter.

GETTING THERE:

Buses connect Vence with Nice by way of St. Paul at nearly hourly intervals. The trip takes a bit less than one hour. See the previous chapter for details.

By car, follow the directions to St. Paul and continue on for three more miles to Vence. A faster route, bypassing St. Paul, is to take the A-8 Autoroute or coastal roads to Cagnes-sur-Mer, then the D-236 north to Vence. It is 14 miles northwest of Nice. The most convenient place to park is at Place du Grand Jardin.

WHEN TO GO:

Vence may be visited at any time. The nearby Chapel of the Rosary is usually open on Tuesdays and Thursdays (except in November) only, but possibly more frequently during the summer or by special arrangement. Ask the tourist office about this.

FOOD AND DRINK:

Vence has several restaurants and outdoor cafés in and around the Old Town. Some of the better selections include:

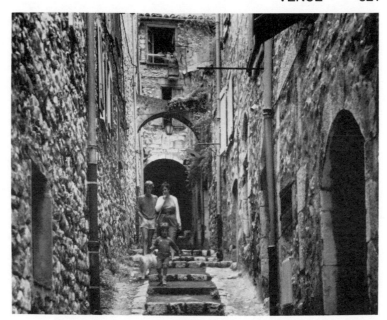

Rue Ste.-Luce in the Old Town

Auberge des Seigneurs (Place du Frêne) An old inn with superb food. X: Sun. eve., Mon., mid-Oct. to early Dec. $$$
Les Portiques (6 Rue St.-Véran, 1 block east of Place Godeau) Long a local favorite. For reservations phone 93-58-36-31. X: Sun., Aug. $$
La Farigoule (15 Ave. Henri-Isnard, 2 blocks northwest of the tourist office) Authentic regional cuisine in a lovely garden restaurant. X: Fri. in low season. $$
Closerie des Genets (1 Impasse Maurel, 4 blocks southwest of the cathedral) A charming country inn with family-style cooking. X: Mon. off season. $ and $$

TOURIST INFORMATION:
The local tourist office, phone 93-58-06-38, is located at Place du Grand Jardin, near the bus stop.

SUGGESTED TOUR:
Leave the **bus stop** (1) and stroll over to the **tourist office** (2), where you can ask about seeing the famous Chapel of the Rosary (7), designed and decorated by the artist Henri Matisse.

Place du Peyra (3), on the site of the ancient Roman forum, is reached via a medieval gateway standing next to a 15th-century tower. This delightful little square in the Old Town is enlivened by a gurgling urn-shaped fountain and several outdoor cafés.

Turn right and follow the map to the 11th-century former **Cathedral** (4), which still retains parts of its 5th-century predecessor, erected on the site of a Roman temple. The present structure was greatly altered during the 17th century. To the left of the main door there is an ancient inscription in honor of the 3rd-century Roman emperor Gordianus. Step inside to see the wonderfully satiric carvings on the 15th-century choir stalls. These are in a gallery that is sometimes open—just ask if it isn't.

Now follow the map around to **Place Godeau** (5), at the center of which stands a Roman column dedicated to the god Mars. Continue on and pass through the Porte d'Orient gate, then turn left and follow the line of the walls, re-entering the medieval quarter by way of Rue Pisani.

Meander along through the ancient narrow streets and exit the Old Town at the 13th-century Levis Portal. **Place du Frêne** (6), also known as Place Thiers, is noted for its enormously thick, centuries-old ash tree. Legend has it that this was planted in 1538 to commemorate a visit by François I. From the north end of the square you can get a good view of the nearby mountains and, if you can pick it out, the Chapel of the Rosary. The 15th-century **Château des Villeneuve**, near the Peyra Gate, is now restored and used for art exhibitions. It is open in the afternoons, but not in November.

You may want to walk—or drive—to the nearby **Chapel of the Rosary** (7, off the map), a bit less than one mile away. Although this is the best-known attraction in Vence, it is generally open only on Tuesdays and Thursdays, from 10–11:30 a.m. and 2:30–5:30 p.m., but not in November. Visits on other days may be possible, especially during the summer, but be sure to check with the tourist office before making the trek. Designed and decorated by the noted artist Henri Matisse around 1950, this simple chapel is considered to be a great masterpiece of modern art and architecture. To get there just follow Avenue Henri-Isnard and Avenue des Poilus, then turn right on Avenue Henri-Matisse across a bridge and uphill to the Chapelle du Rosaire.

Var Valley

Little known to foreign visitors, the narrow-gauge rail line through the Var Valley offers a magnificent visual treat coupled with an exciting ride. The private railway, properly known as the *Chemins de Fer de la Provence,* operates along a spectacular mountain route in the lower Alps between Nice and Digne. This same trip can also be made by car.

GETTING THERE:

Trains of the private railway depart from the Provence Station *(Gare du Sud)* in Nice, just a few blocks north of the main station. It is necessary to get to the station before 8:30 a.m. if you plan to make a whole day of it. Eurailpasses are accepted, and holders of the France Railpass or InterRail Pass are granted a 50% fare reduction. Be sure to pick up a current schedule to determine which stops can be made— and for how long. Schedules are also available at the main Nice station.

By car, you can cover most of the same route by following the N-202 north from the Nice Airport. There are difficult mountain roads between Scaffarels and St.-André-les-Alpes, but these can be bypassed by sticking to the N-202.

WHEN TO GO:

Trains operate all year round, although on a reduced schedule in winter. The castle at Entrevaux is usually open from mid-June to mid-September, but closed on Mondays.

FOOD AND DRINK:

There are simple restaurants and cafés at each of the stops. Some of the better choices are:

> **Le Grand Hôtel** (by the station in St.-André-les-Alpes) Good food in a convenient location. X: winter. $
>
> **Hôtel du Parc** (Place de l'Eglise in St.-André-les-Alpes) A comfortable inn near the old church. X: Mon. off season. $ and $$

The Train at St.-André-les-Alpes

Grand Hôtel Grac (Place du Germe in Annot) Good food in an old inn. X: Dec. to mid-Mar. $

De l'Avenue (in the village of Annot) A small country inn with meals. X: Nov. through Mar. $

Le Vauban (by the main road in Entrevaux) A simple inn with Provençal cooking. $

TOURIST INFORMATION:

The tourist office in Entrevaux, phone 93-05-46-72 (in winter call the Town Hall at 93-05-40-04), is inside the town gate. The phone number in Nice for the Provence Railway is 93-88-28-56 or 93-84-89-71.

SUGGESTED TOUR:

Board the train in **Nice** (1) and ride it all the way to **St.-André-les-Alpes** (2), a trip of about 2½ hours, or 74 miles. Along the way you will climb through narrow gorges to an elevation of 3,353 feet, then begin a short descent to the pleasant little mountain resort. This is a fine place for a delightful country lunch, or you may decide to take the next train back to Annot or Entrevaux and eat there, depending on the schedule.

The Entrance to Entrevaux

The wonderfully picturesque old town of **Annot** (3), founded in the 12th century, is another excellent place to have lunch. If you do stop there, be sure to check the schedule so you don't miss out on seeing Entrevaux.

The most visually exciting town along this route is **Entrevaux** (4), an ancient walled fortress approached via a drawbridge over the Var stream. Once a frontier between France and the Kingdom of Savoy, its present ramparts were built in 1695 by Vauban, Louis XIV's great military engineer. Wander through the unspoiled passageways to the 12th- and 17th-century former **Cathedral**, known for its richly-decorated interior. Perched high above the village is the mighty **Citadelle**— a castle that may be visited in summer by asking at the tourist office *(Bureau d'Accueil)*. There is also an interesting small **museum** of motorscooters in the village, open daily in July and August.

If time permits, you may want to make a stop at **Puget-Théniers** (5) before returning to Nice. This lovely old town, dominated by the ruins of an ancient castle, has a fine 13th-century church and an attractive square. It is also a well-known center for **steam-train** activities.

TO DIGNE

St.-André -les-Alpes ●

2979

②

Thorame ●

3320

VERDON

3106

2312

N-202

Annot ● ③

Méailles ●

Scaffarels ●

N

VAR

1551

Entrevaux ●
④

The N-202 road parallels the rail line, starting at the Nice-Côte d'Azur Airport. This bypasses the mountainous region between Scaffarels and St.-André-les-Alpes. *Elevations of the rail line above sea level are shown in feet.*

1335

Puget-Théniers ●
⑤

Villars ●

853

CAGNES-SUR-MER

456

Plan du Var

VAR

St.-Martin du Var

213 ● Castagniers

Colomars ●

SNCF MAIN LINE

PROVENCE RAILWAY

Airport

①

NICE

Var Valley

Not to scale. It is 74 miles by rail from Nice to St.-André-les-Alpes.

Index

Cathedrals, Châteaux, Glossaries, Museums, Paris, and Roman Relics are listed individually under those category headings. Names of persons are in italics.

DAYTRIPS

TRAVEL GUIDES BY EARL STEINBICKER

● OTHER TITLES NOW AVAILABLE ●

DAYTRIPS IN BRITAIN

Most of Britain's best attractions lie within easy daytrip range of London, Edinburgh, or Glasgow. This remarkable new guide—successor to the popular *Daytrips from London*—takes a close look at 60 of the most exciting destinations and shows you, in step-by-step detail, exactly how best to explore them on your own. 352 pages, 65 large maps, and 107 photos.

DAYTRIPS IN HOLLAND, BELGIUM AND LUXEMBOURG

There's more to the Low Countries than just Amsterdam, Brussels, and Luxembourg City. Experience what most tourists miss in the 40 daytrips described in this new guidebook. Many unusual destinations are covered, along with all of the favorites including the three major cities. Rail and road glossaries in Dutch and French, 44 maps, 65 photos, 288 pages.

DAYTRIPS IN ITALY

Features 40 one-day adventures in and from Rome, Florence, Milan, Venice, and Naples. It includes walking tours of the major cities as well as many smaller destinations, and has a large section on getting around in Italy—complete with rail and road glossaries. 304 pages, 47 maps, 63 photos.

DAYTRIPS IN GERMANY

50 of Germany's best attractions can be enjoyed on delightful daytrips from Munich, Frankfurt, and Hamburg. Walking tours of the big cities are included as well, as are glossaries. 56 maps and 92 photos. Third edition, 304 pages.

"Daytrips" travel guides by Earl Steinbicker describe the easiest and most natural way to explore Europe on your own. Each volume in the growing series contains a balanced selection of thoroughly enjoyable one-day adventures that can be taken from a major base city. Some of these are to famous attractions, while others feature little-known discoveries.

For every destination there is a suggested do-it-yourself tour, a local map, full travel directions, time and weather considerations, restaurant recommendations, photos, and just enough background material to make the day's experiences more rewarding.

Since all of the daytrips can be made by public transportation, the books are especially useful to holders of the various popular railpasses. Road directions are included for those who would rather drive.

SOLD AT LEADING BOOKSTORES EVERYWHERE

Or, if you prefer, by mail direct from the publisher.
Use the handy coupon below or just jot down your choices on a separate piece of paper.

━━━━━━━━━━━━━━━━━━━━━━━━━━━━━━━━━━

Hastings House
141 Halstead Avenue
Mamaroneck, NY 10543

Please send the following books:

_____copies	DAYTRIPS IN BRITAIN @ $12.95 (0-8038-9301-9)	_____
_____copies	DAYTRIPS IN FRANCE @ $12.95 (0-8038-9326-4)	_____
_____copies	DAYTRIPS IN ITALY @ $10.95 (0-8038-9292-4)	_____
_____copies	DAYTRIPS IN GERMANY @ $12.95 (0-8038-9327-2)	_____
_____copies	DAYTRIPS IN HOLLAND, BELGIUM AND LUXEMBOURG @ $12.95 (0-8038-9310-8)	_____

New York residents add tax: _____

Shipping and handling @ $1.50 per book: _____

Total amount enclosed (check or money order): _____

Please ship to: _____

_____

_____